D1043753

Artists & Writers Colonies

Retreats, Residencies, and Respites for the Creative Mind

Artists & Writers Colonies

Retreats, Residencies, and Respites for the Creative Mind

Researched, edited, and written by
Robyn Middleton, Mindy Seale,
Martha Ruttle, Emily Stephens,
Stacey Loomis, Nicole Peterson

LIBRARY
FASHION INSTITUTE OF
TECHNOLOGY
227 WEST 27th STREET
NEW YORK, NY 10001

Blue Heron Publishing • Portland, Oregon

Artists and Writers Colonies:
Retreats, Residencies, and Respites for the Creative Mind

Copyright © 2000 by Robyn Middleton, Mindy Seale, Martha Ruttle, Emily
   Stephens, Stacey Loomis, Nicole Peterson.

All rights reserved. No part of this book may be reproduced, stored
in a retrieval system, or transmitted in any form or by any means
without permission in writing from the publisher, except by a
reviewer, who may quote briefly in review.

Printed and bound in the United States of America.

Cover design: Sue Tencza

Published by
Blue Heron Publishing
420 S.W. Washington St.
Suite 303
Portland, Oregon 97204
503.221.6841
info@blueheronpublishing.com
www.blueheronpublishing.com

ISBN 0-936085-45-2

Publisher's Cataloging-in-Publication Data

Middleton, Robyn and Mindy Seale, Martha Ruttle, Emily Stephens,
Stacey Loomis, Nicole Peterson.
   Artists and Writers Colonies / by
      Middleton et alia — 2nd ed.
         p.   cm.
   Includes appendices.
   ISBN 0-936085-62-2
   1. How-to. 2. Artists and writers colonies.
3. Reference   I. Title

Ref.St
NX
110
.B69
2000

M1D 2003   12/27/02

Publisher's Note

The compilation of this new edition of *Artists & Writers Colonies* has been a remarkable experience. When Gail Bowler, who researched and wrote the first edition, contacted us to say she would be unable to do the needed revision, I was at first dismayed. I couldn't imagine how we'd accomplish the necessary work in-house, given the other responsibilities that too few of us shoulder at this small press.

The solution to this unexpected situation resulted in a wonderful book and also afforded us the opportunity to redesign our intern program, which we have always valued highly and striven to improve. A book like this one is a perfect project for teaching book publishing, since it includes research, interviewing, writing, editing, designing, and marketing. But clearly, this would be too much for any single intern to manage, so we reevaluated our entire intern program. We'd always had only one intern at a time, and we wondered if we could handle more than that. We shouldn't have worried. The team approach was the right one, and the interns whose names appear on this book became an extraordinarily talented and collaborative publishing group. They assumed full responsibility for the production of this new edition, short of the physical layout of the book, and created a rational division of labor among themselves. The clear focus of the book's needs provided a natural structure for the classes I teach about the different aspects of publishing.

I want to thank them here for their efforts. I hope they benefitted from the experience. I know that I did, as did the press. Our internships will never be the same. Certainly, these six are the first Blue Heron interns to have produced a complete book. They are its authors, but they are more than that around here. They are heroes. Thank you, Robyn Middleton, Mindy Seale, Martha Ruttle, Emily Stephens, Stacey Loomis, and Nicole Peterson. It was a joy to work with you.

Dennis Stovall, Publisher

Acknowledgments

We would like to thank Gail Hellund Bowler for entrusting us with the second edition of what began as her book, *Artists & Writers Colonies*, the first edition. Also, thanks to Dennis Stovall and Daniel Urban at Blue Heron Publishing for their support, guidance, and faith in us.

Thanks, of course, are extended to all of the colonies listed in this book for sending us information. Without your cooperation and enthusiasm, this book would not have been possible. Thanks also to the proprietors, caretakers, and staff members at all of the colonies and centers for persevering despite limited funds. In a time of waning financial support for the arts, your dedication to fostering the creative endeavors of your fellow artists is an inspiration.

Many thanks to the artists who contributed narrative accounts of their experiences. Your stories make this a richer book.

And finally, thanks to everyone who contributed to this book. Like many creative endeavors, this book was a collaborative effort, fostered by a sense of community and shaped by new ideas and voices.

Robyn Middleton, Mindy Seale,
Martha Ruttle, Emily Stephens,
Stacey Loomis, and Nicole Peterson

Contents

PACIFIC COAST COLONIES

MIDDLE ATLANTIC COLONIES

INTERNATIONAL COLONIES

APPENDIX (colonies and retreats by subject and discipline)

LIST OF ARTISTS' ESSAYS ON THEIR RETREAT EXPERIENCES

Introduction

Artists and writers colonies are a well-kept secret. The colonies themselves rarely advertise because the ratio of applicants to residencies is already so high—what artist doesn't crave time and seclusion to concentrate intensely on her or his work? While most artists have a vague knowledge of the existence of colonies, either from magazine articles or from a citation on the acknowledgements page of a treasured book, the scarcity of detailed information about colonies can make them intimidating. They are considered by many to be inaccessible, only for the elite. This is simply not true.

The word *colony*, with its undertones of exclusivity, eccentricity, and even secrecy, is perhaps misleading. All kinds of opportunities exist for artists of any discipline, level of professionalism, or income bracket. The programs and facilities featured in this book are many and varied—from relatively expensive retreats that offer total seclusion and complete amenities to fully subsidized residencies in artistic or academic communities. They differ in atmosphere, cost, degree of seclusion, competitiveness, and length. Many that do charge fees are able to offer financial assistance to artists who qualify for it. Others will waive a portion of the fees in exchange for teaching services or labor. If you read this book carefully, you will most certainly be able to find a number of programs that are appealing and realistic possibilities for you.

As you read this book, think about what you would like from the experience you hope to have. How long can you afford to stay away from your "real life"? Can you afford to travel far from home? What do you hope to accomplish during this time away? How much solitude and seclusion can you handle? Do you have any skills or the time to exchange for fees? Thinking carefully about your expectations, goals, and needs before you apply to programs will help you to have the most fulfilling artistic experience and will be a valuable way to warm up before filling out lengthy application forms. You may want to read some of the first-hand accounts of residency and retreat experiences that are included in this book. Some artists write about how their specific goals affected their choice of program: a longer, more secluded retreat may be more constructive if you want to explore new ways of making art, while a shorter retreat may be just what you need to really focus on and complete a specific project. One sculptor writes about the difference between a very secluded colony and a highly social artists' community. In seclusion, he had the time and freedom to be introspective. As part of a larger community, he felt inspired by the other artists at times, but often felt overwhelmed. Consider how these factors might affect you, but also be open to the unexpected. There will certainly be surprises, and the unexpected can be a source of inspiration.

How to Use This Book

Artists & Writers Colonies includes residency, retreat, and fellowship opportunities for all types of creative people, including artists, writers, performers, and scholars. This book focuses on opportunities that provide either the time, space, or money for you to work on creative projects that the conditions of your everyday life prevent you from completing. Artists and writers are simply in search of a place where they have the luxury to make art their top priority. Luckily, there are people who understand this and have made a career out of supporting the creative efforts of their fellow artists by maintaining these colonies and programs.

There are five types of listings in this book (and some variations on those). The following definitions are general, not literal, and sometimes overlap:

Residencies: Residencies are a specific allotment of time awarded to an applicant to complete a project that was probably clearly defined during the application process. Most residencies are served on the campus or grounds of a colony, foundation, university, art center, museum, or estate. Residencies provide various levels of physical and financial support for the artist. Some charge minimal fees for food, housing, materials, or studio space. Some are free.

Retreats: Retreats are various commercial and noncommercial enterprises that cater to artists. They range from bed and breakfast houses and private lakeside cabins to monasteries and villas. Most retreats offer a private room with a private or shared bath. Some offer access to communal kitchens and studios. All charge a fee, but because they house artists for long periods of time, most offer substantial discounts for long-term guests, especially during the winter. Some retreats have an application process so that they can screen candidates and assure residents the atmosphere, privacy, and quiet they have a right to expect; others are simply booked on a first-come, first-served basis. Retreats are good for those who face deadlines and do not have time to go through the application, selection, notification, acceptance, and scheduling processes of colonies. Some retreats cost less than colonies and residencies.

Fellowships and Grants: Fellowships are awards to artists, usually as a combination of a residency and stipend. Most fellowships require fellows to participate in the promotional activities of the sponsors and to interact with staff, community, and students. Many expect fellows to teach classes, donate works of art, or allow the sponsors to advertise their affiliation with the artist. The amount of support for the artist varies, but it can be quite substantial. In some cases, it is based on the recipient's pre-award earnings; other times, fellows receive a flat subsistence stipend. Some fellowships and grants provide housing and meals as well. Many are nonresidential.

Opportunities for Playwrights: Because the structure of playwriting programs is a bit different from other programs, we have included those that offer full production, staged readings, or participation in developmental workshops, rehearsals, or playwriting festivals. They do not provide undisturbed time as such, but they do provide playwrights with access to other aspects of their craft, the production experience, and the opportunity to see their work come alive on stage.

Artist-in-Residence Programs: These programs provide studio space, use of the center's equipment, materials, and sometimes room and board for free or at greatly reduced rates for selected artists. Residencies in these programs are usually long-term (from six months to three years). Since few artists have twelve- to fifteen-foot ceilings, overhead cranes, kilns, printing presses, or any of the other highly specialized tools these centers may provide, they are able to work on projects that would not be possible without the programs. Those that do not provide a stipend or living accommodations for the artists realize that most visiting artists must work (at least part-time) in order to survive. Some allow the artists to work at the center for either a wage or an exchange. Others allow the artists to work outside the center as long as they spend a certain number of hours in their studios each week developing their art.

The colonies in this book are grouped by geographic region and listed in alphabetical order. You may note that not all states are included; that is because there are a few states for which we have no listings. The eight regions are:

Midwestern: Includes colonies in Illinois, Indiana, Iowa, Kansas, Michigan, Minnesota, Missouri, Nebraska, North Dakota, Ohio, South Dakota, and Wisconsin.

Rocky Mountain: Includes colonies in Colorado, Idaho, Montana, Nevada, Utah, and Wyoming.

Southwestern: Includes colonies in Arizona, New Mexico, Oklahoma, and Texas.

Southern: Includes colonies in Alabama, Arkansas, Florida, Georgia, Kentucky, Louisiana, Mississippi, North Carolina, South Carolina, Tennessee, Virginia, and West Virginia.

New England: Includes colonies in Connecticut, Maine, Massachusetts, New Hampshire, Rhode Island, and Vermont.

Pacific Coast: Includes colonies in Alaska, California, Hawaii, Oregon, and Washington.

Middle Atlantic: Includes colonies in Delaware, the District of Columbia, Maryland, New Jersey, New York, and Pennsylvania.

International: Includes all colonies located outside of the fifty United States. Colonies in this section are listed in alphabetical order according to the country in which the program is held.

An appendix that lists colonies according to the kinds of artists they host can be found in the back of the book. Colonies are still grouped by region in this appendix so that you can locate them easily in the text. This may be a helpful way for you to navigate the book if you are not restricted by geography.

Each listing provides the colony's name, location, mailing address (be sure to include the name of the colony as well when sending mail), telephone number, and email and Web addresses if available. Other pertinent information is divided into standardized categories. We have outlined the application procedures for most colonies; this information is intended only to give you a sense of what the application process for a particular colony entails. Before you apply, you should request information directly from the colony itself, because the requirements, procedures, and deadlines are subject to change. Also, make sure that you meet all of the eligibility requirements before you apply to any colony or retreat. For instance, some do not accept applications from students, and others will grant funds only to area residents.

You will note that we have listed a number of colonies that have been discontinued. In most cases, someone responded to let us know that the program had been discontinued. In other instances, when repeated attempts to contact colonies by phone, mail, and email failed, we had to assume that they no longer exist. We wanted to provide this information for people who are searching for information about a specific colony that may no longer operate. Colonies have been discontinued for a number of reasons: sometimes it is because the proprietors have retired, but more often it is due to a shortage of funds. We did not use the space to explain each discontinuation or provide old contact information. The names and locations of the terminated colonies should identify them adequately. We did, however, include information about programs that are on hiatus.

We took the opportunity of a second edition to include a number of personal narratives from artists who have spent time at colonies listed in this book. Those narratives are listed in the table of contents and appear beside the colony that the artist attended. While the artists have overwhelmingly positive things to say about their experiences, the inclusion of these pieces is not intended to be an endorsement of any specific colony. We simply hope that they will give you a sense of what some colony experiences are like. We also recommend that you talk to any artists you know who have spent time at colonies. The advice and information of others is valuable and will give you a perspective on a place in a way that the listings in this book simply cannot. If you can't talk to someone who has attended a colony that you're interested in, talk to someone who works at the colony. Always request that they send you information to supplement the information in this book. Reading what they have to say about their own program will give you a more complete sense of what the atmosphere is like. Always provide them with a self-addressed, stamped envelope (SASE) to send any materials you request.

§

While this book is probably the most complete of its kind, it is certainly a good idea to do some research on your own to supplement the information in it. All states, and many cities and towns, have their own arts councils or commissions. Check the government listings in your telephone directory, and call the arts commission or council and ask to be added to their mailing list. See if any of their programs are suitable for you. Also, the National Endowment for the Arts has many programs for artists. We chose not to list them in this book for two reasons: first, the government has so many provisos to their awards that there isn't room to list them; second, because of funding cuts, the future of these programs is uncertain, and the information might soon be out of date. If you're interested in any NEA programs, write for current offerings to the following address:

National Endowment for the Arts
Nancy Hanks Center
1100 Pennsylvania Avenue, N.W.
Washington, DC 20506-0001

If you know the name of the program about which you'd like information, tell them. If you don't, do a little research (at the library, a university, or on the Web) to find out what programs might interest you. If you have no luck, simply tell them what you do and what you're looking for, and they will send you the appropriate booklets. If you have Internet access, visit the NEA Web site (http//arts.endow.gov). The site is surprisingly easy to navigate, and information about programs and grants (including deadlines and applications) is available at http//arts.endow.gov/guide. The Internet has become a wonderful resource for writers and artists over the past few years. Many Web sites for artists, and especially writers, list workshops, retreats, and colonies. There is a lot of information to weed through, but you may turn up something new and exciting. Good luck!

Midwestern Colonies

Illinois
Indiana
Kansas
Michigan
Minnesota
Missouri
Nebraska
North Dakota
Ohio
South Dakota
Wisconsin

Soapstone Creek, Near Soapstone's Retreat in Oregon

MARY ANDERSON CENTER FOR THE ARTS   IN

101 St. Francis Drive, Mount St. Francis, Indiana 47146
Phone: (812) 923-8602; fax: (812) 923-3200
Email: maca@iglou.com

Type of Facility/Award
Residency with or without fellowship.

Who Can Apply
Writers, musicians, dance and performance artists, visual artists, artisans, composers, architects, designers, and scholars.

Provisos
None listed. Center is handicapped-accessible.

Dates of Operation
Open year-round.

Location
The center is located in rural southern Indiana, fifteen minutes north of downtown Louisville, Kentucky.

History
The program for artists' residencies was established in 1989. The Conventual Franciscan Friars initiated the secular program as part of an effort to continue their 700-year heritage of fostering spiritual, cultural, and educational expression. The name and inspiration for the center came from the nineteenth-century Louisville actress Mary Anderson, who originally owned the 400 acres that became Mount St. Francis. By giving the land to the stewardship of the friars, she hoped to preserve its natural environment. The setting provides calm and beauty for body and mind.

What They Offer
The center has a year-round residency and retreat program. Residency terms are from one week to three months; the average stay is one month. Retreats are from one to six days. Residencies are by application. Retreats are by reservation.

The center also has three continuing fellowship programs. Eight Mary Anderson Fellowships are awarded annually. Four fellowships are offered to writers in any genre, three are offered to visual artists and artisans, and one is offered to a musician or composer. This fellowship awards artists at mid-career the opportunity to spend one month in residency. The Senior Fellows Program recognizes artistic excellence in writers, visual artists, artisans who are fifty years old or older. Four awards are made annually, two to artists from Indiana and two to artists from Kentucky. Mentoring

Fellowships for Emerging Artists are designed to recognize talent and potential in artists who do not yet have a significant publication or show record. Other fellowship opportunities provided by various endowments (but not necessarily on an annual basis) are also available each year. Interested artists should contact the center for details on those programs.

Artists and scholars who are accepted are offered a residency that includes a private room, use of studio space (visual artists), and all meals except Sunday and Monday night dinners. If you go out to dinner on Sundays or Mondays, the center will reimburse you up to $6.50 toward your meal if you provide them with a receipt. Breakfast foods are provided but not prepared. Residents must provide their own transportation to the center. Visitors, children, and pets are not allowed. Rooms are not equipped with telephones.

Facility Description

The center shares 400 acres of woodlands with the Mount St. Francis Friary and Retreat Center, though the Mary Anderson Center for the Arts is not affiliated with the Franciscan Order or the Catholic Church. Grounds include a wildlife refuge with trails for hiking and a lake to fish in or to just sit beside and contemplate. The Loftus House, which is handicapped-accessible, contains the center's offices, residents' sleeping rooms, and some studios. Each resident is provided with a sleeping room (with wash basin and mirror), which doubles as a studio for writers and scholars. There are six rooms available, three on each floor. Each floor has one bathroom for residents to share. The Visual Arts Studio, which is near the Great Barn, has two to four studio spaces. The top floor has two Vandercook letter presses; the lower level has a potter's wheel and kiln. The center does not have any radios, televisions, or stereo equipment, nor do they subscribe to a daily newspaper. If you want these things, you must bring them.

How to Apply

Send an SASE for a brochure and application. Submit a $15 nonrefundable application fee and two copies of the following: your completed application form; a description of your project; a list of your publications, performances, exhibitions, or presentation credits; two references who have professional knowledge of your work and who are professionally active in your creative area; and a work sample as follows (with SASE). Writers and scholars: two copies of your prose (maximum thirty pages) or poetry (maximum twenty pages). Visual artists and artisans: one set of ten slides (labeled according to instructions) with accompanying descriptive sheet. Musicians, composers, and performers: one audio or video tape (VHS only) with accompanying narrative sheet.

Deadline

Rolling application process for residencies without fellowship. Decisions made within one month of application. Mary Anderson Fellowships: Visual arts—July 1; Writing—August 1; Music—November 1. Senior Fellowships: September 1. Mentoring Fellowships: Variable.

Be sure to call about other offerings provided during the year. Sometimes the center receives one-time gifts to fund residencies.

Approximate Cost of Program

$15 application fee, transportation, partial meal costs, materials, and incidentals. The suggested minimum is $30 per day. Call the center for details on financial aid and one-time fellowship gifts. Recipients of the Indiana Connection Series Fellowship are required to perform some duties in exchange for the fellowship.

THE ANDERSON CENTER FOR INTERDISCIPLINARY STUDIES   MN

Mailing Address:

P.O. Box 406, Red Wing, Minnesota 55066
Attention: Residency Program

Physical Address:

5354 Tower View Drive, Red Wing, Minnesota 55066
Phone: (612) 388-2009; fax: (612) 388-2528
Email: 102760.760@compuserve.com

Type of Facility/Award

Residency.

Who Can Apply

Artists, writers, scientists, and scholars of all types. Past residents include choreographers, dancers, botanists, folklorists, novelists, poets, archaeologists, composers, sculptors, anthropologists, theologians, painters, historians, photographers, and journalists.

Provisos

Residents must work on a clearly defined project, engage in the interdisciplinary life of the center, and make a substantive contribution to the community in the form of a talk, reading, or appearance at one of the local civic groups or schools.

Dates of Operation

May, June, August, and September.

Location

The center is located about five miles west of downtown Red Wing, at the intersection of Highways 61 and 19.

History

"Dr. Alexander P. Anderson grew up in Spring Creek valley, Featherstone Township, only five miles away from the estate he would later build. Anderson attended a one room school and worked on the family farm until he was eighteen. He attended the University of Minnesota, paying his way by carrying papers, shoveling snow, and tending furnaces. He discovered the process of puffing cereal grains, which led to the commercial products known as 'Puffed Rice' and 'Puffed Wheat'. In 1915 he returned to Red Wing to build the Tower View Estate, known today as The Anderson Center. Since that time the Anderson heirs have donated the property and all of its buildings in hope of preserving the complex for the benefit of humanity."

What They Offer

Since 1995, the Anderson Center has headed a nonprofit, privately funded program aimed at bringing together a rich mix of artistic, scientific, scholarly, and cultural activities. Residents benefit from exploring their subject in relation to a much wider variety of fields than a typical residency offers. Because of the residents' close proximity, shared evening meals, and common areas in which to congregate, the exchange of ideas flows freely. Residencies last two to four weeks and include meals and lodging. Residents have access to studios, classrooms, laboratories, and public meeting spaces, and may attend or participate in readings, workshops, lectures, and publications. The center shares space and equipment with the Environmental Learning Center, Tower View Alternative High School, the Institute for Minnesota Archaeology, and others, and works collaboratively with the Sheldon Theatre, the Public Library, the Goodhue County Historical Society, the Arts Association, and local schools. Residents are expected to participate in some kind of community service which may include lectures, readings, or appearances at one of the local civic groups or area schools.

Facility Description

The center has stood for almost eighty years amidst 330 acres of farm and forest land, surrounded by buildings listed on the National Register of Historic Sites such as the original Anderson Home and the landmark tower on the Tower View property. Today the property offers modern facilities on a large campus that ranges from farmland to river bottoms. The first floor of the Anderson Home includes a newly remodeled kitchen, full dining room, living room, master bedroom and bath, small study, and screen porch. Upstairs includes five bedrooms, three baths, and a sitting room. Tower View is surrounded by a large lawn and is close to the Cannon Valley Bike Trail. Additional facilities include two large conference rooms and a cafeteria.

How to Apply

Send an SASE for an application form.

Deadline
Variable.

Approximate Cost of Program
Transportation, materials, and incidentals.

APOSTLE ISLANDS NATIONAL LAKESHORE WI
Route 1, Box 4, Bayfield, Wisconsin 54814
Attention: Artist-in-Residence Program
Phone: (715) 779-339; fax: (715) 779-3049

Type of Facility/Award
Artist-in-residence program.

Who Can Apply
Writers, composers, visual artists, and performing artists are invited to interpret the island environment through their work.

Provisos
Applicants should be self-sufficient and in good health as the accommodations provided are somewhat primitive and remote. The selection committee will consider all forms of art except those that manipulate or disturb the park's environment. The Wellish Cabin is not handicapped-accessible.

Dates of Operation
Late June through mid-September.

Location
The Apostle Islands are located in western Lake Superior, off Wisconsin's Bayfield Peninsula. The park is 90 miles east of Duluth, Minnesota, 217 miles north of the Minneapolis/St. Paul area, and 352 miles north of Milwaukee, Wisconsin. Access is by private or concession-operated boat.

History
The Apostle Islands Artist-in-Residence Program began in 1994 as part of a continuing tradition by the National Park Service to support professional artists. Painters, photographers, writers, journalists, musicians, and composers (among others) have helped to stimulate interest in the national parks and foster an appreciation of them through artistic expression.

What They Offer
Artists are housed in the Wellish Cabin, located on the southeast shore of Sand Island, about three miles by boat from the Little Sand Bay Ranger Station. Residents must stay for a minimum of two weeks. While basic cooking utensils and fuel are

provided, the artist must bring bedding, personal gear, food, and art supplies—all of which need to be purchased before the residency begins. The cabin is about a half-mile from the boat dock; whatever you bring with you must be carried that distance. Residents are asked to donate a finished piece of work inspired during the island stay to the program.

Facility Description

Twenty-one of the twenty-two Apostle Islands and a twelve-mile stretch of the mainland shoreline make up the 750-square-mile national lakeshore. Wellish Cabin is simple but roomy, with a large living room, three bedrooms, and a screened porch. The cabin has a vault toilet, no electricity, and no running water. Expect cool temperatures, muddy trail conditions, and insects. A forest trail connects the Wellish Cabin with the Sand Island Lighthouse, established in 1881 and now staffed by volunteers. "Along the way are old farmstead clearings, towering white pines that escaped the logger's axe, and stones for skipping over Justice Bay. Early summer's brilliant wildflowers give way to the lush blueberry patches in August. Storms roll in and retreat, leaving rainbows over the low green profiles of neighboring York and Raspberry Islands. The interplay of the land and lake, the song of wood thrushes, and lingering stories of shipwrecks and lightkeepers are among the many sources of inspiration for an artist's creative endeavors."

How to Apply

Send an SASE for an entry form and brochure. Return the completed form with a one- to two-page résumé, a summary of your creative work, a statement describing your ability to meet the selection criteria and what you hope to achieve from a wilderness residency, your preference of dates, and samples of your work (with an adequate SASE for return). Visual Artists: Submit six 35 mm slides in standard mounts (no glass) labeled as specified. Musicians and composers: Send a cassette. Dancers and performing artists: Send a video cassette. Writers and journalists: Submit no more than ten double-spaced, typewritten pages of manuscript.

Deadline

January 15 (postmarked).

Approximate Cost of Program

Transportation, meals, materials, and incidentals.

ART FARM   NE

1306 West 21st Road, Marquette, Nebraska 68854-2112
Attention: Ed Dadey or Janet Williams
Phone: (402) 854-3120; fax: (402) 854-3120
Email: artfarm@hamilton.net

Type of Facility/Award

Artist-in-residence program.

Who Can Apply

Artists working with ceramics, the environment, fiber and installation art, painting, sculpture, and woodworking.

Provisos

Artists must be self-motivated and resourceful. Those skilled with tools will find it a plus.

Dates of Operation

June 1 through November 1 (residency). November 15 through April 30 (rental).

Location

Located in central southern Nebraska, Art Farm is about 130 miles west of Omaha and eighty miles west of Lincoln.

History

Art Farm is a nonprofit organization set up to provide artists with a worksite, resources, support, and time to experiment with new ideas or projects in a rural setting. The artist-in-residence program began in 1993, though ground work began twenty five years ago when Ed Dadey, after graduating from college, moved back to his family's farm near Marquette. In a search for studio space, he noticed a number of barns in the area and, over a seven year period, began moving them to his parents' farm. The work at Art Farm of restoring, repairing, and converting barns for studio space continues today.

What They Offer

Summer residencies include living accommodations and studio space for up to three artists at a time in exchange for fifteen hours of labor each week (three hours each day for five days a week). Labor can be any of the following: general construction, deconstruction, and carpentry (renovating barns, roofing, concrete pouring, etc.); maintenance (upkeep of grounds, mowing, tending the vegetable garden, fixing equipment and machinery, running errands, etc.); or office work. Because it takes a while to adjust to the environment at Art Farm, a residency of at least two months is recommended. Artists are responsible for their own bed linens, towels, and telephone charges. Residencies are also available in the winter months for a fee.

Facility Description

Art Farm is a working farm, growing everything from hybrid corn to eighty species of prairie grass. The environs are part of a drainage basin forming the headwaters of the Big Blue River. The surrounding landscape, mainly cornfields, varies from flat to

Art Farm
Visual Art

Samantha Fields

I attended Art Farm in June and July of 1996. I had earned my B.F.A. the year before and was on my way to graduate school in the fall. I was accepted as a visiting artist at both Chataqua and the Vermont Studio Program for the same summer. I chose the residency at Art Farm over these other programs because I wanted privacy and seclusion to create a body of work to serve as a springboard into graduate school. I wanted to hit the ground running, so to speak.

At Art Farm I created my own schedule; the only requirement was that I work 15 hours a week for room and board. In Nebraska, it gets pretty hot in the summer, so my schedule was much different from my "normal" life. My focus was art-making—there were no distractions like paying bills, answering the phone, all the things that eat up the day. I would get up around 5 a.m., and work in the studio for 2 hours. Around 7 or 8 a.m. I would work with Janet and Ed, the owners and caretakers of Art Farm, for work exchange renovating the wood storage shed and the art gallery. It was hard work, but we always had a blast, and I learned how to lay shingles and put up drywall. (Useful skills for any artist!) Around 11 a.m. we would finish and I would go for a swim with the other

gently rolling hills to shallow wetlands. Two miles northwest of the farm is the Platte River where the flat landscape changes into clay bluffs. Besides the twenty outdoor acres, the old farmstead comprises about ten buildings. The Granary Studio is 500 square-feet with wood floors, white paneled walls, and high ceilings. It is also suitable

resident at a nearby pond and have lunch. Usually, we would siesta or run errands during the hot part of the day. I would then eat dinner and go back to the studio and work until 11 p.m. or so. There is no work exchange on weekends, so I would work in the studio all day.

I was able to create an entire body of work (25 pieces) in less than three months at Art Farm. At the end of summer, the other resident and I had a two person show in the newly renovated gallery. The time I spent at Art Farm allowed me to focus intently on my work, and gave me a considerable head-start on my graduate work. It eased the transition between working 9–5 and full-time graduate work in the studio, which was just what I wanted. The seclusion gave me the space, both physically and mentally, to consider what I wanted to achieve in the coming two years, and it was a joy to walk into grad school with a new body of work.

Art Farm is completely different from where I normally work. It is an intensely secluded place....there are absolutely no distractions, so if you are a person who needs lots of social activity, this may not be the place for you. I did four times more work per day than I do now, because I was there solely to make art. In my regular life, I send out slides, shoot work, teach classes, go to openings, work the scene, etc......but at Art Farm, I just made paintings, which is what a residency program is for.

For other artists, I would describe Art Farm as a beautiful, rustic, secluded environment. The nearest town is just a few blocks long, and is twenty minutes away. The roads are mostly dirt and go on and on in straight lines as far as the eye can see. We grew most of our own vegetables, and had fresh eggs from a nearby farm. The studios are rustic; one of them is open air. There is a lot of land for large sculpture pieces and environmental work, and lots of "found" material all over the farm. It's very quiet and serene, and the giant barn configuration that Ed has been working on is incredible. The whole experience is one I look back on with great fondness, and I continue to stay in touch with Ed and Janet.

as a small installation space. Pig Pottery Studio (a former hog house turned pottery studio) is 800 square-feet with concrete floors, low ceilings, and unfinished walls. Lone Pine Studio is 800 square-feet with an earth floor, unfinished walls, and an open end. The Schoolhouse/District 62 Gallery (a renovated and winterized 1873 rural schoolhouse) is 600 square-feet with white-painted drywalls and high ceilings; it also doubles as a public events and exhibition space. Additionally, there is a 12,000-square-foot building currently being renovated for functional woodworking, metal-working, printing, photography, and computers facilities. Artists are housed in a nineteenth-century farmhouse that accommodates up to three people and comes equipped with pots, pans, kitchen utensils, and laundry facilities. The farmhouse and schoolhouse are available for a monthly winter rental. For further information and costs, please contact Art Farm. Buildings are smoke-free and no pets are allowed. Visitors may come for short periods depending upon space availability.

How to Apply

Send an SASE for an application and brochure. Return your completed application form with a current résumé and ten slides (labeled according to instructions and with an adequate SASE for their return).

Deadline

April 1 for summer residencies. September 1 for winter residencies.

Approximate Cost of Program

Transportation, meals, materials, and incidentals.

BADLANDS NATIONAL PARK   SD

PO Box 6, Interior, South Dakota 57750
Attention: Artist-in-Residence Program

Type of Facility/Award

Artist-in-residence program.

Who Can Apply

Professional artists.

Provisos

Art forms that manipulate or disturb the park's environment or that is disrespectful to any race or gender will not be accepted.

Dates of Operation

September 1 through October 31 and March 15 through May 15.

Location

Badlands National Park.

History

"Badlands National Park was established as a National Monument in 1939 to protect dramatic scenery created through geological processes and some of the world's most extensive mammal fossil beds. Today, the park also educates on the mixed grass prairie ecosystem and a rich human history extending back over 11,000 years." The artist-in-residency program was founded in 1996.

What They Offer
Residencies last from four to six weeks and include housing in a small apartment complex at park headquarters. Apartments are fully furnished, including basic cooking supplies. Bedding, personal gear, food, and art supplies are the responsibility of the residents. Badlands offers reimbursement for all expenses up to $300. Any costs above $300 are the responsibility of the artist. Artists have access to the park library and computers and are required to present two sessions at a local school to introduce art and an interpretation of the Badlands to students. The park provides a government vehicle for transportation to school programs. The park also provides bicycles for artists' use. Each artist is asked to contribute a mutually agreed upon work of art that represents the residency within one year of completion. Artists are enrolled in the park's Volunteers in the Parks program and are covered by worker's compensation for any injuries incurred during the residency.

Facility Description
Applicants should be aware that weather conditions can be rough in the park, including blizzards, temperatures above one hundred degrees Fahrenheit, and high winds.

How to Apply
Send an SASE for a brochure. Submit your current résumé, a summary of your creative works, a statement of what you hope to gain from your residency and what you hope to incorporate into your classroom presentations, and up to three choices of beginning and end dates for your residency. Visual artists: Submit at least six 35 mm slides with title, medium, and image size (height and width); mark slides with your name and a number corresponding to your list; and indicate the top of the slide with a letter *T*. Slides should show only the actual work (backgrounds, mats, or frames should not be included). Writers: Submit no more than ten double-spaced, typewritten pages of your manuscript. Performing artists: Submit audio and video-tapes which are indexed to identify your five-minute segment for jury review.

Deadline
Fall residency: July 15. Spring residency: December 31.

Approximate Cost of Program
Transportation, meals, materials, and incidentals. Housing and reimbursement of up to $300 are provided.

BEMIS CENTER FOR CONTEMPORARY ARTS

724 South Twelfth Street, Omaha, Nebraska 68102-3202
Attention: Ree Schonlau, Residency Coordinator
Phone: (402) 341-7130; fax: (402) 341-9791
Web site: www.novia.net/bemis
Email: bemis@novia.net

Type of Facility/Award
Residency.

Who Can Apply
Visual artists.

Provisos
None listed.

Dates of Operation
Open year-round.

Location
The Bemis facility is housed in two urban warehouses and a half-block of open urban property in downtown Omaha, Nebraska.

History
Bemis Center for Contemporary Arts (originally titled Alternative Worksite) was established in 1981 by a group of artists in Omaha as a unique opportunity for ceramic artists. The major portion of the project took place at a functioning brick factory, the Omaha Brick Works. Between 1981 and 1984, more than one hundred artists came to work at the site, the direct outgrowth being the Bemis Center for Contemporary Arts—a nonprofit organization dedicated to supporting exceptionally talented visual artists of all types. It is supported by the efforts of private and corporate donors and public funding.

What They Offer
For three to six months, artists are provided with a well-equipped studio space, living accommodations, and a monthly stipend ranging from $200 to $1,000 per month. Part of the residency may be spent on a farm or in studios in the small, historically-preserved town of Brownville. The residency should be directed toward exploration and self-challenge rather than production for a possible show. Residents are expected to give an informal slide presentation of their work sometime during their stay and leave one piece of work done during the residency as a donation to the center. The artist and director together will select the piece to be donated. Ask about their summer programs at the Art Farm and the studios in Brownville.

Facility Description

The Bemis Center is located in a large warehouse. Space has been divided to form several studio apartments averaging 1,800 square-feet with twelve- to sixteen-foot ceilings. Each unit has good natural light, heating, air conditioning, a kitchen, and bath. Sculptors and ceramic artists receive slightly smaller studio apartments and share a 6,000-square-foot workspace on the ground floor. (Since this description was provided, the center has moved its base to another building one block away, adding a new sculpture facility and general offices. The old location now focuses on works by Midwest artists.) All work-related equipment is provided, as well as 200-, 100-, and 20-cubic-foot kilns, an overhead bridge crane, two forklifts, and welding equipment. Facilities include a woodshop with tools, ample metalworking equipment, the new sculpture facility, and a small photographic darkroom with film cameras and projectors, a videotape camera, and editing equipment. Access to printmaking equipment is also available. The center has a gallery that annually carries eight exhibitions of contemporary art in all media. Work from some of the residencies may be included in the shows. The center hosts receptions, performances, concerts, and lectures. The center houses a fine collection of books, videos, and magazines in the Clare Haas Howard Art Library.

How to Apply

Send an SASE or obtain an application from the Web site. Return the completed application with a $25 nonrefundable application fee, ten slides (labeled according to instructions) of work you have completed within the last two years, a list of three references who are authorities in your field and are familiar with your work, and a résumé. You may include any reviews, catalogs, or other support materials for the selection committee's evaluation, but they will not be returned. Include an adequate SASE for return of the slides.

Deadline

April 30 and September 30.

Approximate Cost of Program

$25 application fee, transportation, meals, materials, and incidentals—offset by $200–$1,000 monthly stipend.

BLUE SHORES   WI   **DISCONTINUED**

THE GOSHEN COLLEGE PEACE PLAY CONTEST IN

Goshen College, Goshen, Indiana 46526
Attention: Doug Liechty Caskey, Professor of Communication and Theater
Phone: (219) 535-7393; fax: (219) 535-7600
Web site: www.goshen.edu/communication/playcontest.shtm
Email: douglc@goshen.edu

Type of Facility/Award
Opportunity for playwrights.

Who Can Apply
Playwrights.

Provisos
The one-act play contest is open to everyone, but the college is especially interested in scripts from college students and historical peace churches. As the contest title suggests, plays with contemporary peace concerns are encouraged. Preference is given to plays that "present nonviolent alternatives, the tragedy of violence, or seek understanding and reconciliation across the boundaries that divide the human community."

Dates of Operation
October (even-numbered years only).

Location
Goshen, Indiana.

History
Goshen College is a Mennonite college. The contest is held every other year on even-numbered years. All winning plays have been produced by the college. Some have gone on to tour various off-campus settings.

What They Offer
The winning entry will receive a cash award of $500 and full production of the play.

Facility Description
The Umble Center at Goshen College. No details were provided.

How to Apply
Send an SASE for guidelines. Submit your one-act play, no longer than thirty minutes (with an adequate SASE for its return), to the address above before the deadline.

Deadline
December 31 (odd-numbered years). Notification around June 1.

Approximate Cost of Program
Not applicable for this listing.

THE GUEST HOUSE AT NEW LIGHT STUDIOS   WI

1610 Town Hall Road, Beloit, Wisconsin 53511
Attention: Rolf Lund, Proprietor
Phone: (608) 362-8055

Type of Facility/Award

Retreat.

Who Can Apply

Artists, writers, musicians, or anyone seeking solitude in a peaceful, rural setting.

Provisos

Best suited for those seeking a quiet, nurturing atmosphere.

Dates of Operation

Open year-round.

Location

Beloit is located two hours north of Chicago, an hour and a half southwest of Milwaukee, and forty-five minutes south of Madison, Wisconsin, at the interchange of highways 40 and 43. Take the VanGalder bus to Beloit from Chicago's O'Hare Airport. Transportation from the bus stop at Beloit College is available if prearranged.

History

The three hosts are working artists: a musician, a writer, and a sculptor. In 1992, they established the Guest House at New Light Studios as a retreat center for artists and writers seeking solitude. They have hosted large groups and teams of writers who work together, as well as countless others who have created a rich history of art.

What They Offer

Available year-round for periods of either one or two weeks, the Guest House is a self-sufficient cottage with two bedrooms, a kitchen, a bathroom with shower, and a living room. For the duration of their stay, guests enjoy use of the entire house, as well as local and long-distance phone calls. The hosts of the Guest House will be glad to help with arrangements and accommodations for exhibits or readings on the premises.

Facility Description

The house is one story with enough available seating for small readings or house concerts. It is equipped with cooking appliances, utensils, a refrigerator, a furnace, and a wood stove. Guests must supply their own food and should bring their own towels and bedding if possible. There are private guest rooms available down the road at the studio of another artist. Rooms have chalkboards, desks, and space for drawing or painting. Guests may enjoy a swim in the pool, a game of basketball or ping-pong, or a hike or drive through the countryside. Additionally, there are creeks nearby for canoeing, and the prairie provides an excellent place for cross-country skiing in the winter.

How to Apply

Send a sample of your work, an outline of how you plan to use your time there, the dates you can attend, and an SASE. The Guest House is booked on a first-come, first-served basis, but plan to book at least two months in advance.

Deadline

None.

Approximate Cost of Program

There is a nonrefundable deposit of $25, and the hosts accept donations in excess of that amount. In the past, the hosts have accepted paintings and readings as partial payment of guests' bills. Work exchange (practical things like painting the barn, gardening, etc.) is also an option if prearranged. If you go, plan on paying for your stay. Guests cover the costs of transportation, meals, materials, and incidentals.

INDIANA DUNES NATIONAL LAKESHORE   IN

Artist-in-Residence Program, 1100 N. Mineral Springs Rd., Porter, Indiana 46304
Attention: Elizabeth Hertel
Phone: (219) 926-7561 ext. 225
Web site: www.nps.gov/indu/arp.htm

Type of Facility/Award

Artist-in-residence program.

Who Can Apply

Visual artists, video artists, filmmakers, writers, poets, photographers, landscape architects, and others.

Provisos

None listed.

Dates of Operation

June through September.

Location

The park is located on Lake Michigan in the northern part of Indiana.

History

The program was founded on the belief that artistic endeavors and natural settings are intimately connected. For over a century, artists of all kinds have played a key role within the national park system, helping to record and preserve landscapes through their writings, photographs, paintings, and films. The Indiana Dunes National Lakeshore Artist-in-Residence Program has provided a place of both creative inspiration and natural beauty for a long, distinguished list of artists, including poet Carl Sandberg, painter Frank V. Dudley, and landscape architect Jens Jensen.

What They Offer

Two- to four-week residencies provide housing within the park in the form of either a house or a campsite. The resident house includes a furnished bedroom, lamps, housewares, and a kitchen fully equipped with appliances and utensils. Bed linens are not provided. The campsite offers restroom and shower facilities, paved roads, and a parking lot. Currently no stipend is provided, although a modest reimbursement for in-park travel may be available. In exchange for accommodations, participants are expected to donate a sample of their art to the park collection. The donation should accurately reflect the artist's style and her/his experience with the program. Artists must also be prepared to set aside a few hours of their time in the park to interact with interested patrons and staff members.

Facility Description

Dunes rise nearly two hundred feet above the southern shore of Lake Michigan. The lakeshore is surrounded by beach areas, marshes, swamps, and prairie remnants open for exploration. Historic sites include an 1822 homestead and a family farm erected around the turn of the century.

How to Apply

Send an SASE for a brochure and application. Submit the application with your current résumé (one to two pages); samples of your recent work (which may include 35 mm slides labeled with your name, half-inch VHS or $3/4$-inch u-matic videotape, or six copies of either a manuscript excerpt, short story, or poetry, not to exceed six pages); a statement concerning what you hope to achieve during your residency; a statement concerning what public activities you envision; a list of your residency preferences (be sure to include a specific length of time between two to four weeks as well as what housing accommodations you prefer, and specify three choices of actual dates you intend to complete your presentation or park program); and an adequate SASE for the return of submitted materials. Do not send original work or irreplaceable items.

Deadline

March 30.

Approximate Cost of Program

Transportation, meals, materials, and incidentals. A modest reimbursement of in-park travel costs may be provided.

ISLE ROYALE NATIONAL PARK   MI

800 East Lakeshore Drive, Houghton, Michigan 49931
Attention: Artist-in-Residence Program
Phone: (906) 482-8753
Email: ISRO_PARKINFO@nps.gov

Type of Facility/Award

Artist-in-residence program.

Who Can Apply

Writers, composers, and all visual and performing professional artists.

Provisos

Writers, composers, and all visual and performing professional artists whose work
can be influenced by the Northwoods wilderness are invited to apply. The directors
will consider all forms of art except those that manipulate or disturb the park's environment. Applicants should be self-sufficient, in good health, and well prepared.

Dates of Operation

Mid-June through mid-September.

Location

Isle Royale is an island wilderness in Lake Superior. It is forty-five miles long and
eight and a half miles wide. The park—fifteen miles from Grand Portage, Minnesota, seventy-three miles from Houghton, Michigan, and fifty-six miles from Copper Harbor, Michigan—has no roads. Transportation is by boat or foot.

History

"Isle Royale's cultural history includes prehistoric Native American copper mining,
lighthouses, fisheries, and maritime culture. Some of these resources are accessible
from Rock Harbor via 165 miles of maintained trails or by various boat services.
With Isle Royale's vast and varied cultural and natural resources, it presents itself as
the ideal place for creative endeavors. The solitude and serenity of the island inspire
creativity."

What They Offer

Each year four to five artists are selected for a two- to three-week residency period.
Artists are housed in a rustic cabin (former summer residence of the Dassler family)
in Tobin Harbor, two miles by boat or trail from the park's major development at
Rock Harbor. The cabin sleeps two. A guest house at the site can serve as a work-
room and/or storage space. The accommodations are simple—a pit toilet and no
electricity or running water. Basic cooking equipment, bedding, and fuel are provided, but the artist needs to bring personal gear, food, and art supplies. Food for the
entire stay needs to be purchased before the trip. A canoe is provided for transporta-

tion. Expect cool temperatures, solitude, and simplicity. Isle Royal is a remote wilderness and all visitors must be well prepared. The artist should be self-sufficient and in good health. Selection is based on artistic integrity, ability to reside in a wilderness environment, a willingness to donate a finished piece of work inspired on the island, and the artist's ability to relate and interpret the park through their work. Transportation to the island is provided at no cost to the artist on the *Ranger III*, a 165-foot ship operating out of Houghton, Michigan.

Facility Description
The island is quite picturesque with its wave-washed shores, boreal forests of spruce and fir, miles of ridge and valley topography, fascinating mammals including wolves and moose, and colorful birds. Hundreds of interesting plants and wildflowers grow in the forests. Ninety-nine percent of the island is wilderness, which is designated an International Biosphere Reserve. The facility is not wheelchair accessible

How to Apply
Send an SASE for a brochure. Return the entry form with your résumé (one to two pages in length), a summary of your creative works, a statement explaining what you hope to achieve from a wilderness residency, preferred dates between June and early September (two to three weeks), and support materials. These may include 35 mm slides (in standard mounts and labeled according to instructions) of your recent work, an audio cassette, a video cassette, a manuscript excerpt, a short story, or an article. Include an adequate SASE for return of your support materials.

Deadline
February 16 (postmarked). Notification April 15.

Approximate Cost of Program
Transportation, meals, materials, and incidentals.

THE JOHN MICHAEL KOHLER ARTS CENTER　　　　　　　WI
608 New York Avenue, P.O. Box 489, Sheboygan, Wisconsin 53082-0489
Attention: Arts/Industry Coordinator
Phone: (414) 458-6144; fax: (414) 458-4473

Type of Facility/Award
Artist-in-residence program.

Who Can Apply
Visual artists (all disciplines).

Provisos
Applicants, whether emerging or established artists, need not be trained ceramists or metal sculptors. However, they must be capable of mastering industrial technologies

quickly once the residency begins. Artists may work in the pottery, the foundry/enamel shop, or both depending upon space availability.

Dates of Operation
Open year-round.

Location
The John Michael Kohler Arts Center is fifty miles north of Milwaukee and 150 miles north of Chicago in Sheboygan, Wisconsin, which is just five miles from the Kohler Company in the village of Kohler.

History
"Arts/Industry is undoubtedly the most unusual ongoing collaboration between art and industry in the United States. Conceived and administered by the John Michael Kohler Arts Center of Sheboygan, Wisconsin, the program makes industrial technologies and facilities available to artists through long-term residencies, short-term workshops, tours, and other programming so that they may further their artistic explorations. Major funding is provided by Kohler Company and the National Endowment for the Arts." The program generally serves four resident artists at a time, supporting approximately fifteen artists per year. Since its inception in 1974, the Arts/Industry Program at Kohler has served hundreds of artists.

What They Offer
Residents may work in the Kohler Co. Pottery, iron and brass foundries, and the enamel shop to develop a number of projects.

Two- to six-month residencies include studio space accessible round-the-clock, free materials, use of equipment, technical assistance from industrial craftspeople and engineers, photographic services, housing, basic round-trip travel expenses within the continental United States, and a modest stipend for food, personal expenses, and shipping finished work. Housing includes a room in a furnished, four-bedroom house located near the site. Artists are encouraged to bring their own cars. Upon arrival, artists receive an extensive orientation on the use of professional industrial equipment. Tools and materials not normally used at the factory must be provided by the artists, who are asked to pay minimal amounts for the use of brass in excess of one hundred pounds and for "A-1" company products. Although all work produced during the residency belongs to the artist, residents are expected to donate one work each to both the John Michael Kohler Arts Center and to the Kohler Company. Much of the residency work is documented on 35 mm slides by the program. Artists receive a copy of the slide documentation. Additionally, artists are asked to give one day per month to educational activities such as slide lectures, video interviews, tours of their work space, or other activities.

Facility Description

The pottery: "The primary studio space for work in clay is located in the casting shop of Kohler Co.'s Pottery, the largest pottery in the world under one roof. Artists use a strong, off-white vitreous china clay which is once-fired in oxidation to 2400° F (cone 10). A kiln fired to 2100° F (cone 5) is also available. The clay is superb for slip casting and carving but is less effective for throwing and hand building. It is in slip form and is piped under pressure to the artist's studio space. Artists use plaster to make their own molds for slip-casting their work. Discarded production molds and ware also can be utilized. Cast pieces can be assembled in various ways before or after firing. Even the plaster is sometimes used to create sculpture. Artists are encouraged to experiment with the range of glaze possibilities. Color variations may be made by adding ceramic stains (no oxides) to a variety of clear and white glaze bases. Kohler Co. has an extensive Research and Development Laboratory where artists are able to develop glazes."

The iron foundry: "The Kohler Co. Iron Foundry, the largest in Wisconsin, allows artists to cast or free-pour iron shapes. Artists may create their own patterns and molds, use production discards, or incorporate scrap metal into their work. An array of materials is available for making patterns, including wood, plaster, clay, metal, urethane, Styrofoam, and found objects. Artists may use pep-set, green sand, or natural sand for making molds and cores. Enamel-base iron is used for casting. Welding and cutting facilities may also be used at certain times. Artists working in the Iron Foundry may have periodic access to the Brass Die Cast area where they may cast forms in brass using pep-set or greensand molds. At times, they may also add sprayed metal surfaces to the iron. Carpentry shops are available for fabricating supports, patterns, and armatures."

The enamel shop: "The Enamel Shop allows artists to use enamel powders directly on red-hot cast iron in single or multiple applications. The Enamel Shop contains 36 large enameling ovens; the use of one oven is usually reserved for artists. The Enamels Laboratory allows artists to experiment with and test the brilliant vitreous enamels available. Past artists-in-residence have developed liquid and paste enamels for use on somewhat cooler iron and with a variety of stencils."

How to Apply

Send an SASE for an application and brochure. Return completed application with a current résumé; twenty slides of your recent work, packaged and labeled according to instructions (slides will not be returned); catalogues, reviews, and/or other publications about your art; a cover letter describing the work you propose to undertake during your residency, reasons why the industrial facility is appropriate for your work, the extent of your experience with the materials and processes you wish to use, and a brief statement about your work (e.g. aesthetics, working methods); a list of three alternative residency periods, two to six months in duration, in order of your preference; and a page of six references. Drawings of the proposed work may be helpful but are not mandatory.

Deadline
August 1 (received) for residencies beginning the following year.

Approximate Cost of Program
Meals and incidentals—offset by stipend.

LAKESIDE ART AND CULTURE INTERNATIONAL   MI
DISCONTINUED

THE LAKESIDE STUDIO   MI
15486 Red Arrow Highway, Lakeside, Michigan 49116
Attention: John Wilson
Phone: (616) 469-1377; fax: (616) 469-1101
Web site: www.members.tripod.com/lakesideGAL/
Email: lakesidegal@triton.net

Type of Facility/Award
Artist-in-residence program.

Who Can Apply
Visual artists, particularly ceramists.

Provisos
None listed.

Dates of Operation
April through October.

Location
The studio is located in the most southwestern part of Michigan, one hour from Chicago.

History
Since 1968, Lakeside Studio has been the publisher of Limited Edition Prints. In 1987, the studio inaugurated its international artist-in-residence program, with an emphasis on ceramic work. The Lakeside Gallery exhibits a wide collection of residential work, along with a variety of current exhibitions.

What They Offer
Residencies of up to three months include studio space and housing. Studios can be rented daily ($20), weekly ($100), monthly ($375), or tri-monthly ($1000). A stu-

dio apartment can also be rented daily ($20), weekly ($100), or monthly ($350) and comes complete with a kitchen and living room.

Facility Description

Work done at the studio is mostly ceramic, but facilities can also accommodate painting. Wheels, kilns (electric and gas), salt firing, clay mixing, and a glaze room are provided. There is a gallery show at the end of the residency.

How To Apply

Send an SASE for an application and brochure. Submit your completed application with eight slides of your current work (with a catalog or reviews), a description of your proposed project, and your desired time period.

Deadline

At least two months in advance of desired dates for residency.

Approximate Cost of Program

Transportation, rent, meals, materials, and incidentals.

THE LOFT-McKNIGHT AWARDS   MN

The Loft Literary Center, 66 Malcolm Avenue Southeast, Minneapolis, Minnesota 55414
Attention: McKnight Fellowships for Writers
Phone: (612) 379-8999; fax: (612) 951-4423
Web site: www.loft.org
Email: loft@loft.org

Type of Facility/Award

Fellowship.

Who Can Apply

Writers of creative prose and poetry.

Provisos

Applicants must have been legal residents of Minnesota for twelve months prior to application. Past winners of the Loft-McKnight Awards may not reapply in the same genre. Past winners of the Loft-McKnight Award of Distinction may not reapply. Applicants may only apply for one award—the Loft-McKnight Award or the Loft-McKnight Award of Distinction. Those applying for the Award of Distinction must have published at least one book or three stories in at least two different magazines.

Dates of Operation

Not applicable in this listing.

Location
Not applicable in this listing.

History
"The Loft-McKnight Awards and the Loft-McKnight Awards of Distinction were created to provide Minnesota writers of demonstrated ability with an opportunity to work for a concentrated period of time on their writing."

What They Offer
"The Loft offers two types of awards in the McKnight Artist Fellowships for Writers program: the $10,000 Loft Awards in Poetry and Creative Prose and the $20,000 Loft Awards of Distinction in poetry and creative prose. The five Loft Awards will be given to two poets and three prose writers. Creative prose includes fiction and literary nonfiction, such as a memoir, autobiography or personal essay. These fellowships do not support nonfiction, technical or playwriting." Awards of Distinction rotate annually between poetry and prose. Winners are paid in equal monthly installments and their work is published in an anthology, with editorial input from Graywolf Press, and distributed to agents and publishers throughout the country, as well as Minnesota schools and libraries.

Facility Description
Not applicable in this listing.

How to Apply
Send an SASE for application guidelines. Follow the detailed instructions provided. There is a nonrefundable $10 processing fee for nonmembers.

Deadline
Mid-November. Deadline may vary.

Approximate Cost of Program
$10 application fee, if a nonmember.

THE MILTON CENTER'S POST GRADUATE FELLOWSHIPS   KS
The Milton Center, Kansas Newman College, 3100 McCormick Avenue,
    Wichita, Kansas 67213-2097
Attention: Esie Sappenfield
Phone: (316) 942-4291 ext. 326 or (800) 736-7585; fax: (316) 942-4483
Web site: www.ksnewman.edu
Email: miltonc@newmanu.edu

Type of Facility/Award
Fellowship.

Who Can Apply
Writers of fiction and nonfiction.

Provisos
Christian writers only.

Dates of Operation
Academic year (September through May).

Location
Wichita, Kansas.

History
The Milton Center was founded in 1986 to "support work by writers who seek to animate the Christian imagination, foster intellectual imagination, and explore the human condition with honesty and compassion." The fellowship, first granted for the 1994/95 academic year, was designed to give Christian writers an opportunity to complete their first book-length manuscript of fiction or poetry.

What They Offer
The center provides living expenses (housing is not prearranged) and a stipend of $11,000 that is disbursed over nine months. Two fellowships are awarded each year. In exchange, fellows will work no more than ten hours each week at the center, helping with the newsletter, planning conferences, etc. Peer review of manuscripts in progress is available. The fellow is also invited to become part of the worshipping community at Kansas Newman College while in residence. Fellows will have the opportunity to work with writing mentors as well.

Facility Description
College campus. Fellows arrange for their own living accommodations.

How to Apply
Send an SASE for an application and brochure. Return your completed application with a $15 nonrefundable application fee, a résumé, three letters of reference, a two- or three-page book proposal, two sample chapters or ten poems, and a one-page statement explaining what you aim to accomplish at the Milton Center. None of these items will be returned to you.

Deadline
March 1.

Approximate Cost of Program
$15 application fee, transportation, meals, materials, and incidentals—offset by $11,000 stipend.

NEW YORK MILLS ARTS RETREAT   MN

24 North Main Avenue, P.O. Box 246, New York Mills, Minnesota 56567
Attention: Eric Graham
Phone: (218) 385-3339; fax: (218) 385-3366
Web site: www.kulcher.org
Email: nymills@uslink.net

Type of Facility/Award

Artist-in-residence program.

Who Can Apply

Writers, poets, musicians, and artists.

Provisos

The New York Mills Arts Retreat focuses on support for emerging artists. Applicants may not have an extensive list of previous grants and awards. They should be at a developing stage in their arts career, committed to a life in the arts, and under-recognized.

Dates of Operation

September through December and January through May. Summer residencies are sometimes available.

Location

The town of New York Mills, Minnesota (population 900) is situated among the 1000 lakes of Otter Tail County and is located along the Continental Divide.

History

"The New York Mills Arts Retreat was once a working dairy farm surrounded by cornfields and cows. Now it's a country retreat for writers, poets, musicians, and artists, and it's still surrounded by cornfields and cows. The purpose of the Arts Retreat is to provide residents a peaceful, rural setting for their work while they share their creativity with the community. Resident artists have taken portraits of the townspeople, taught in the local school systems, and even composed a symphony about the town."

What They Offer

Four to seven artists are accepted during each nine-month residency season. Two-week residencies include a $750 stipend. Four-week residencies include a $1,500 stipend. Residents receive room and board in a small house, which was recently renovated, and studio space. Each artist is scheduled to spend up to eight hours per week interacting within the community.

Facility Description

The main studio space, located at the regional cultural center, is a large, bright room with lots of natural light that is good for painting and writing but not suited to sculpture. Other studio spaces are available. The house for visiting artists includes cooking facilities, one bedroom, and a modest amount of studio space. Artists sometimes stay at the Whistle Stop Inn, a bed and breakfast located in an old Victorian-style home in New York Mills. Artists may dine at the local cafe, and there is a small grocery store within walking distance of the retreat house.

How to Apply

Call or send an SASE for an application and brochure. Return the completed application along with your résumé, a description of your work, a condensed description of the purpose of the retreat, a community outreach plan, a sample of your work, and an adequate SASE if you want your work samples returned. Finalists are required to submit two letters of recommendation and additional work samples. Visual artists: Send twelve slides. Writers: Send a maximum of twelve pages. Musicians: Send a minimum of one cassette or CD. Filmmakers/videographers: Send a minimum of one cassette.

Deadline

April 1 (postmarked) for retreats from September through December. October 1 (postmarked) for retreats from January through May.

Approximate Cost of Program

Transportation, meals, materials, and incidentals—offset by stipend.

NEWBERRY LIBRARY   IL

60 West Walton Street, Chicago, Illinois 60610-3380
Attention: Committee on Awards
Phone: (312) 255-3666
Web site: www.newberry.org
Email: research@newberry.org

Type of Facility/Award

Fellowships.

Who Can Apply

Postdoctoral scholars, certain college instructors, women of Native American heritage, and others.

Provisos

Postdoctoral scholars; scholars holding a Ph.D. or equivalent; independent scholars who have demonstrated excellence in their field (appropriate to Newberry) through publications, etc.; certain college instructors; women of Native American heritage with at least an undergraduate degree; and others who might benefit from research in the library's holdings are invited to apply. See "What They Offer" below.

Dates of Operation
Each fellowship has its own timeline.

Location
Chicago, Illinois.

History
The Newberry Library was founded in 1887. It is an independent research library; admission is free, and it is open to the public. "In addition to developing and caring for its extensive collections, and serving the needs of individual scholars, the Newberry fosters the productive use of its resources by developing educational projects and centers where extended research is conducted by a community of scholars."

What They Offer
The Newberry Library offers research opportunities in the form of fellowships to scholars of various levels. Because each fellowship has its own award criteria, they are listed by name only. If you are interested in any of these fellowships, please contact the library directly.

- National Endowment for the Humanities Fellowships
- Lloyd Lewis Fellowships in American History
- Monticello College Foundation Fellowship for Women
- Mellon Postdoctoral Research Fellowship
- Spencer Foundation Fellowship in the History of Education
- Rockefeller Foundation Fellowship in Gender Studies in Early Modern Europe
- Newberry Library Short-term Fellowships
- Newberry Library/American Antiquarian Society Short-term Fellowship
- American Society for Eighteenth-Century Studies Fellowship
- Frances C. Allen Fellowship
- Arthur Weinberg Fellowship for Independent Scholars
- South Central Modern Language Association Fellowships
- The Audrey Lumsden-Kouvel Fellowship
- Lester J. Cappon Fellowship in Documentary Editing
- Short-term Fellowship in the History of Cartography
- Newberry/British Academy Fellowship for Study in Great Britain
- Herzog August Bibliothek Wolfenbüttel Fellowship
- Weiss/Brown Publication Subvention Award
- Ecole des Chartes Exchange Fellowship

Facility Description

The library houses more than one and a half million volumes and five million manuscripts in the humanities. The Newberry's collections concern the civilizations of Western Europe and the Americas from the late Middle Ages to the early twentieth century. Bibliographic holdings are extensive and certain special collections are internationally noted.

How to Apply

Send an SASE for a *Fellowships in the Humanities* brochure. Then write for additional information on specific fellowships.

Deadline

Each fellowship has its own deadline.

Approximate Cost of Program

Each fellowship has its own stipend/award provisions.

NIANGUA COLONY   MO   **DISCONTINUED**

NORCROFT: A WRITING RETREAT FOR WOMEN   MN

32 E. 1st Street, Duluth, Minnesota 55802
Attention: Tracy Gilsrik
Phone: (218) 727-5199; fax: (218) 727-3119

Type of Facility/Award

Artist-in-residence program.

Who Can Apply

Women writers.

Provisos

Norcroft is a feminist endeavor with feminist-funded projects. The application process anticipates work that is respectful toward and supportive of women. Applicants must be at least twenty-one years of age.

Dates of Operation

May through October.

Location

Norcroft is located roughly ninety miles northeast of Duluth, Minnesota, on the shores of Lake Superior.

History

"Founder Joan Drury has spent countless hours benefiting from the splendor of this location and established Norcroft as part of her ongoing commitment to providing more choices and opportunities for women and enabling feminist social change."

What They Offer
Residencies range in duration from one to four weeks. Each artist is provided with her own bedroom and a shed for writing and meditating. Each shed comes with a desk, chair, dictionary, thesaurus, and rocking chair. A fully-stocked kitchen is also supplied in an area shared by resident artists.

Facility Description
Norcroft's main lodge is surrounded by ten acres of woods and was built over fifty years ago.

How To Apply
Call or write for an application.

Deadline
October 1.

Approximate Cost of Program
Transportation, materials, and incidentals. Room and board are provided.

NORTHWOOD UNIVERSITY   MI
Alden B. Dow Creativity Center Fellowships
3225 Cook Road, Midland, Michigan 48640-2398
Phone: (517) 837-4478 or (517) 837-4468
Email: creativity@northwood.edu

Type of Facility/Award
Fellowship.

Who Can Apply
People working in all disciplines and areas of interest, including the arts, sciences, and humanities, are invited to apply.

Provisos
The structure of the program requires that artists possess the maturity to work independently and live cooperatively. International citizens are invited to apply, provided they can communicate in written and spoken English. The center is looking for new and innovative ideas that have the potential for impact in their field. No creative area will be overlooked when a project idea may result in a significant advance.

Dates of Operation
Mid-June through mid-August.

Location

The Alden B. Dow Creativity Center is located in the Saginaw Valley area of central Michigan, about 125 miles north of Detroit.

History

Alden B. Dow was born in Midland, Michigan, in 1904, the son of Grace A. and Herbert Henry Dow, founder of the Dow Chemical Company. He studied mechanical engineering and earned a degree in architecture. He studied and worked with Frank Lloyd Wright at Taliesin in Wisconsin. Dow returned to Midland and opened his own architectural offices in a studio/home of his own design. He was commissioned to design many homes, churches, schools, college campuses, business complexes, art and civic centers, and one entire town. Dow received many awards and honors, including the 1937 Diplome de Grand Prix for residential architecture, a fellowship from the American Institute of Architects, an honorary doctorate from Northwood Institute in 1969, and in 1982, he became the first recipient of the Frank Lloyd Wright Creativity Award. In 1983, he was named architect laureate of his home state of Michigan.

The Northwood Institute was founded in 1959 by Drs. Arthur E. Turner and R. Gary Stauffer. With Mr. Dow, they shared a devotion to quality and innovation. In 1978, they founded the Creativity Center to encourage individual creativity and to preserve the work and philosophy of Alden B. Dow.

What They Offer

Four ten-week fellowships are awarded annually and include travel to and from Midland. Expenses for international artists will be covered from their point of entry into the continental U.S. Fellows are encouraged to drive in order to have a car available. If fellows travel by air, some shipping expenses may be assumed by the center. Residents are housed in large, furnished apartments and receive board through a per diem allowance. Weekday lunches are provided at the Creativity Center. A stipend of $750 is provided for each awardee to be applied to the cost of project materials, travel during the summer, or incidental expenses. No at-home expenses are covered. Families and pets cannot be accommodated. Upon completion of the residency, fellows make oral presentations about their projects to a selected audience including Creativity Center board members, evaluators, Northwood University staff, and invited guests.

Facility Description

Northwood University's Alden B. Dow Creativity Center provides residents with individual apartments in a wooded environment. Each apartment is furnished and has a fully-equipped kitchen. Laundry facilities are available on campus.

How to Apply

Send for a brochure and application guidelines. The center begins considering applications in the fall of each year. In addition to a project proposal (maximum two pages), submit a cover page containing your name, address, and telephone number. Also include a $10 nonrefundable application fee, a list of facilities and equipment you would request the Creativity Center to provide, a résumé, three references (with contact information), and any materials that would aid in the evaluation of your project—such as writing samples, slides, or tapes. Enclose an adequate SASE for return of materials.

Deadline

December 31 (postmarked). Notification by April 1.

Approximate Cost of Program

$10 application fee, materials, and incidentals—offset by $750 stipend.

OX-BOW: A SUMMER SCHOOL OF ART AND ARTIST'S RESIDENCY   MI

Saugatuck, Michigan
Phone: (616) 857-5811

Winter Address/Administration/Applications:

The School of the Art Institute of Chicago, Ox-Bow, 37 South Wabash, Room 35,
    Chicago, Illinois 60603
Attention: Professional Artists Residency Program
Phone: (800) 318-3019; fax: (312) 899-1453
Email: oxbow@artic.edu

Type of Facility/Award

Artist-in-residence program.

Who Can Apply

Professional and practicing visual artists.

Provisos

Applicants should enjoy working in a secluded, natural environment unencumbered by the outside world. Students are ineligible.

Dates of Operation

June through August.

Location

Ox-Bow is between Lake Michigan and the Kalamazoo River near Saugatuck, just three hours from Chicago. The nearest airport is in Grand Rapids. Bus and train services run through the area. Ox-Bow itself provides parking for those who bring their cars.

History

Founded in 1910, Ox-Bow is a nonprofit artists' colony and summer school operating in association with the School of the Art Institute of Chicago. "The mission of Ox-Bow, in keeping with its history, is to sustain a haven for nurturing the creative process, through instruction, example, and community. Ox-Bow provides professional and amateur artists with lifelong learning opportunities, and offers accredited instruction to degree-seeking students. Ox-Bow seeks to foster an appreciation of art in the surrounding community, while preserving the natural environment that has energized Ox-Bow since its founding."

What They Offer

Residencies are for one week only. They start on Sunday afternoon and end on Saturday morning, without exception. Room and board are provided for $380, which must be paid upon arrival. Residents are encouraged to present a slide lecture of their work and to participate in discussions.

Facility Description

Working facilities include a large studio (with northern light) for painting and drawing. There are separate studios for papermaking, glassblowing, ceramics, and printmaking. There is also an open-air studio for sculpture. Ox-Bow's inn provides dining and housing. The dining hall, a lecture room, the gallery, and two large screened-in porches are located on the first floor. Upstairs are the shared guest rooms and bathrooms with showers.

How to Apply

Send an SASE for an application and brochure. Return your application with ten slides of your current work, a letter of intent on use of the residency, and a current résumé.

Deadline

May 5.

Approximate Cost of Program

$380 plus transportation, materials, and incidentals.

PEWABIC POTTERY MI

Pewabic Society, Inc., 10125 East Jefferson Avenue, Detroit, Michigan 48214
Attention: Susan Beiner, Director of Education
Phone: (313) 822-0954 ext. 17; fax: (313) 822-6266
Web site: www.pewabic.com
Email: pewabic@pewabic.com

Type of Facility/Award
Artist-in-residence program.

Who Can Apply
Ceramic artists.

Provisos
None listed.

Dates of Operation
Open year-round.

Location
Detroit, Michigan.

History
"Founded in 1903 during the height of the Arts and Crafts Movement in America, Pewabic Pottery is today a nonprofit organization dedicated to the preservation of the Arts and Crafts ideals while advancing contemporary ceramic arts through its full curriculum of educational programs, its support of individual artists, outreach to various communities, and leadership in the exhibition of contemporary and historic collections and archiving of scholarly research."

What They Offer
At the core of the program is the belief that an exchange of ideas and knowledge within a supportive environment helps to inspire the creativity and growth of the residents and others who work at the pottery. The twelve-month residency includes studio space, clay, glazes, firing, and access to kilns and equipment. A resource committee of professionals periodically reviews studio work in progress and offers critical guidance. Residents work at the pottery at least sixteen hours each week doing gallery or design work, work in tile and vessel production, or teaching. Residents are expected to allocate at least twenty-four hours each week to individual studio time. The residency culminates with an exhibit of work at Pewabic Pottery and at area galleries.

Facility Description
Studios are located in a historic firehouse equipped with tables, a slab roller, electric kilns, and storage. Gas, wood, and soda kilns are available at the main building.

How to Apply
Send an SASE for a brochure. Submit your résumé, twenty slides (and an adequate SASE for their return), a letter of intent stating your personal goals and interest in the program, and two letters of recommendation (sent directly to Pewabic by their authors). For more information, contact Susan Beiner, Director of Education.

Deadline
April 30.

Approximate Cost of Program
Transportation, housing, meals, and incidentals—offset by wage.

PICTURED ROCKS NATIONAL LAKESHORE   MI
Artist-in-Residence Program, P.O. Box 40, N 8391 Sand Point Road, Munising,
    Michigan 49862-0040
Phone: (906) 387-3700
Web site: www.nps.gov.piro

Type of Facility/Award
Artist-in-residence program.

Who Can Apply
Visual artists.

Provisos
Professional two-dimensional visual artists whose work can be influenced and enhanced by the superb Lake Superior coastal scene are encouraged to apply.

Dates of Operation
September and October.

Location
The park is located in the central Upper Peninsula of Michigan on Lake Superior and stretches forty-two miles along the southern coast between Munising and Grand Marais. The Upper Peninsula's largest city, Marquette, is located forty miles west of the park.

History
"Begun in 1996, the inaugural Artist-in-Residence year, the program provides artists the opportunity to capture the many moods of Pictured Rocks National Lakeshore in their particular medium."

What They Offer
The park offers a rent-free park residence for up to four weeks during the months of September and October. Limited reimbursement is available for in-park mileage and

other out-of-pocket expenses incurred during the artist's stay. In return, artists are asked to contribute an example of their work and provide a minimum of two interpretive programs which will help advance the park's mission. Residents will be enrolled in the National Park Service Volunteer in Parks Program which provides advantages to both parties, including compensation for work related injuries. The artist should bring personal gear, food, and supplies. Art and photo supplies may be available in Marquette.

Facility Description

The topography ranges from towering sandstone cliffs, rising some two hundred feet above Lake Superior, to upland beech-maple forests. At the east end of the park, the Grand Sable Dunes suggest a moonscape that harbors unique vegetation while other areas hold large wetlands. The lakeshore is studded with inland lakes and rushing trout streams.

Artists may choose from three options for their accommodations. Final approval rests with the park staff depending on other staff housing needs. Sullivan's Creek Cabin is located along Twelvemile Beach. This rustic 1940s cabin has photovoltaic powered lights, gas appliances, a fireplace, running water, two bedrooms, and a bath. Phones are not provided. Sand Point Residence is located adjacent to park headquarters, Sand Point beach and Marsh Trail. The small 1950s-era house has a kitchen, living room, bath, and three bedrooms. There is no phone, but one can be installed at the artist's expense. The Grand Marais Dorm is a former U.S. Coast Guard station on Canal Street in Grand Marais.

How to Apply

Send an SASE for a brochure. Send the following items contained in a single envelope: your résumé (maximum two pages), no more than eight slides of your recent work that best convey your style and ability, a list of the size and media of your work samples, a statement of what you hope to gain from the residency with a specific explanation of how you propose to assist the lakeshore to further its mission, your preferred accommodation, and an adequate SASE for return of the slides.

Deadline

December 31 (postmarked).

Approximate Cost of Program

Transportation, meals, and incidentals.

THE PLAYWRIGHTS' CENTER   MN

2301 Franklin Avenue East, Minneapolis, Minnesota 55406-1099
Attention: Playwright Services Director
Phone: (612) 332-7481; fax: (612) 332-6037

Type of Facility/Award
Fellowships/grants. Opportunities for playwrights.

Who Can Apply
Playwrights.

Provisos
All applicants must be U.S. citizens. For some of the awards listed below, applicants must also be residents of Minnesota.

Dates of Operation
Open year-round.

Location
Minneapolis, Minnesota.

History
"Since 1971 the Playwrights' Center has fueled the contemporary theater by providing services that support the development and public appreciation of playwrights and playwriting. The Center is committed to artistic excellence; playwright initiative and leadership; the practice of cultural pluralism; the discovery of emerging artists; advocacy of playwrights' work; and new visions of theatre."

What They Offer
The center offers a number of fellowships, grants, and opportunities for playwrights.

The Jerome Fellowships: The center annually awards five emerging American playwrights fellowships of $7,200 each. Fellows spend a year in residence developing their skills through readings, workshops, and developmental programs.

Many Voices: This program serves writers of color with culturally focused playwriting roundtables, multicultural collaboration grants, and residencies.

The McKnight Advancement Grants: Minnesota playwrights may apply for these $8,500 grants (three are awarded annually), which are intended to significantly advance the recipients' art and careers. Winners are allowed access to the center's developmental programs. In exchange, they must participate in the center's educational outreach program.

The McKnight Fellowships: Each year, two American playwrights whose work has made a significant impact on contemporary theater are each awarded $10,000. Additionally, fellows spend a month in residence at the center participating in its developmental programs and contributing to the artistic community.

PlayLabs: These intensive workshops provide thirty to forty hours for the development of four or more unproduced, unpublished scripts by American playwrights. Playwrights refine scripts with professional directors, dramaturges, and actors. Each play receives a public reading followed by an optional audience discussion.

Young Playwrights Summer Conference: Student writers between the ages of fourteen and eighteen create original stage plays and screenplays in a lively, supportive environment with a faculty of nationally recognized playwrights and theater professionals, including staff from the conference cosponsor, Hamline University. No previous playwriting experience is necessary. Students receive on-going mentorship and support through a one-year membership in the Playwrights Center.

Detailed information about each of these programs can be obtained by sending an SASE to the center during the months specified below.

Facility Description
Theater center.

How to Apply
Send an SASE for an application form and brochure. Applications for the Jerome Fellowships are available each year in July. Many Voices applications for grants and residencies are available each year in July. The McKnight Advancement Grants applications are available each year in December. Applications for the McKnight Fellowships are available each year in November. PlayLabs applications are available each year in October. YPSC applications are available each year in December.

Approximate Cost of Program
Transportation, housing, meals, materials, and incidentals—some offset by fellowship or grant awards.

PUDDING HOUSE WRITERS RESOURCE CENTER   OH
60 N. Main Street, Johnstown, Ohio 43031
Attention: Jennifer Bosveld, President
Phone: (740) 967-6060
Web site: www.puddinghouse.com
Email: pudding@johnstown.net

Type of Facility/Award
Retreat and residency.

Who Can Apply
Poets and writers.

Provisos

None listed.

Dates of Operation

Open year-round.

Location

Pudding House is twenty miles northeast of downtown Columbus and Ohio State University, and fourteen miles southeast of I-71 on State Route 37 at its crossroads with U.S. 62.

History

Pudding House Publications started in Columbus, Ohio, in 1979 as an outgrowth of Jennifer Bosveld's writing workshops and various poetry involvements in central Ohio. In 1987, Jennifer and her husband Jim added Pudding House Writers Resource Center to the already existing Pudding House Publications, Pudding House Bed and Breakfast for Writers, and the Pudding House Writers Workshops.

What They Offer

Any writer can stay at the regular rate. Writers must apply in order to be granted writer-in-residence status. Rooms are equipped with a desk. Writers have access to an electronic typewriter and all the paper they can use while at the house. The house provides many comfortable spaces to read, write, and edit. There is a fireplace in the gathering room, a dining room for casual dining, a wonderful library, a guest computer available by appointment, and a spoken word audio library. One-on-one consultations for writers of various abilities working in any genre are offered. Each guest has kitchen privileges. Guests are expected to spend one hour per day performing a household service.

Facility Description

Pudding House is a stately, twelve-room home one block from Johnstown's old town hall, public library, post office, restaurants, laundromat, drugstore, and other conveniences. Two blocks away is a community park. The house is fifteen minutes from Denison University in Granville and Otterbein College in Westerville, seven minutes from Morris Woods State Nature Preserve, and ten minutes from Hoover Reservoir (for boating and fishing). The house is on two bike paths. Antiques are abundant in Sunbury, Granville, and New Albany, all within about twelve minutes. Johnstown also has a large antique mall, and Jennifer and Jim are antique dealers. Pudding House has a twenty-four-hour writer's workshop (and a wonderful library) on the premises where you can type, work on revisions and submissions, research, read, and purchase books and writers' supplies.

How to Apply

Call for reservations or send an SASE for information about the writer-in-residence program. Reservations are made based on availability. If you are applying for a residency, send six to ten pages of your poetry or prose, a literary résumé or bio, and a letter explaining why you wish to attend. Explain how you would like to use your time and what you could do as a volunteer for one hour a day while you are in residence (gardening, weeding, landscaping, painting, cleaning, repairs, filing, Web site management, computer work, etc.).

Deadline

None.

Approximate Cost of Program

$100 a week plus meals, transportation, materials, and incidentals.

RAGDALE FOUNDATION   IL

1260 North Green Bay Road, Lake Forest, Illinois 60045
Phone: (847) 234-1063; fax: (847) 234-1075
Web site: nsn.nslsilus.org/lfkhome/ragdale
Email: ragdale1@aol.com

Type of Facility/Award

Residency.

Who Can Apply

Writers, composers, visual artists, playwrights, and screenwriters.

Provisos

None listed.

Dates of Operation

Early January through April 30. June 1 through December 15.

Location

Thirty miles north of Chicago near Lake Michigan, Ragdale is accessible from O'Hare International Airport by limousine service and by rail through Chicago with a transfer to the Metra Kenosha commuter line to Lake Forest.

History

Ragdale is on the National Register of Historic Places. Ragdale House and the Barnhouse were designed and built in 1897 by Howard Van Doren Shaw, a leader in American Arts and Crafts architecture. The Shaw family later established a haven for artists by creating an outdoor theater on the grounds and staging productions for the enjoyment of their friends and the community. In 1976, Shaw's granddaughter, Alice

Ragdale Foundation
Screenwriting

April Dammann

Ten years ago J spent time at a colony for women writers on Whidbey Jsland in Washington State. J packed up my laptop, printer and warm duds and left my husband and two children for a 3-week retreat to complete a screenplay. The experi-

ence of quiet solitude and the creativity it spawned convinced me to seek out other such retreats. J discovered then and subsequently (in very productive stays at Ragdale in Lake Forest, Jllinois) that few screenwriters attend artists' colonies. J think we are a fairly paranoid bunch; leaving L.A. for 3 or 4 weeks, no matter that there is a reasonable expectation of returning with a finished script, puts one out of the loop. Agents go a little crazy when a client is ensconced in a mysterious "colony" with other artists far from home. What, they wonder, goes on there?

What goes on is unique to each writer or artist, but J can say this: at Ragdale my work was treated with the utmost respect; J was given the freedom to create in an almost painfully beautiful environment; and the other residents — my fellow co-conspirators in the creation of art — became my friends. That the Ragdale Foundation would offer me a private room in a mansion for a month on Lake Forest's Shaw Prairie at almost no expense to myself, moves me profoundly. All for the purpose of doing what J love most: writing.

One stay and J was hooked. The place is highly selective but equally welcoming to new, emerging and established writers and artists. J read a short description of Ragdale in Gail Bowler's Artists & Writers Colonies and decided to apply, because J had spent a good part of my childhood in Chicago. So far, J've been the only screenwriter in residence during my stays. And the only California girl.

The Ragdale experience has become so precious to me, that I cannot imagine a time when I will not want to return. I have walked the historic meadow and prairie in deep winter and in spring, as every living thing — from the lowest weed to the highest-soaring bird — reaches for the light. The light at Ragdale has inspired my writing. Infused it. As a writer for the screen, I am as concerned with image as I am with language. At Ragdale the confluence of river, lake, tree, sky and grass just beyond my Barnhouse window reminds me that every story is placed somewhere. For me Ragdale embodies the power of place. I have completed two screenplays there: An Un-American Childhood and Heart of my Heart. In both pieces, the settings take on the significance of another character. The peace and grace of Ragdale are in my work.

One certainly feels an obligation to give something back to places like Ragdale. I led writing workshops for seniors and Lake Forest High students while in residence. I would do it again, in a minute. I completed a 3-week retreat in October. This time I worked on a full-length stage play, The Man Upstairs. Once again, I gave myself over to the charms of the two magnificent houses, the town, the folks who run Ragdale and keep it humming. For the curious literary agents and other who ask, "why go there?" I need only compare daily life in my office in Hollywood to the sweet, uninterrupted quiet of the artists' colony. Happily, I can have both.

Judson Hayes, created the Ragdale Foundation; in 1980, the foundation, formally incorporated and tax-exempt, bought back the barn and expanded Ragdale to accommodate twelve residents.

What They Offer

Ragdale offers residencies for two weeks, four weeks, six weeks, or eight weeks, beginning on either the first or fifteenth of each month. The Ragdale House can accommodate twelve artists at a time. For six nights a week, residents are provided with an evening meal. Breakfast and lunch supplies are stocked in communal kitchens, allowing residents to set their own schedules. The foundation sponsors readings, concerts, workshops, art exhibitions, and seminars in poetry and fiction writing. Additionally, the Frances Shaw Fellowship is offered for women writers whose serious work began after the age of fifty-five. Other fellowships are available when funding allows. There is currently assistance available for artists from twelve under-served

Ragdale Foundation
Musical Composition

Morgan Powell

Arriving at Ragdale for the first time in 1991, I was struck by the beautiful and affluent area of Lake Forest spilling over with mansions and limos. My first thought was that I would be stopped, questioned, and escorted out of town. Not the case. The Foundation itself, it turns out, is well-respected and supported by everyone in town, regardless of tax bracket.

I was likewise impressed by the way in which the staff introduced its residents to the world that is Ragdale. We were handed sheets of paper with simple drawings and writings explaining basic information: where the studio was, what time we ate — and not much else. Other answers I needed came from either staff or other residents with previous Ragdale experience. It was a pleasant way to meet the other people and it really set the tone for me. I knew this place would give me the hands-off freedom I needed to work on my music.

While strolling the grounds a short time later, taken in by the remote, quiet openness and beauty of the setting, I remember finally thinking, quite simply, "I can actually work here." To the west were a prairie and miles of foot paths that passed through meadows and woods, and ran along a creek — places to wander during those times away from pen and paper.

I have returned to Ragdale since that initial visit, spending many more enjoyable hours sitting on the porch of the Friends Studio, smoking a cigar, having a cocktail, and watching a bird fly from tree to tree while my colleagues played croquet below. Inside, the building is divided into two studios — the smaller being primarily used by composers. I have spent a lot of time there pinning pre-compositional charts and drawings to its sky-lit walls, and scattering books, papers, pens, and erasers over its tables. There is even a beautiful grand piano attended to by an old school technician. He tunes it entirely by ear over the course of several hours, resulting in the richest sound you could imagine.

The larger studio is normally used by visual artists, but the new music ensemble, Tone Road Ramblers, of which I am a member, rehearses there during annual residencies. We use the space now to talk, construct forms, improvise, and rehearse composed pieces — six to eight hours each day. The room is large enough for the six of us to spread out our instruments, including a large percussion set, stands, music, and mutes. And the acoustics are perfect for presenting informal concerts to an audience of residents, staff, and friends who crowd around the ensemble or climb into the loft — our Children of Paradise. From these residencies has come our latest CD, "Tone Road Ramblers: The Ragdale Years, 1994-1999," released on Einstein Records in February 2000.

Each of my residencies has had its own dynamic. There have been periods of intense focus when contact with other residents has been minimal. On other occasions, I've been entertained by boisterous frivolity or intrigued by serious discussion at the dinner table — discussion which has in turn contributed to the development of my work. It has always been a surprise and delight to discover the varied dynamics of the different groups gathered for each residency. The Foundation becomes a sort of microcosm of The Arts World.

As do other colonies, Ragdale provides that unworldly escape from everyday responsibilities which are, under normal living conditions, inescapable. It is a time of freedom and openness to dream, think, and work — all made possible through the work of an extraordinarily capable and wonderful staff who do their best to support each artist's needs and shield him or her from outside concerns.

states and for economically stressed artists from the Chicago area. (Separate brochures are available for these programs; send an SASE if you are interested.)

Facility Description

There are five available rooms in the Ragdale House for writers. The Barnhouse includes three rooms for writers and two rooms for visual artists. Both houses have large kitchens and living rooms for communal use, informal libraries, and laundry facilities. The Friend's Studio can accommodate two additional visual artists or one visual artist and one composer. All studios have plenty of working space and skylights. The beautifully landscaped property adjoins fifty-five acres of virgin prairie.

How to Apply
Send an SASE or email for an application and brochure. Ask for information on fee-waivers and special programs if you are interested. Return the completed application with your $20 nonrefundable application fee and the names and addresses of two references. Writers: Include four copies of a description of your proposed project (no longer than 250 words), four copies of a work sample (one short story, essay, chapter of a novel, act from a play or script, or ten poems) that is representative of the genre in which you intend to work, and one copy of a current résumé or vita. Manuscripts should include a cover sheet with your name, address, and title of the work submitted. Do not include an SASE—manuscripts will not be returned. Visual artists: Include one copy of a description of your proposed project (no longer than 250 words) indicating whether you have any special studio or equipment needs, one set of ten slides (packaged and labeled according to instructions) accompanied by a descriptive sheet, one copy of a current résumé or vita, and an SASE for return of materials. Composers: Include three copies of a description of your proposed project (no longer than 250 words) indicating whether you have any special studio or equipment needs, two identical sets of tapes and scores of one recent composition, one copy of a current résumé or vita, and an SASE. Other disciplines: Ragdale has limited space for performance artists, filmmakers, and choreographers. Call for details on applying in these disciplines.

Deadline
January 15 for residencies from June 1 through December 15; June 1 for residencies from January 2 through April 30.

Approximate Cost of Program
$20 plus transportation, materials, and incidentals. Full and partial fee waivers may be available. Full fellowships (with application) may be available.

ROPEWALK WRITERS RETREAT   IN
University of Southern Indiana, 8600 University Boulevard, Evansville, Indiana
  47712
Attention: Linda Cleek
Phone: (812) 464-1863 or (800) 467-8600; fax: (812) 465-7061
Web site: www.usi.edu/extserv/ropewalk
Email: lcleek@usi.edu

Type of Facility/Award
Retreat.

Who Can Apply

Most applicants are serious writers with at least some academic background and formal training. Undergraduate students are not encouraged to apply unless they are of a nontraditional age (twenty-five plus). All applicants must be at least eighteen.

Provisos

New Harmony, where the retreat is held, is a historic site and many of the buildings are not fully handicapped-accessible. Though most events are held in fully accessible facilities, anyone using a wheelchair is advised to call first.

Dates of Operation

June 11 through June 17.

Location

The retreat is held in New Harmony, Indiana, which is roughly thirty miles northwest of Evansville and the nearest airport. It is south of Interstate 64, about three hours from both Louisville, Kentucky, and St. Louis, Missouri.

History

RopeWalk was founded in 1989 to take advantage of the atmosphere of New Harmony and to encourage writers in the Midwest. Participants have come from across the country, but most are from Indiana, Illinois, Kentucky, Michigan, and Ohio.

What They Offer

RopeWalk is a week-long writers' retreat featuring workshops, conferences, lectures, and public readings. Writers participate in three group workshops and individual meetings with their workshop leaders. The retreat has a faculty of four to six nationally recognized writers. $435 tuition includes breakfasts and lunches; participants are responsible for suppers. Lodging ranges from $100–$500 for the week, and camping is available. A limited number of full and partial scholarships are awarded based on merit.

Facility Description

The Barn Abbey, a rustic retreat center, offers housing in bunk-bedded double rooms at $20 per night. A block of rooms are reserved at the New Harmony Inn and Conference Center.

How to Apply

Send an SASE for a brochure in February, or check the Web site.

Deadline

May 15. Scholarships April 15.

Approximate Cost of Program

$550–$950. Transportation, partial meal costs, materials, and incidentals.

SLEEPING BEAR DUNES NATIONAL LAKESHORE   MI

9922 Front Street, Empire, Michigan 49630-9797
Attention: Artist-in-Residence Program
Phone: (616) 326-5134

Type of Facility/Award

Artist-in-residence program.

Who Can Apply

American writers, composers, and visual artists.

Provisos

Artists must be healthy, self-sufficient, and able to work closely with the park rangers
to meet the goals of the residency.

Dates of Operation

The program operates twice a year in three-week blocks from September 12 through
October 2 and October 3 through October 23.

Location

The park includes fifty-seven kilometers of land along the east coast of Lake Michigan between the towns of Frankfort and Leland.

History

"The National Lakeshore's cultural history includes prehistoric use by American In-
dians, lake steamer fueling stations, logging, farming, commercial fishing, lighthouses,
U.S. Life-Saving Stations, and other maritime activities. Because Sleeping Bear Dunes
National Lakeshore offers so many varied cultural and natural resources, it is an ideal
location for a creative endeavor."

What They Offer

The program is designed to provide artists with inspiration from the Michigan landscape. Housing is provided rent free, and residents have a choice between a campsite or
a park house located near the village of Empire. Residents are responsible for bringing
their own gear, materials, bedding, and food. Supplies can be purchased in nearby
towns. A moderate stipend is available for mileage and other out-of-pocket expenses
incurred within the park during the residency. Artists are expected to be in good health,
self-sufficient, and able to work closely with the park rangers to meet the goals of the
residency. Artists must also donate to the park an original piece of work that was produced during the residency. This piece will be displayed in the park or shared with the
visiting public through other appropriate means. During the last week of the residency
artists are also asked to provide a demonstration, reading, slide talk, etc. of their work
for the public. Artists must also be willing to interact with the park's visitors when

encountering them in the field. Residents will be enrolled in the Volunteers in the Parks program, which includes compensation for injuries.

Facility Description
The national lakeshore is a hilly region consisting of coastal plateaus, sand dunes, clear lakes, tree-lined streams, beech-maple forests, and bluffs above Lake Michigan.

How to Apply
Send an SASE for a brochure. The application must include six copies of your résumé (no more than two pages long), six copies of a summary of your creative work, six copies of a statement of what you hope to gain through your residency, six copies of a statement of your willingness to present a program to the public and interact with visitors, a work sample, your preference for a period of residence and accommodation, and an SASE large enough for return of materials. For work samples, visual artists should send eight 35 mm slides in standard mounts (labeled with your name, medium, image size, and an indication of the top of the slide). Composers should send a cassette recording, and writers and journalists should send six copies of a brief (no more than six pages) manuscript excerpt, short story, essay, poem, or other work.

Deadline
April 15. Selections are made by early June, and the artists will be notified as soon as possible.

Approximate Cost of Program
Transportation, meals, materials, and incidentals—offset by a moderate stipend for mileage and other out-of-pocket costs incurred within the park during the residency.

JAMES THURBER RESIDENCY PROGRAM   OH
The Thurber House, 77 Jefferson Avenue, Columbus, Ohio 42315
Attention: Michael J. Rosen, Literary Director
Phone: (614) 464-1032; fax: (614) 228-7445
Web site: www.thurberhouse.com
Email: thurberhouse@thurberhouse.org

Type of Facility/Award
Artist-in-residence program.

Who Can Apply
Writers, playwrights, and journalists.

Provisos
Applicants must be published and have college-level teaching experience.

Dates of Operation
Residencies are based on Ohio State University academic quarter dates.

Location
The Thurber House is within walking distance of downtown Columbus, Ohio.

History
James Thurber's boyhood home, the Thurber House, was opened as a literary center in 1984. It is unique in its combination of historic preservation of Thurber archives, literary programming, bookstore, children's writing academy, and writers' residencies. Since 1984, more than a dozen residents have spent time living and working at the house. The center also sponsors a lecture series called Evenings with Authors. In the summer they sponsor literary picnics.

What They Offer
The award includes housing (and work space) in a furnished, third-floor apartment of the Thurber House and a stipend of $6,000 for the academic quarter. Each resident will have limited responsibilities. Writers will teach a class in fiction, poetry, or creative nonfiction in the Creative Writing Program at the Ohio State University; participate in a writing residency with a community agency; and offer a public reading. Playwrights will teach one class in playwriting in the Theater Department at Ohio State University (two afternoons each week) and will have one play considered for a public reading, mounting, or production by the school's Theater Department. Journalists will teach at the Ohio State University School of Journalism (one afternoon each week), give a public reading, and conduct a community writing workshop.

Facility Description
The Thurber House is listed on the National Register of Historic Places. It is a "faithfully restored version of a nineteen-teens dwelling for a family of modest means. Mission oak furniture, oiled pine flooring, beveled glass windows, and lace curtains characterize this home."

How to Apply
Send an SASE for a brochure and guidelines. Then submit a letter of interest with your curriculum vitae to the literary director any time before December 15. A field of writers will be selected in each genre to complete an official application form and to send writing samples. Selected writers will be brought to Columbus for an interview. Final choices will be announced in March.

Deadline
December 15 (postmarked) for letter of interest. January 1 for application and samples (if requested). Notification in March.

Approximate Cost of Program

Transportation, meals, materials, and incidentals—offset by stipend.

UNIVERSITY OF NEBRASKA NE
Great Platte River Playwrights' Festival

University of Nebraska, Theatre, UNK, Kearney, Nebraska 68849
Attention: Jack Garrison
Phone: (308) 234-8406; fax: (308) 865-8806
Email: garrisonj@platte.unk.edu

Type of Facility/Award

Opportunity for playwrights.

Who Can Apply

Playwrights.

Provisos

Though the competition is open to all kinds of subject matter, plays dealing with Great Plains themes are of particular interest. Plays must be original and unpublished in play form. Works in progress are encouraged. The festival reserves the right to developmental readings and staging of submitted plays without payment of royalties. Cash awards serve as royalties for initial full productions.

Dates of Operation

June through July.

Location

University of Nebraska campus, Kearney, Nebraska.

History

The year 2000 will be the eleventh season for producing new works.

What They Offer

Winners of the competition receive cash awards of $500 for first place, $300 for second place, and $200 for third place. In addition, winners have their plays developed and produced by the university. Winning playwrights also receive travel expenses and lodging on the university campus while the play is in production. The festival reserves the right to withhold awards in any category.

Facility Description

University campus.

How to Apply

Send an SASE for guidelines. Submit two copies of your original, unpublished play (or play in progress) for entry in one of the following categories: (1) Adult—drama or comedy, (2) Children—drama or comedy, (3) Musical—drama or comedy, or (4) Historical—drama or comedy. You may submit more than one entry. If submitting a musical, send a tape. Do not send the original or only copy. Include an adequate SASE for return of your materials.

Deadline
April 1. Notification by July 31.

Approximate Cost of Program
Meals and incidentals.

UNIVERSITY OF WISCONSIN   WI
Wisconsin Institute for Creative Writing
Department of English, Helen C. White Hall, 600 North Park St., University of
    Wisconsin, Madison, Wisconsin 53706
Attention: Ron Kuka
Phone: (608) 263-3374; fax: (608) 263-3709
Web site: www.polyglot.lss.wisc.edu/english
Email: rfkuka@facstaff.wisc.edu

Type of Facility/Award
Fellowship.

Who Can Apply
Poets and fiction writers.

Provisos
Those who have completed an M.A., M.F.A., or equivalent degree in creative writing and who are working on a first book of poetry or fiction are invited to apply.

Dates of Operation
Academic year (August 15 through May 15).

Location
University of Wisconsin in Madison, Wisconsin.

History
The Institute for Creative Writing was created in 1986.

What They Offer
Fellows receive time, space, an intellectual environment, and a fellowship of $22,000 for the academic year. Five awards are given annually. Fellows must teach one introductory creative writing workshop per semester and give one public reading from

their work-in-progress. Fellows may also participate in other English Department programs.

Facility Description
University campus.

How to Apply
Send an SASE for a brochure. Submit your résumé, two letters of recommendation, one story of up to thirty pages in length (typed, double-spaced, and stapled) or ten pages of poetry (typed, single-spaced, and stapled), and one manuscript cover sheet including your name, address, telephone number, social security number, and titles of submitted works. Your name must not appear on any page of the manuscript except the cover sheet. Letters of recommendation may arrive under separate cover, but must be received in February. Include a business size SASE for results.

Deadline
Applications are accepted throughout the month of February. Notification May 1.

Approximate Cost of Program
Transportation, housing, meals, materials, and incidentals—offset by $22,000 fellowship.

URBAN INSTITUTE FOR CONTEMPORARY ARTS   MI
DISCONTINUED

ROCKY MOUNTAIN COLONIES

Colorado
Idaho
Montana
Nevada
Utah
Wyoming

ACTS INSTITUTE   ****DISCONTINUED****

ANDERSON RANCH ARTS CENTER   CO

P.O. Box 5598, 5263 Owl Creek Road, Snowmass Village, Colorado 81615
Attention: Jeremy Swanson, Artists Residency Program
Phone: (970) 923-3181; fax: (970) 923-3871
Web site: www.andersonranch.org
Email: info@andersonranch.org or artranch@rof.net

Type of Facility/Award
Residencies and artist-in-residence programs.

Who Can Apply
Visual artists (woodworkers, photographers, painters, sculptors, ceramists, printmakers, book artists, etc.).

Provisos
Anderson Ranch Arts Center seeks artists who have a commitment to exploration in the studio and a willingness to communicate formally and informally with other artists in a broad range of media.

Dates of Operation
October 15 through April 15.

Location
Anderson Ranch Arts Center is located in the resort community of Snowmass Village, ten miles west of Aspen and two hundred miles west of Denver. United Airlines serves Aspen's airport, which is seven miles from the ranch. Taxi or bus service is available to Snowmass Village. Denver International Airport is a four-hour drive away. Limousine service is available through Aspen Limo. Travel discounts are available if you book your ticket through Aspen Travel.

History
Founded in 1966, Anderson Ranch Arts Center has developed from an informal arts program into a nationally recognized visual arts community. It is a nonprofit educational organization that brings top national artists together with student artists of all ages and levels of accomplishment.

What They Offer
Visiting artists are granted short residencies at the ranch during which they are encouraged to experiment with their art forms. Longer residencies of two, three, or six months in duration are granted to artists-in-residence. Guests are welcome to stay during the summer months and may attend workshops. The center also holds summer assistantships in the following fields: children's workshops, ceramics, woodworking/furniture,

painting, sculpture, photography, digital imaging, gallery, grounds-keeping, and administration. The ranch provides assistants with room, board, and a modest stipend. Contact the center directly for more information. Modest housing options are provided at prices ranging from $400 to $1025. Only workshop students are expected to pay for their own housing. Anderson Ranch offers full and partial scholarships to those artists who would not be able to attend without financial assistance. Participants in the visiting artists, artists-in-residence, and assistantship programs are provided with housing and are awarded modest stipends.

Facility Description

The ranch covers over four acres. Old West farm buildings house state-of-the-art studios and workshops—artists work in hay lofts, barns, and on outdoor patios. Facilities for specific disciplines are large and well-equipped. Ceramics studios cover more than 10,000 square feet in three separate buildings and are furnished with electric and kick wheels, slab rollers, and a manual Randall Extruder. Salt and soda kilns, reduction kilns, a wood kiln, two test kilns, and a number of electric kilns are also available. Glazes and instruments are provided. Sculpture facilities cater to those working with metals, ceramics, wood, plaster, found objects, and installation projects. Sculptors have access to welders, torches, saws, a drill press, a chop saw, a plasma cutter, a tig welder, band saws, an air compressor, pneumatic tools, a bead blast cabinet, a small metal foundry for aluminum and bronze, and hand tools for grinding, shaping, carving, texturizing, and finishing. Facilities for woodworking and furniture, painting and printmaking, photography, and digital imaging are similarly well-equipped. Artists are invited to bring additional materials and tools they might need. The center also includes a volleyball court and a large white tent for slide shows and gatherings. The ranch cafe offers meals at reasonable prices to guests. Vegetarian fare is always available.

How to Apply

Write or call for the brochure and application form. Submit your completed application with ten to twenty 35 mm slides of your work, a descriptive sheet of the slides, your résumé, a brief statement of your career goals and reason for applying, three references who can be reached by phone and your relationship to each, and an SASE for return of the slides.

Deadline

Mid-September for visiting artists residencies. Mid-March for artists-in-residence. Call or write for specific dates.

Approximate Cost of Program

Modest housing options are provided at prices ranging from $400 to $1025. Only workshop students are expected to pay for their own housing. Anderson Ranch offers full and partial scholarships to those artists who would not be able to attend without financial assistance. Participants in the visiting artists, artists-in-residence, and assistantship programs are provided with housing and are awarded modest stipends which offset the costs of transportation, meals, incidentals and, materials.

THE ARCHIE BRAY FOUNDATION   MT

The Archie Bray Foundation for the Ceramic Arts, 2915 Country Club Avenue,
    Helena, Montana 59601
Attention: Josh DeWeese, Resident Director
Phone: (406) 443-3502

Type of Facility/Award
Artist-in-residence program.

Who Can Apply
Ceramists.

Provisos
None listed.

Dates of Operation
Open year-round.

Location
The foundation is three miles from downtown Helena on the twenty-six-acre site of the former Western Clay Manufacturing Company.

History
The Archie Bray Foundation was founded in 1951 as a nonprofit public educational foundation by Archie Bray, Branson Stevenson, and Pete Meloy. It is dedicated to the enrichment of the ceramic arts. The list of ceramic artists who have worked at the Bray is a Who's-Who of American ceramists.

What They Offer
Full-time residencies for up to two years provide each artist with a studio for which they are required to pay $75 per month in rent. Short-term residencies are also available primarily in the summer months at $150 per month. Glazing and kiln facilities are shared. The cost of fuel and materials is the responsibility of the artist, but the foundation does offer discount rates to residents. Artists may consign their work to the foundation gallery for a one-third commission. Residents are expected to be self-motivated and willing to help with various jobs around the studio to maintain the Bray Foundation. Resident artists teach throwing and handbuilding classes for the community. No housing is provided, although residents usually find reasonable accommodations in Helena. Residents are advised to bring their own vehicles.

Facility Description
In addition to several studios and workshops, which include extensive kiln facilities and limited wood- and metal-working tools, the facility maintains a gallery space to exhibit and sell works produced there. The foundation also operates a retail ceramic supply business with an extensive inventory of pre-mixed and dry clays, studio equipment, glaze materials, and ceramic literature.

How to Apply
Contact the foundation for application materials and guidelines.

Deadline
March 1.

Approximate Cost of Program
$75–$150 per month plus $20 application fee, transportation, housing, meals, materials, and incidentals.

DENVER CENTER THEATRE COMPANY   CO
The Denver Center for the Performing Arts, US WEST TheatreFest or The
    Francesca Primus Prize, 1050 13th Street, Denver, Colorado 80204
Attention: Bruce K. Sevy, Associate Artistic Director
Phone: (303) 446-4856; fax: (303) 825-2117
Web site: www.denvercenter.org/index.html
Email: bsevy@star.dcpa.org

Type of Facility/Award
Opportunity for playwrights.

Who Can Apply
Playwrights.

Provisos
The company seeks full-length plays that have not yet gone through a professional production, and will accept only one script per playwright per year. One-acts, single-character plays, adaptations, and translations are ineligible. No musicals will be considered for the Francesca Primus Prize.

Dates of Operation
Variable.

Location
Denver, Colorado.

History

Since 1984, Artistic Director Donovan Marley has led the Denver Center Theatre Company in its presentation of quality work that includes classic and contemporary drama as well as new works, many of which have been developed through the new play program. A distinguished theatre recognized for its outstanding performances and work, DCTC received the 1998 Tony Award® for Regional Theatre.

U S WEST TheatreFest, the Denver Center Theatre Company's annual festival of new plays, was established in 1985. The Francesca Primus Prize is named in memory and honor of Francesca Ronnie Primus, who was for many years a columnist and theatre critic for *Back Stage*.

What They Offer

Opportunities for new play development at DCTC consist of two options: playwrights may submit their plays for U S WEST TheatreFest or for the Francesca Primus Prize, (the latter of which applies only to female playwrights).

Each play chosen for use in U S WEST TheatreFest receives a one-week rehearsal, using professional actors and directors, and a public reading of the play. Selected scripts are optioned for production at DCTC. Playwrights are awarded a $1,000 option fee, round trip transportation to Denver, and housing for the duration of festival rehearsal and performance time.

The Francesca Primus Prize is awarded annually to one woman playwright who receives $3,000, a residency period, and a rehearsed public reading of her play by a professional director and actors in U S WEST TheatreFest. DCTC retains the option to mount a full production of the play in its next subscription season.

Facility Description

"The DCTC performs in four distinctive theatres. *The Stage* is a 700-seat thrust. *The Space* is a theatre in the round—all of its 427 seats are within 27 feet of center stage. *The Ricketson* is a proscenium house seating 250, while *The Source* has an intimate 200-seat thrust design. All four theatres are located in the *Helen Bonfils Theatre Complex*."

How to Apply

Send an SASE for more information about new play development. Then send your clean, legible, securely bound script with a cover letter, a résumé of your experience as a writer, and a brief description of any readings, workshops, or amateur productions the script has received. Be sure to include your name, address, and telephone number on the title page. Unsolicited manuscripts will only be accepted from residents of Arizona, Colorado, Idaho, Iowa, Minnesota, Montana, Nebraska, New Mexico, North Dakota, Oregon, South Dakota, Utah, Washington, and Wyoming. Residents of other states should send a letter of inquiry before sending a script. All submissions should be sent to Bruce Sevy at the address listed, but make sure to specify either U S WEST TheatreFest or the Francesca Primus Prize above the address. Any scripts submitted for U S WEST TheatreFest that were written by women playwrights will automatically be considered for the Francesca Primus Prize, so please do not send two copies of your script. Only scripts accompanied by a large SASE will be returned.

Deadline
U S WEST TheatreFest: December 31 (postmarked). The Francesca Primus Prize: July 1 (postmarked). Playwrights will be notified by April 30. Scripts postmarked after these dates will be considered for the following year.

Approximate Cost of Program
Not applicable for this listing.

LADAN RESERVE   CO   **DISCONTINUED**

MONTANA ARTISTS REFUGE   MT
Box 8, Basin, Montana 59631
Attention: Jennifer Pryor, Administrative Coordinator
Phone: (406) 225-3500; fax: (406) 225-9225

Type of Facility/Award
Artist-in-residence program.

Who Can Apply
Artists of all disciplines.

Provisos
None listed.

Dates of Operation
Open year-round.

Location
The refuge is located in downtown Basin, Montana, where the Basin and Cataract Creeks flow into the Boulder River. It is twelve miles from Thunderbolt Mountain and the Continental Divide. Solitude can be found just ten minutes out of town in any direction.

History
The town of Basin (pop. 250) was established as a gold camp in 1862. It has two bars, a cafe, a tiny grocery, a production pottery, a post office, and a one-room school. MAR is an artist-led residency program which was established to build a wider, more diversified arts community in a rural environment, as well as to provide a refuge for

61

artists to relax, create, and rejuvenate. To date, MAR has provided refuge to over thirty artists from as close as Bozeman and as far away as South Africa. Artists have included writers, sculptors, painters, ceramic artists and composers/musicians from twenty-two to seventy-four years young.

What They Offer

The program is simply a chance to work in a relaxed, unpretentious atmosphere. Montana Artists Refuge provides the opportunity for solitude, collaboration with others, the exchange of ideas, and recovery from the hectic pace and demands usually placed upon the urban artist.

Facility Description

Facilities include a large, two-story brick building that was, in previous incarnations, the Hewett State Bank and a Masonic hall. The lower floor houses a 20' x 30' studio and a large apartment with a high ceiling. The second floor is a spacious, two-room apartment with an adjoining 20' x 30' space suitable for performance, dance, weaving, painting, or other art projects. A dry goods store next door houses the MAR office, a studio apartment, and a one-bedroom apartment which has been soundproofed to house a musician/composer. The refuge is housed in old buildings and operates on a limited budget, so the spaces are not barrier-free. All spaces are smokefree. Pets are not allowed.

How to Apply

Send an SASE for a brochure and application guidelines. Submit a résumé and a statement of intent, including desired length of residency, what you expect from the refuge, what you want to accomplish during your stay, and the materials you will be using (to help decide which space is most suitable). Also send support materials according to your discipline: ten slides for visual artists, tapes for performance artists, and manuscripts for writers. If seeking financial aid, indicate the amount needed and why you think you would be a worthy recipient.

Deadline

Rolling application process.

Approximate Cost of Program

Transportation, reduced-rent housing/studio space, meals, materials, and incidentals. Rents range from $260 to $450 per month depending upon facilities. From time to time, the refuge provides financial assistance to artists-in-residence to defray rent. Rent can be shared by the number of people using the space.

PIKES PEAK WRITERS' RETREAT   CO

4400 Martindale Avenue, Cascade, Colorado 80809
Attention: Micheline Cote/Anthony Lanza
Phone: (719) 684-0953; fax: (719) 684-2257
Web site: www.WritersRetreat.com
Email: cotlanza@ix.netcom.com

Type of Facility/Award
Retreat.

Who Can Apply
Writers, editors, and publishers.

Provisos
None listed.

Dates of Operation
Open year-round.

Location
Cascade, Colorado, is ten miles west of Colorado Springs. The retreat center is located atop Pikes Peak.

History
Pikes Peak Writers' Retreat was founded in 1998 by Anthony Lanza, Program Director. The idea was born out of his desire to find a place to write at short notice and for an inexpensive rate.

What They Offer
This is a year-round writing retreat facility which includes a main lodge where writers can gather together to discuss ideas and foster camaraderie. Guests receive comfortable and inspiring accommodations, as well as work space. Airport transportation is provided. Retreats may be booked for any duration. Rates run from $400–$600 per week for studio space with bathroom facilities. Inquire about discounts.

Facility Description
The retreat includes fifteen studios spread among four fully equipped homes set in the pines. The grounds are peaceful with a Colorado rustic style, boarded by Pikes National Forest. Dishes and linens are included. Residents are responsible for their own food; kitchens are fully equipped. Guests and pets are not allowed. Each home has a fireplace and a telephone with modem capabilities. There are stores and restaurant deliveries available in close proximity. Computer and car rentals are available upon request. Residents have access to the in-house literary agent (New York) and the screenwriting consultant (Los Angeles). Both of them are published and have national reputations.

How to Apply
Reservations are made on a first-come, first-served basis. No application process is required. Call or write for a brochure or make your reservations on-line.

Deadline
None.

Approximate Cost of Program
$400–$600 per week, transportation, meals, materials, and incidentals.

ROCKY MOUNTAIN NATIONAL PARK   CO
1000 Highway 36, Estes Park, Colorado 80517
Attention: Artist-in-Residence Coordinator
Phone: (970) 586-1206

Type of Facility/Award
Artist-in-residence program.

Who Can Apply
All professional artists, including literary, visual, and performing artists. Housing is not fully accessible for those with disabilities.

Provisos
Applicants must be working at a professional level and are expected to donate one piece of artwork inspired by their residency. The copyright of this piece will be given to Rocky Mountain National Park. In addition, artists must give a public presentation.

Dates of Operation
June through September.

Location
Rocky Mountain National Park.

History
"Currently used as the 'home' of Rocky Mountain National Park's Artist-in-Residence program, the rustic cabin on the hill overlooking Moraine Park was the summer retreat of William Allen White from 1912 to 1943. A nationally recognized journalist and editor of the *Emporia Gazette* (Kansas), the spirit of this Pulitzer Prize-winning author lives on with the contemporary artists who work in his cabin today."

What They Offer
From June to September, the Park Service offers the use of the historic William Allen White cabin for periods of two weeks. Artists are allowed to pursue their particular art form while surrounded by the inspiring landscape of the park. In return, each artist is asked to donate to the park's collection a piece of work representative of her or his style

and stay in the park. Works will be displayed on a rotating schedule for public viewing. Artists must also participate in a public presentation such as a demonstration, talk, exploratory hike, or performance. This is expected to consume only a few hours of the artist's stay. Eight or nine finalists will be chosen each year, based solely on merit.

Facility Description
The cabin has a living and dining area with high-beamed ceilings and a large fireplace. There is one bedroom, a bath, and a small kitchen. The cabin is fully furnished, including linens and kitchenware, but some artists choose to bring some of their own belongings with them. The cabin is not fully accessible for those with disabilities, and there is no central heat. Call the program coordinator to discuss individual needs.

How to Apply
Send an SASE for a brochure. Submit four copies of a one- to two-page résumé and summary of your creative works, four copies of a brief statement of what you hope to achieve from your residency, and a sample of your recent work as follows. Visual artists: six slides. Musicians and composers: a cassette recording. Dancers and other performing artists: a $\frac{1}{2}$" VHS video tape. Writers and journalists: no more than six pages of a manuscript excerpt, a short story, an article, or poetry. Enclose an adequate SASE for return of your work sample.

Deadline
Usually January, but deadline is variable. Contact coordinator for current date.

Approximate Cost of Program
Transportation, meals, materials, and incidentals.

ROCKY MOUNTAIN WOMEN'S INSTITUTE   CO
7150 Montview Boulevard, Denver, Colorado 80220
Attention: Angela Brayham
Phone: (303) 871-6923; fax: (303) 871-6922
Email: rmwi@ecentral.com

Type of Facility/Award
Artist-in-residence program

Who Can Apply
Literary artists, media artists (film/video), performing artists, visual artists, and scholars pursuing independent study.

Provisos
Applicants must be permanent Denver-area residents within commuting distance of the institute. Students enrolled in a degree-granting program are not eligible.

Dates of Operation
One year, beginning in September.

Location
Denver, Colorado.

History
The Rocky Mountain Women's Institute was founded in 1976 in honor of the sentiment expressed in *A Room of One's Own* by Virginia Woolfe. The institute continues to promote the intellectual and artistic accomplishments of women through the creation of an artists' community.

What They Offer
Annual associateships are offered to six to ten artists to assist in the creation of new work. Associates meet monthly and present their work to the public in a showcase held at the end of each year. The institute provides $1,250 for the full year.

Facility Description
None provided.

How to Apply
Send an SASE for a prospectus in the fall. Submit a completed application form accompanied by a project proposal, a list of prior achievements or experience in the area of your proposed project, and a statement of your need and desire to work in a women-oriented, cross-disciplinary environment.

Deadline
March 15.

Approximate Cost of Program
Transportation, housing, meals, some materials, and incidentals—offset by $1,250 stipend.

MARIE WALSH SHARPE ART FOUNDATION   CO/NY
711 North Tejon Street, Suite B, Colorado Springs, Colorado 80903
Attention: Joyce E. Robinson, Vice President and Executive Director
Phone: (719) 635-3220; fax: (719) 635-3018
Email: sharpeartfdn@sprintmail.com
Studio space located in Manhattan.

Type of Facility/Award
Artist-in-residence program.

Who Can Apply
Visual artists.

Provisos
Applicants must be at least twenty-one years of age and citizens or permanent residents of the U.S. Students and artists who presently have a studio space of 400 square feet or larger in New York City are not eligible.

Dates of Operation
Spaces available after September 1 for a period of up to one year.

Location
Manhattan, New York City.

History
The foundation was established by Marie Walsh Sharpe in 1985 to benefit visual artists. The Artists Advisory Committee, formed in 1988, developed two programs for artists: The Space Program and a national toll-free information hotline (in cooperation with the American Council for the Arts) for visual artists, which began on October 1, 1990. This referral service provides artists with information on programs and services available to them.

What They Offer
The Space Program provides non-living studio space, rent-free, for the making of new art. No stipend, equipment, or materials are provided.

Facility Description
Fourteen studios are available (from 450 to 500 square feet with eleven-foot ceilings).

How to Apply
Send an SASE for information and application guidelines. Work samples can be in the form of either eight 35 mm slides (no glass slides) of recent work (labeled according to instructions) with accompanying description sheet, or a video that portrays art work (must be three minutes or less) with a brief paragraph describing the work, including the date of its creation. Also include a résumé, a brief statement (no more than one page) indicating why studio space is needed, a specific desired start date (must be after September 1) and length of stay (up to one year), and an adequate SASE for return of your slides.

Deadline
January 31. Notification by the end of April.

Approximate Cost of Program
Transportation, housing, meals, materials, and incidentals.

A Snowy Day in Ucross, Wyoming, Home of the Ucross Foundation

THE UCROSS FOUNDATION RESIDENCY PROGRAM   WY

30 Big Red Lane, Clearmont, Wyoming 82835
Attention: Sharon Dynak, Executive Director
Phone: (307) 737-2291; fax: (307) 737-2322
Email: ucross@wyoming.com

Type of Facility/Award

Residency.

Who Can Apply

Painters, poets, sculptors, photographers, printmakers, composers, authors, playwrights, storytellers, filmmakers, video artists, and interdisciplinary artists.

Provisos

Quality of work is the primary consideration, but projects that promise to be of major significance in their fields are given priority. Facilities are handicapped-accessible.

Dates of Operation

Open year-round.

Location

The colony is located on a 22,000-acre working cattle ranch "at the confluence of Piney, Clear, and Coal Creeks in Ucross, Wyoming." The retreat is twenty-seven miles southeast of Sheridan in the rugged foothills of the Big Horn Mountains.

Sheridan is served by commuter airlines via Denver, Colorado. By car, Ucross is located at the point where U.S. Highways 14 and 16 intersect, seventeen miles north of Buffalo, Wyoming.

History

"The Ucross Foundation was incorporated as a nonprofit organization on June 1, 1981. Its primary objectives include the restoration of the historic Clear Fork head-quarters of the Pratt & Ferris Cattle Company, known as Big Red and built in 1882, the promotion of the preservation of other historical sites in the area through educa-tion and conferences, and the provision of facilities and program activities for an artists-in-residence project. The Ucross Foundation Residency Program opened its doors in 1983 and has to date provided fellowships for over 750 artists and writers from all disciplines."

What They Offer

Approximately sixty residents are selected each year. The foundation provides eight residents at a time (four writers and four visual artists) with studio space, living accommodations, and meals. Residency terms are from two to eight weeks. Meals are prepared by a professional kitchen staff and served in the School House Dining Room. Residents must provide their own transportation to the colony. While there is no charge for the residency, the Ucross Foundation depends on both public and private support to continue to provide an optimum retreat environment.

Facility Description

"Ucross is situated in a complex of buildings known as Big Red, which is on the National Register of Historic places. The largest building is the Big Red Barn, which houses four studios, including one with an etching press, a gallery, and a conference area in the loft. Additional studios are in the Kocur Writer's Retreat along the bank of Clear Creek. The Depot provides living quarters and two writer's studios with pri-vate bedrooms attached. All studios have natural light, running water, and private entrances. The Ucross School House has private bedrooms, laundry facilities, and the main kitchen and dining room. The facility is handicapped-accessible."

How to Apply

Send an SASE for an application and brochure. Return four copies of each of the following: the completed Ucross Application Form (one copy must be the original), a résumé, a project proposal, three letters of personal reference (two from authorities in your field), and a sample of your recent work. Include an adequate SASE for return of your materials. Appropriate work samples vary by category of art. Writers, scholars, and scientists: Send ten pages of poetry or twenty pages of other work (work must be recent—published or unpublished). Musicians and composers: Send a cassette, record, or other audio form of work. Visual artists: Send a representative selection of ten to fifteen slides of your recent work (packaged and labeled according to instructions) with an accompanying descriptive sheet. Submit one work sample and four full sets of all other materials. If you would like notification that your application and materials were received, please include an SASP. Collaborators must apply separately.

Deadline

October 1 for February to early June. March 1 for August to early December.

Approximate Cost of Program

Transportation, materials, and incidentals.

SOUTHWESTERN COLONIES

Arizona
New Mexico
Oklahoma
Texas

ARIZONA COMMISSION ON THE ARTS   AZ

Creative Writing Fellowships, 417 W. Roosevelt, Phoenix, Arizona 85003
Attention: Jill Bernstein, Literature Director
Phone: (602) 229-8226
Email: jbernstein@ArizonaArts.org

Type of Facility/Award
Cash award.

Who Can Apply
Fiction writers and poets.

Provisos
Applicants must be residents of Arizona, at least eighteen years of age, and not enrolled in school.

Dates of Operation
Annual event.

Location
Not applicable in this category.

History
None provided.

What They Offer
The category rotates each year between fiction and poetry. $5,000 to $7,500 are awarded to an undefined number of applicants. Because every winner receives the same dollar amount, and because panelists generally want to offer more applicants awards rather than less, the award usually ends up being $5,000 each. Awards are given based on artistic excellence.

Facility Description
Not applicable in this category.

How to Apply
Contact Jill Bernstein directly by mail or email.

Deadline
September 16. Awards received by April.

Approximate Cost of Program
Not applicable in this category.

THE GLASSELL SCHOOL OF ART   TX

5101 Montrose Boulevard, Houston, Texas 77006
Attention: The Core Program
Phone: (713) 639-7500

Type of Facility/Award
Fellowship.

Who Can Apply
Visual artists.

Provisos
Visual artists who are just finishing their undergraduate or graduate fine arts training are invited to apply. Certificates of achievement may be earned in painting, drawing, printmaking, sculpture, ceramics, photography, and jewelry.

Dates of Operation
September through May.

Location
Montrose/Museum District of the city of Houston, Texas.

History
The Glassell School of Art (formerly the Museum School) was founded in 1927 as part of the Houston Museum of Fine Arts. Established in 1982, the Core Program provides talented young artists with a stimulating work environment between formal school training and professional life. The focus is on intensive studio experience and self-motivated investigation of the visual arts.

What They Offer
Up to eight Core fellows may be selected each year. Fellows work in close proximity to each other in order to promote dialogue and the exchange of ideas. Each fellow receives approximately 450 square feet of studio space (with twenty-four-hour access), critiques with visiting artists and critics, and an annual group exhibition. Included is a $5,000 stipend dispersed in monthly increments over the course of the stay. Tuition waivers are also available. In exchange, fellows give five hours each week in service to the school or museum. The school does not provide housing, but affordable housing is usually available within walking distance. Most fellows find it necessary to take part-time employment. Eighty percent of the Core fellows apply for a second and final year in the program.

Facility Description
The school is located in a spacious, modern building next to the Lillie and Hugh Roy Cullen Sculpture Garden and across the street from the Museum of Fine Arts and the

Contemporary Art Museum. There are a 4,600-square-foot indoor/outdoor sculpture shop, a 3,000-square-foot indoor/outdoor ceramics shop, a fully equipped printmaking shop for lithography and intaglio, a state-of-the-art light metals and jewelry shop, a gang-style darkroom, studios (for drawing, painting, and design), a lecture hall, and a main gallery with a 33-foot atrium and mezzanine exhibition space.

How to Apply
Send an SASE for a brochure. Submit twelve slides of recent work labeled according to specifications (a video of work is also acceptable), a résumé, a statement of intention, three letters of recommendation, and an adequate SASE for return of your slides.

Deadline
April 1 for the following September to May program. Notification by May 1.

Approximate Cost of Program
Transportation, housing, meals, materials, and incidentals—offset by $5,000 stipend dispersed in monthly increments over the course of stay. Tuition waivers are also available.

HAWK, I'M YOUR SISTER   NM
P.O. Box 9109, Santa Fe, New Mexico 87504-9109
Attention: Beverly Antaeus
Phone: (505) 984-2268
Web site: www.womansplace.com
Email: hawk@womansplace.com

Type of Facility/Award
Retreat/respite.

Who Can Apply
Always women, sometimes men and children.

Provisos
All participants are expected to be in good general health. Some trips are more strenuous than others. Some trips are restricted to women only, others are co-ed, and others include children.

Dates of Operation
Trips are at various times throughout the year.

Locations
Upcoming events include a writing retreat/canoe trip for women only in Montana; a women-only excursion to the Ecuadorian Amazon, Machupicchu, and the Peru-

vian Andes; another women-only retreat to Fiji and New Zealand; and a co-ed trip to Norway. There might be other trips available. Contact Beverly Antaeus for further information.

History

"Beverly Antaeus, founder of Hawk, I'm Your Sister, has guided river trips since 1975. Her decision to specialize in women's wilderness and international journeys, evolved from the satisfaction of sharing the growth and enthusiasm of women exploring the Earth as independent people of competence and power. Beverly has paddled over 20,000 miles on oceans, lakes, and rivers in Canada, Mexico, Russia, Peru, and 16 of the United States. She has studied river rescue techniques and holds the Emergency Response Certification. She holds a BA from the Goddard Program of Vermont College and graduated from the Bonnie Prudden School of Physical Fitness and Myotherapy."

Hawk, I'm Your Sister also runs a nonprofit scholarship fund for women through Dragon Farm, Inc. and a nonprofit fund for animals called Sister Hawk. The original Sister Hawk fund went specifically towards raptor rehabilitation at the Wildlife Center in Espanola, New Mexico, and gifts sent for this purpose are still forwarded to the center. Sister Hawk, however, has expanded its mission. In partnership with the Heart and Soul Animal Sanctuary and the Espanola Animal Shelter, Sister Hawk also fosters abandoned and orphaned dogs and puppies and finds them new homes when they are healthy, socialized, and neutered or spayed. Sister Hawk raises additional funds for various organizations that care for animals in need.

What They Offer

Hawk, I'm Your Sister organizes and leads unique canoe expeditions all over the world. Some are for women only, while others include men and/or children. Many have a theme (such as their writing retreat). Unlike the other programs for writers listed in this book, this program speaks to the other side of writing—the side that requires thought, experience, and time with the elements. This is a respite for which participants must pay, as they would for any other vacation.

The trips are fully staffed with an interesting array of people who do everything from cook to dive. Some have various first aid, CPR, and lifesaving certifications. Writing affiliates of note (such as Deena Metzger, Sharon Olds, Michael Ortiz Hill, and Milly Sangama) often join on the expeditions and share their experience and knowledge with other participants.

Participants will be taught appropriate skills for the trip: how to read the weather, camp safely, and prepare camp meals that are both nutritious and tasty. Vegetarian diets may be accommodated when requested in advance. Members share daily tasks of cooking, cleanup, filtering water, loading/unloading canoes, and dealing with latrines.

Hawk, I'm Your Sister provides all major equipment: canoes, paddles, life jackets, tents, cooking and eating utensils, and toilet tissue. Participants provide their own sleeping bags and personal gear. (Hawk, I'm Your Sister provides a recommended list of useful gear and clothing.) Trips involve physical effort, so participants are encouraged to reach a reasonable level of fitness beforehand. Trips range from seven to seventeen days.

Facility Description
Variable.

How to Apply
Send a size ten SASE for their application or Dragon Farm/Hawk Fund scholarship application. A nonrefundable deposit of $300 for U.S. trips and $500 for international trips will reserve your place. After your application has been accepted you will be expected to complete and sign medical and liability release forms in order to participate.

Deadline
Different for each trip.

Approximate Cost of Program
Prices vary according to length of trip and location. Current prices range from approximately $950 to $4200. You are responsible for the cost of transportation to designated airport(s), as well as meals and lodging before and after the trip. Purchasing travel insurance is also encouraged.

ROSWELL MUSEUM AND ART CENTER   NM
100 West 11th Street, Roswell, New Mexico 88201
Attention: Artist-in-Residence Program Director
Phone: (505) 622-6037
Email: rswelair@dfn.com

Type of Facility/Award
Residency/grant.

Who Can Apply
Artists involved in painting, drawing, sculpture, printmaking, and other studio-based arts are invited to apply.

Provisos
The center does not accept performance artists or production crafts artists. Applicants must be U.S. citizens or permanent residents.

Dates of Operation
Open year-round.

Location

At an elevation of 3,560 feet, Roswell is a high plains community of about 47,000 people. Albuquerque and Santa Fe are each approximately 200 miles away. Roswell is served by bus or by Mesa Airlines commuter service. Local attractions include the Roswell Museum and Art Center, Bitter Lakes Wildlife Refuge, Bottomless Lakes State Park, Carlsbad Caverns, White Sands National Monument, and the Ski Apache ski area.

History

The center's program was established in 1967 to provide professional studio artists with the opportunity to concentrate on their work in a supportive, communal environment. "The Artist-in-Residence Program serves as a contemporary counterpoint to the traditional arts of the Southwest, reinforces the Program's interest in strengthening the vitality of art in New Mexico, and has been a catalyst in broadening community understanding of modern art."

What They Offer

Each resident is provided with her or his own house, studio, and stipend of $500 per month. Utilities, repairs, and routine maintenance costs are covered by the program. $100 per month is available for each dependent living with the resident. Residents are responsible for the cost of their materials and for their phone bills. Dogs are not allowed. It is recommended that residents have some form of transportation, as public transportation in Roswell is quite limited.

Facility Description

The studios measure approximately 25' x 25' x 12'. They are well-lighted, open spaces convertible to artists' requirements (within reason). There is a printmaking facility set up for lithography and etching. Housing includes a complex of six houses and nine studios on five acres. The buildings are close to one another, and houses can accommodate a single person or a family. Each house is partially furnished with major furniture items, appliances, and utensils. Vacuum cleaners and laundry facilities are available for shared use.

How to Apply

Send an SASE for application and brochure. Submit your completed application with fifteen to twenty 35 mm (thin mount, not glass) color slides of at least ten works completed within the last two years and a slide information sheet (check brochure for specifications of both). Artists who require long production periods are permitted to submit slides of fewer than ten works. Installation artists should submit evidence of the widest range of their most recent work. A current résumé, copies of reviews, and any other material should be limited to no more than ten pages stapled together independent of the other application materials. You need not submit letters of recommendation; references listed on the application form will suffice. Include an adequate SASE for return of materials.

Deadline
May 1 (postmarked). Deadlines may vary.

Approximate Cost of Program
Transportation, meals, materials, and incidentals—offset by monthly stipend.

SONTERRA CONDOMINIUMS   NM
206 Siler Road, Box 5244, Taos, New Mexico 87571
Attention: Sharon Fredericks, Owner
Phone: (505) 758-7989
Web site: www.heartlink.com/sonterra

Type of Facility/Award
Retreat.

Who Can Apply
Anyone.

Provisos
None listed.

Dates of Operation
Open year-round.

Location
Sonterra is located in the residential area of Taos, four blocks from the historic Taos Plaza.

History
None provided.

What They Offer
Ten one-bedroom condominiums are available on a daily, weekly, or monthly basis. Call for current rates. Participants may bring up to four extra guests (including children) for an additional charge. Taxes are additional, and maid service is available for an added fee.

Facility Description
The town of Taos offers breathtaking scenery, over eighty art galleries, unusual historic sites (including the Taos Pueblo), and premier skiing. Units at Sonterra under 450 square feet are individually furnished in a warm, Southwestern style; some have traditional kiva fireplaces. Bedrooms open onto a private patio. Bathrooms have

showers only. Units are not air-conditioned. Amenities include a generously equipped kitchen, color cable television, and a guest laundry. Surrounded by an adobe wall and latilla fence, the condominiums face an inner courtyard with a graceful Mexican fountain and flower gardens. Pets are not allowed. Also available are the Wild Rose Casita, the Columbine Casita, and a 2100-square-foot main house, all located on a six-acre compound near the mouth of the Valdez Valley.

How to Apply
Call or write for reservations, which are made on a first-come, first-served basis.

Deadline
None.

Approximate Cost of Program
Current rent rates, transportation, meals, materials, and incidentals.

THE SYVENNA FOUNDATION   **TX**   ****DISCONTINUED****

UNIVERSITY OF ARIZONA   **AZ**
Poetry Center
Poetry Center, 1216 N. Cherry Avenue, Tucson, Arizona 85721-0410
Attention: Residency Program
Phone: (520) 321-7760; fax: (520) 621-5566
Email: poetry@u.arizona.edu

Type of Facility/Award
Residency.

Who Can Apply
Writers.

Provisos
The University of Arizona Poetry Center is looking for writers who, at the time of submission, have not published more than one full-length work (self-published works and chapbooks are excepted). Unpublished writers are encouraged to apply.

Dates of Operation
June 1 through August 31 (dates are negotiable).

Location
University of Arizona campus.

History
None provided.

What They Offer

A one-month residency for an individual writer.

Facility Description

The recipient is housed in an historic adobe guest cottage two blocks from the University of Arizona campus and two houses away from the Poetry Center.

How to Apply

Send an SASE for guidelines. To apply, you will need to submit a letter with your name, address, phone number, and titles of the work you're submitting; your current résumé; three copies of no more than ten pages of poetry or twenty pages of prose; and an SASE for a reply. Manuscripts will not be returned.

Deadline

Send materials between February 15 and March 15. Notification by May 1.

Approximate Cost of Program

Transportation, meals, materials, and incidentals.

UNIVERSITY OF NEW MEXICO   NM
D.H. Lawrence Fellowship   **DISCONTINUED**

Department of English Language and Literature, Humanities Building 217,
   Albuquerque, New Mexico 87131-1106
Attention: Scott P. Sanders, Chair, Department of English
Phone: (505) 277-6347

> *Notice: The D.H. Lawrence Fellowship has been suspended, but will be reinstated at some undefined date. "The University of New Mexico may commit itself to any of several changes in its stewardship of the facilities currently available at the D.H. Lawrence Ranch north of Taos, New Mexico. Given the uncertainties, we have suspended the D.H. Lawrence Fellowship—as it has been administered and defined for the past two decades—indefinitely. We will reinstate the fellowship, changed no doubt in some ways to reflect changes in the ranch itself, as soon as possible. When the fellowship is reinstated, it will be announced to the literary community in the appropriate listings."*

UNIVERSITY OF TEXAS AT AUSTIN   TX
The Dobie Paisano Fellowships
702 East Dean Keeton Street, Austin, Texas 78705
Attention: Audrey N. Slate, Ph.D., Director of the Dobie Paisano Project
Phone: (512) 471-8542; fax: (512) 471-9997
Web site: www.utexas.edu/ogs/Paisano.pdf
Email: aslate@mail.utexas.edu

Type of Facility/Award
Fellowship.

Who Can Apply
Writers.

At the Paisano Ranch

Provisos
The program is offered exclusively to writers who are native Texans, writers living in Texas, writers who have previously lived in Texas for two or more years, writers whose lives and published works have been substantially identified with Texas, or writers whose published works focus on a Texan subject. (For native, current, and past Texas residents, there is no restriction on subject matter.)

Dates of Operation
Open year-round. Fellowships are awarded for six-month periods: One begins September 1. The other begins March 1.

Location
The late J. Frank Dobie's ranch Paisano is located just west of Austin, Texas.

History
More than fifty writers and artists have won the fellowship since it was established in 1967. The Texas Institute of Letters and the University of Texas at Austin offer two residencies each year to stimulate the creative endeavor by making it possible for a person to work without distractions. One is the Ralph A. Johnston Memorial Fellowship; the other is the Jesse H. Jones Writing Fellowship.

What They Offer
The University of Texas Office of Graduate Studies selects two people each year to spend six months in residence at the Paisano ranch. Fellowships begin in September

Dobie Paisano Fellowship
Writing

Katherine Hester

I applied to the Dobie-Paisano Program for a 1999 residency because I wanted to embark on a series of short stories I suspected would be shaped by the geography and history of Texas; because, as an "expatriate" of the state, I welcomed the opportunity to spend six months in the Hill Country around Austin; and, above all, because a residency at the Paisano Ranch, the former 250+ acre ranch of writer J. Frank Dobie, offers that commodity always so precious to writers: time.

Photo credit: Werner Weitzel © 2000

But I also have to admit that curiosity played at least some part in my decision to apply. I'd been warned there could sometimes be a "dark" side to a residency at Paisano: a creek that, when it flooded, could strand residents on the property for days at a time and had been fierce enough to, upon occasion, sweep away or damage cars; four-foot rattlesnakes (and they were always four-foot, never smaller) periodically seen in the vicinity of the house; a rural location that, though only twenty miles outside of

and March and include housing on J. Frank Dobie's 265-acre ranch and a $1,200 monthly stipend. Fellows must provide their own linens and personal belongings.

Facility Description

The house is simply but adequately furnished. All utilities and maintenance are provided by the University of Texas at Austin, excluding long-distance phone charges.

How to Apply

Send an SASE for an application and brochure. Entries should be submitted on the Application for Fellowship at Paisano. Applications can also be accessed by visiting www.utexas.edu/ogs/Paisano.pdf. With an application fee of $10 made out to the

Austin, could be, by turns, both invigorating and isolating. These aspects of Paisano intrigued me. I loved the country but had spent the past few years in cities. Could I cut it?

Now that I'm midway through a Dobie-Paisano residency, I can safely say that Paisano is not only a unique opportunity for writers, but one that is difficult to describe.

Because a residency here lasts six months, I've been able to sink my teeth into the project I had hoped to work on, and I've been able to make progress on it of a sort I would have been hard-pressed to manage elsewhere.

But perhaps more importantly, because I'll spend six months here, the Paisano Ranch has become more than just a place to write, as wonderful as having a place to write might be. It has become a home, and it's one where I feel lucky to have lived. Because it lacks some of the built-in camaraderie of other residencies, where writers and artists meet over meals, I've developed what I only know to call a personal relationship with the house and property. The wildlife of Paisano — the graceful white-tailed deer, the armadillo, the four-foot snakes, the clamorous coyote — have graciously shared their home with me, asking only that I understand I am their guest while here. Through subtle changes of season and weather, the land itself has taught me the necessity of stillness, and of slowing down. I've come to realize that the very nature of a Paisano residency — its length, its isolation — requires and fosters a particular kind of noticing, and that it is from that noticing, which usually lies beneath the white noise of our daily lives, that much of our most thoughtful writing springs.

University of Texas at Austin, return in triplicate the completed application, an outline of your project, and examples of your work (no more than fifty pages in length).

Deadline
January 21, postmarked.

Approximate Cost of Program
$10 application fee plus transportation, meals, materials, and incidentals—offset by monthly stipend of $1,200.

The Farm House at Paisano Ranch

VALLECITOS RETREAT **NM** ****DISCONTINUED****

THE HELENE WURLITZER FOUNDATION OF NEW MEXICO   NM
P.O. Box 1891, Taos, New Mexico 87571
Attention: Noel Simmons, Office Manager
Phone: (505) 758-2413; fax: (505) 758-2559
Email: hwf@taosnet.com

Type of Award
Residency.

Who Can Apply
Painters, poets, writers, playwrights, sculptors, composers, photographers, and other creative artists.

Provisos
None listed.

Dates of Operation
April 1 through October 30. Also open on a limited basis between November 1 and March 31.

Location
Taos is located one hour from Santa Fe and two and a half hours from Albuquerque and the international airport. Bus and shuttle services provide transportation to and from the airport, and local shuttle services are also available.

History

Since 1954, the foundation has provided furnished studio residencies to persons engaged in creative fields in all media.

What They Offer

Residencies are normally made for three months, but this period is flexible and may be shortened or lengthened if conditions are mutually satisfactory. Residents are provided with rent-free/utility-free housing in separate, individual houses. Residences are secluded and private. Artists may work without any expectation or pressure to leave with a finished product. There is no stipend for living expenses or supplies. Residents are expected to clean their own houses, do their own laundry, and to purchase, cook, and serve their own meals. Space is limited, so the foundation's bookings for approved residencies run about two years into the future.

Facility Description

Eleven fully furnished residences are located on eighteen acres of land and within walking distance from the main downtown Taos plaza. Facilities are handicapped-accessible.

How to Apply

Send an SASE and a written request for an application. Submit your completed application, references, a résumé that includes your educational background, and some samples of your work (photographs, transparencies, manuscript, etc.). If you want your work samples returned, include an adequate SASE. Also include a cover letter stating your choice of residency dates and the length of residency you desire.

Deadline

Rolling application process. If you do not file an application within six weeks of requesting information, your file will be closed. Still, with residencies booked so far in advance, plans change and cancellations make space available.

Approximate Cost of Program

Transportation, meals, materials, and incidentals.

Chickens at the Walden Residency

SOUTHERN COLONIES

Alabama
Arkansas
Florida
Georgia
Kentucky
Louisiana
Mississippi
North Carolina
South Carolina
Tennessee
Virginia
West Virginia

ALTERNATE VISIONS

c/o Alternate ROOTS, 1083 Austin Avenue, N.E., Atlanta, Georgia 30307
Attention: Lisa Grady-Willis
Phone: (404) 577-1079

Type of Facility/Award
Fellowship/grant.

Who Can Apply
Artists (all disciplines).

Provisos
Applicants must be residents of Georgia, Kentucky, Tennessee, North Carolina, Florida, Alabama, Louisiana, Mississippi, Virginia, West Virginia, the District of Columbia, or South Carolina. All residency activities must take place within the service area. High school students, students enrolled full-time in a degree-granting program, and grant recipients from the most recent year are not eligible. Staff and executive committee members of Alternate ROOTS are ineligible.

Dates of Operation
Open year-round.

Location
This is a nonresidential grant.

History
Alternate ROOTS is a regional membership organization that supports the creation and presentation of original, community-based performing arts in the Southeast. Services include communication, networking, artistic development, audience/community development, and regional and national liaisons. "The Community/Artists Partnership Project (CAPP) is an initiative founded in 1993 to provide artist and community training, technical assistance, and residency/project support in the field of community-based arts. All CAPP activities are meant to foster exemplary and equitable partnerships between artists and the communities they serve."

What They Offer
ROOTS has a maximum of approximately $15,000 to award for each round of CAPP grants. You may request up to $5,000. Funds must be matched dollar-for-dollar with either cash or in-kind support. There must be at least one artist and one community partner. Community partners may include community service organizations, arts presenters, housing agencies, schools, or churches. Intercultural projects are particularly encouraged. All projects must be two weeks or longer (all at once, or over a span of time). Grants will not fund projects that are already completed, work used toward the completion of a degree program, work conceived primarily as an educational project or

student production, travel to other countries, or projects that consist solely of documentation of work (for example, a video of previously produced work).

Facility Description
No facility or studio description is provided.

How to Apply
Send an SASE for an application and brochure. Return the original and nine additional copies of the completed application form and the Project Budget Proposal Form, typed or printed neatly. Include ten copies of a one-page résumé, career summary, or bio for yourself and any collaborators. Then submit a one-page collaborators' statement, describing the relationship between the artists (ownership of completed work, division of responsibilities) and the role of each in the creative process, signed by all collaborators. Also send a sample of your work (collaborators must provide a work sample from each collaborator). Include no more than two of the following forms: a ¹/₂" VHS video tape cued to a continuous five minute sample; a cued audio tape (each work on a separate tape); ten collated copies of five typed pages of a manuscript; up to ten slides (labeled according to instructions) per artist accompanied by a descriptive sheet; compact discs (with track number indicated); or clearly labeled sketches, photos, site maps, etc. No long-playing record albums will be accepted with proposal. Do not include original artwork or slides. Optional inclusions with your submission are: an SASE adequate for return of your support materials; one copy each of up to three examples of other support materials such as past reviews, press coverage, letters of support, etc.; and an SASP if you want Alternate ROOTS to acknowledge receipt of your proposal.

Deadline
Currently, December 15, but deadlines may vary. Notification by January 15.

Approximate Cost of Program
Transportation, housing, meals, and incidentals—offset by award of up to $5,000.

ARROWMONT SCHOOL OF ARTS AND CRAFTS   TN
P.O. Box 567, 556 Parkway, Gatlinburg, Tennessee 37738-0567
Attention: Artist-in-Residence Program
Phone: (865) 436-5860; fax: (865) 430-4101
Web site: www.arrowmont.org
Email: arrowmnt@aol.com

Type of Facility/Award
Residency.

Who Can Apply
Visual artists.

Provisos
Arrowmont is looking for pre-professional, self-directed visual artists with "team spirit" who enjoy working independently as well as with staff, visiting faculty, and other residents. Interaction with community, conferences, children's programs, high-school programs, and Elderhostel art classes is encouraged.

Dates of Operation
Residencies begin in mid-September.

Location
The school is located just three miles from the entrance to the Great Smoky Mountains National Park in eastern Tennessee. Knoxville, Tennessee, and Asheville, North Carolina, are within easy driving distance. Atlanta and Nashville are approximately four hours by car.

History
Arrowmont School, an internationally known visual arts complex, was established in 1945.

What They Offer
Three to five artists are selected annually for residencies lasting from nine to eleven months. Participation in Arrowmont's other programs is encouraged. Artists live on campus in a new building with their own bedroom, bathroom, and shared living and dining areas. They receive access to private studios in the resident artist studio complex for a monthly fee of $200 (covers housing and studio space). Access to Arrowmont's main studio (with specialized equipment) is available for a nominal fee. There is also an opportunity to work with visiting artists of national/international reputation. At the end of the residency, a group exhibition at the Arrowmont Atrium Gallery features work made by the artists during their residencies. In addition to pursuing their own work, residents are required to work for Arrowmont eight hours each week in one of the following capacities: community outreach (Artists in Schools), studio maintenance, gallery installation, instruction for other Arrowmont programs, food service, book/supply store, photography, or office/computer work. Work assignments are established according to the resident's skills and interests before the residency begins. A scholarship for women in need (Trabue Professional Arts Program for Women) is available.

Facility Description
Situated on seventy acres of wooded hillside, the setting alone is a source of visual stimulation and inspiration. Arrowmont has large, well-equipped studio facilities for ceramics, jewelry, metalworking, textiles, weaving, papermaking, book arts, paint-

ing, drawing, photography, and woodturning. Arrowmont's resource center includes a wide assortment of books and periodicals for residents to use.

How to Apply
Send an SASE for an application and brochure. Return the completed application with a $20 nonrefundable application fee, twenty slides of your most recent work (with an adequate SASE for their return), two letters of recommendation, and a personal statement of your present and future goals and what you expect to gain from a residency at Arrowmont. If you are applying for the Trabue scholarship (women only), include a letter explaining your financial need, plus a letter of support.

Deadline
April 30.

Approximate Cost of Program
$220 per month, $20 application fee, transportation, meals, materials, and incidentals.

ATLANTIC CENTER FOR THE ARTS   FL
1414 Art Center Avenue, New Smyrna Beach, Florida 32168
Attention: Residency Program
Phone: (904) 427-6975; fax: (904) 427-5669

Type of Facility/Award
Artist-in-residence program.

Who Can Apply
Associates-in-Residence: artists, musicians, dancers, choreographers, and composers.
Masters-in-Residence (by invitation): distinguished contemporary artists.

Provisos
Associates are described as "mid-career."

Dates of Operation
Open year-round. There are five residency programs held per year. Each residency is three weeks long.

Location
The center is located on the east coast of central Florida.

History
This interdisciplinary arts facility was chartered in 1979 to bring together mid-career writers, artists, musicians, and composers (associates) with master artists (distinguished contemporary artists) in an informal interdisciplinary residency where they have the opportunity to interact, work, and perhaps collaborate with one another.

What They Offer

The center offers five three-week residency sessions each year. Each of the three master artists of different disciplines chooses ten associate artists through his or her own selection process. During the residency period, associates spend half their time on weekdays working with the masters in different ways: meetings, workshops, casual conversations, and occasionally participating in recreational activities. The rest of their time is free to spend pursuing their own projects. A session fee of $800 includes tuition and an on-site private room and bath. No meals are provided. Nonresident tuition is $300. Some scholarships are available. Contact the center for scholarship information and updated fees.

Facility Description

The center includes an administration/gallery complex, a multipurpose workshop, a fieldhouse/commons building, three cottages for the resident master artists, associate housing, and an outdoor amphitheater. Each associate is provided with a private room with a bath and small refrigerator, as well as acces to a communal living room and kitchen space. The center has a pay phone and laundry facilities for residents' use. The 12,000 square feet of studio workspace includes studios for music, painting, sculpture, and dance. In addition, there is a black-box theatre and a resource library. The center is air-conditioned and handicapped-accessible.

How to Apply

Send an SASE for a brochure. Choose the session you'd like to attend and then send for an application form and submittal guidelines. Each master-in-residence selects his or her own associates and sets the selection criteria. Applications should be submitted at least three months prior to residency period desired.

Deadline

Three months prior to residency desired. See brochure for dates.

Approximate Cost of Program

$800 for tuition and housing plus transportation, meals, materials, and incidentals.

CREEKWOOD WRITERS COLONY   AL   **DISCONTINUED**

HAMBIDGE CENTER FOR CREATIVE ARTS AND SCIENCES   GA

P.O. Box 339, Rabun Gap, Georgia 30568
Attention: Bob Thomas, Executive Director
Phone: (706) 746-5718; fax: (706) 746-9933
Web site: www.rabun.net/~hambidge
Email: hambidge@rabun.net

Type of Award
Residency.

Who Can Apply
Writers and visual artists of all types.

Provisos
Applicants must be twenty-one years of age or older. Self-sufficient emerging artists, as well as mature professionals seeking to engage in creative work or research, are invited to apply. Residents of Fulton County, Georgia, may be eligible for a fellowship through the Fulton County Arts Council (inquire directly).

Dates of Operation
September through February. March through August.

Location
The Hambidge Center is 3 miles from Dillard, 120 miles from Atlanta, and 90 miles from Asheville, North Carolina.

History
The center was founded in 1934 by Mary Crovatt Hambidge. Hambidge serves approximately one hundred fellows each year. Since 1974, over one thousand artists have lived and worked at the center.

What They Offer
The Hambidge Center for Creative Arts and Sciences offers stays of two weeks to two months. Residencies begin on a Monday and end on a Friday. The center provides housing, either in individual dwellings/studios or in the Rock House. From May through October, weeknight dinners are prepared and served at the Rock House, but residents must provide their own breakfasts, lunches, and weekend meals. Bed and bath linens are provided. A car is not necessary, but helpful. Financial aid may be available for those in dire need. Inquire when applying. The center also offers workshops, speaker's forums, and gallery exhibitions that are open to the public.

Please note: No meals are provided for residencies taking place during the months of November, December, March, and April.

Facility Description
The Hambidge Center is listed on the National Register of Historic Places. Located in the Blue Ridge Mountains, it includes six hundred acres of unspoiled, wooded land in a mountain valley with several creeks and waterfalls. Numerous nature trails alive with wild flowers cross the property. The center offers guided nature walks throughout the year. There are seven isolated and private individual cottage/studios for residents' use, each with its own fully-equipped kitchen and bath. The Rock House (a large stone house with five bedrooms and two and a half baths) is where residents are served their

evening meals. Residents using the pottery studio may be housed in the Rock House. Rock House residents share use of the bathrooms and the main kitchen. The center also has a gallery (and a small shop) that hosts five or six shows each season.

How to Apply

Send an SASE for an application and brochure. Return the completed application with a $20 processing fee and a résumé of your education and/or training—note any awards, honors, grants, exhibitions, or performances to help the committee to understand your commitment to your field. Append publicity materials, such as copies of reviews, notices, etc., that your work has received, a list of your five most significant professional achievements, three letters of recommendation from people in your field who are familiar with your work, and some samples of your work. Visual artists: Send at least ten slides of your recent work. Choreographers, dancers, and film and video artists: Send video tapes of your recent work. Poets and writers: Send three copies of a manuscript or a published work. If you send a published book, one copy will suffice. Attach a separate page telling the selection committee why a stay at the center would be helpful to your career. Include an adequate SASE if you want your samples returned.

Deadline

May 1 for September through February residencies. November 1 for March through August residencies. Notification in six to eight weeks.

Approximate Cost of Program

$320–$1020, transportation, some meals, materials, and incidentals.

LYNCHBURG COLLEGE IN VIRGINIA   VA
Richard H. Thornton Endowment

Lynchburg College in Virginia, English Department, 1501 Lakeside Drive,
    Lynchburg, Virginia 24501-3199
Attention: Thomas C. Allen, Chair
Phone: (804) 544-8267
Web site: www.lynchburg.edu/public/academic/english/thornton.html

Type of Facility/Award

Fellowship.

Who Can Apply

Writers.

Provisos

Fiction writers, playwrights, or poets who have published at least one book are eligible. Applicants are expected to be qualified for teaching.

Dates of Operation
Academic semesters (fall or spring).

Location
Lynchburg, Virginia.

History
None provided.

What They Offer
Eight-week fellowships include housing and meals at the college and an $8,000 stipend. Fellows must also teach a weekly seminar to advanced-level undergraduate writers, give one public reading on campus, and visit classes as a guest speaker.

Facility Description
Lynchburg College campus.

How to Apply
Send an SASE for application guidelines. Submit your updated curriculum vitae and a cover letter outlining your qualifications.

Deadline
March 1 for fall term. September 1 for spring term.

Approximate Cost of Program
Transportation, materials, and incidentals—offset by $8,000 stipend.

MAITLAND ART CENTER   FL   **DISCONTINUED**
The Maitland Art Center, 231 Packwood Avenue, Maitland, Florida 32751-5596
Attention: Julie M. Mimms, Assistant to the Director
Phone: (407) 539-2181
> *Notice: Maitland's residency program was discontinued in 1984 for lack of funding. The program may be reinstated in 2002. If you inquire, please be sure to include an SASE.*

GEORGE MASON UNIVERSITY   VA
Institute for Humane Studies
3401 N. Fairfax Drive, Suite 440, Arlington, VA 22201-4432
Contact: Nonresidential Fellowships for Professionals
Phone: (703) 993-4880 or (800) 697-8799; fax: (703) 993-4890
Web site: www.mason.gmu.edu/~ihs/
Email: IHS@mason1.gmu.edu

Type of Facility/Award
Nonresidential fellowship.

Who Can Apply
College juniors, seniors, graduate students, or recent graduates interested in the "classical liberal" tradition of individual rights and market economies.

Provisos
Applicants must intend to pursue a career in journalism, film, writing (fiction or nonfiction), publishing, or market-oriented public policy and must have arranged or applied for an internship, training program, or other short-term opportunity related to their intended career. Nonresidential fellowships cannot be awarded for tuition or living expenses associated with pursuing a degree.

Dates of Operation
Operates year-round.

Location
This is a nonresidential fellowship.

History
"Humane Studies Fellowships, begun in 1983 as Claude R. Lambe Fellowships, are awarded by the Institute for Humane Studies to support the work of outstanding students interested in the classical liberal/libertarian tradition. The core principles of this tradition include the recognition of individual rights and the dignity and worth of each individual; protection of these rights through the institutions of private property, contract, and the rule of law, and through freely evolved intermediary institutions; and voluntarism in all human relations, including the unhampered market mechanism in economic affairs and the goals of free trade, free migration and peace."

What They Offer
Each fellowship consists of a stipend of up to $18,000 for the academic year.

Facility Description
This is a nonresidential fellowship.

How to Apply
Submit a proposal of five hundred to one thousand words explaining what specific opportunity or opportunities you have arranged or applied for, how that opportunity would enhance your career prospects, and what financial assistance you may need in order to accept the opportunity. Include a cover letter explaining your interest in classical liberal principles and how that interest fits in with your career plans. Submit a current résumé that includes your educational background (including major field and any academic honors received), your current educational status, your work

experience (including summer positions and internships), and citations of any publications. Submit a writing sample or other samples of your work appropriate to your intended career. Also, provide the names, addresses, and telephone numbers of two academic or professional references.

Deadline
December 31.

Approximate Cost of Program
Not applicable in this category.

MILL MOUNTAIN THEATRE   VA
New Play Competition, Center in the Square, One Market Square SE, Roanoke,
   Virginia 24011-1437
Attention: Literary Manager
Phone: (540) 342-5749; fax: (540) 342-5745
Web site: www.millmountain.org
Email: mmtmail@millmountain.org

Type of Facility/Award
Opportunity for playwrights.

Who Can Apply
Playwrights.

Provisos
The competition is open to playwrights living in the United States. Only one submission per playwright per year is allowed. Only unpublished, unproduced theatrical scripts in English are eligible (no film or television scripts, no translations or adaptations). One-acts are permitted if they are at least twenty-five minutes in length; musicals are permitted if accompanied by a demo tape; plays that have been already developed in a workshop are permitted; and previous submissions are permitted only with substantial revisions. Plays must be agent-submitted or accompanied by a letter of recommendation by a director, literary manager, or dramaturge.

Dates of Operation
Annual competition.

Location
Roanoke, Virginia.

History
"Established in 1986, the Mill Mountain Theatre New Play Competition presents the best of new and innovative theater by emerging American playwrights."

What They Offer

Winner of the competition will receive a $1,000 cash award plus a staged reading with the possibility of full production. Scripts may be for full-length or one-act plays of any subject matter and character variation. No withdrawals, rewrites, or revisions will be accepted after submission except for those plays chosen as finalists that have undergone substantial structural revision. Finalists will be required to sign a statement of authenticity declaring that the play is an original work, it can be publicized as a world premiere, and it is not under consideration for publication or production. By submitting to this contest, the playwright agrees to the submission guidelines and to the production of the submitted script. After the staged reading, the author maintains all rights to the winning play. Winners are announced in the *Dramatists Guild Quarterly* and *American Theatre Magazine*. Mill Mountain reserves the right to withhold the prize and to not declare a winner if no play of merit is found.

Facility Description

None provided.

How to Apply

Send an SASE to the literary manager for a flyer. Then submit your firmly bound, standard letter-sized, typed manuscript including your name, address, and phone number on the title page. Also include a short author's bio and history of the play, a brief synopsis of each scene, an adequate SASP if arrival acknowledgment is needed, and a manuscript-sized SASE if you would like your script returned to you.

Deadline

Submissions are only accepted between October 1 and January 1. Finalists will be announced by August 1.

Approximate Cost of Program

Not applicable in this category.

NEXUS CONTEMPORARY ARTS CENTER   GA

Nexus Press, 535 Means Street N.W., Atlanta, Georgia 30318
Attention: Sam Gappmayer
Phone: (404) 688-1970; fax: (404) 577-5956
Web site: www.nexusart.org
Email: nexusart@mindspring.com

Type of Facility/Award

Residency.

Who Can Apply

Contemporary visual artists.

Provisos

None listed.

Dates of Operation

Open year-round.

Location

Atlanta, Georgia.

History

Nexus Contemporary Arts Center has been providing subsidized studio space for artists for over twenty years.

What They Offer

The Nexus Press offers up to two residencies each year to visual artists who use the facilities at the press to create an artist book. Residencies last from two weeks to two months and include housing in one of two on-site apartments and a stipend. When the book is complete, Nexus Press markets the book, and all proceeds are split between the artist and the press. Nexus Contemporary Arts Center also offers five-year studio leases to visual artists at approximately one-quarter of the market value. Artists are responsible for their own supplies and materials. They are asked to commit eight hours of service each year to the center; many artists fulfill this requirement by teaching a workshop. The center also asks artists to make their studios available for two open houses each year.

Facility Description

Studios are between 224 and 755 square feet in size. All studios are equipped with a sink, but the layout and design of each is unique. Some studios come with shelves, storage racks for paintings, darkroom facilities, or other specific equipment.

How to Apply

Contact the press for information and application materials for residencies. You will be asked to submit a proposal for your book project as part of the application process for the residency. Contact the center for information and application materials for studio rentals.

Deadline

None.

Approximate Cost of Program

Residents are responsible for transportation, housing, meals, materials, and incidentals—offset by stipend.

OSSABAW ISLAND PROJECT   GA   **DISCONTINUED**
P.O. Box 13397, Savannah, Georgia 31406
Phone: (912) 233-5104
Attention: Mrs. Ford West, President
> Notice: Their visual arts project has been suspended. Inquire about possible reopening after 2001.

PENLAND SCHOOL OF CRAFTS   NC
Resident Selection Committee, Penland Rd., Penland, North Carolina 28765-0037
Attention: Dana Moore, Program Director
Phone: (828) 765-2359, ext 19; fax: (828) 765-7389
Web site: www.penland.org
Email: office@penland.org

Type of Facility/Award
Artist-in-residence program.

Who Can Apply
Visual artists working in sculpture, textiles, photography, jewelry, mixed media, books, paper, drawing, iron, metals, printmaking, wood, glass, or clay who are creating nontraditional studio crafts.

Provisos
Applicants must be professional-level, independent artists. Preference is given to former Penland students, studio assistants, visiting artists, and instructors. If you do not have previous Penland experience, write to let them know of your interest in the program, but plan to spend some time at the school in another capacity. Persons interested must be able to support themselves for the duration of the three-year program. They must be able to provide for the costs of rent, utilities, furnishing, equipment, and materials.

Dates of Operation
Open year-round.

Location
The Penland School is located in Mitchell County, North Carolina, fifty miles north of Asheville.

History
The Residents Program was founded in 1963 by Bill Brown. His hope was that the program would encourage craftspeople to settle in the area. Penland offers classes in books and paper, clay, drawing, glass, iron, metals, photography, printmaking, textiles, and wood. The school is supported by a North Carolina Arts Council grant.

What They Offer

Penland offers residencies of two or three years for up to seven artists at a time. The school provides unfurnished housing and studio space for $100 per month, while the resident is responsible for utility costs, which average $125 to $175 per month. Interaction between residents and other school programs is encouraged, including helping to organize occasional group exhibitions of your work. Residents are expected to hold an open house at their studios once each quarter and to maintain an open-door policy toward students and instructors.

Facility Description

Residents live and work at the Sanford Center, which is adjacent to the school. The building has high ceilings, electricity, and running water. Upstairs studios have wooden floors, limiting their use for certain crafts.

How to Apply

Send an SASE for a brochure. Submit your name, address (current and permanent), telephone number, and email address with a nonrefundable application fee of $25 and two letters of recommendation. Include fifteen to twenty slides of your recent work in a carousel for viewing with accompanying descriptive sheet, a résumé, a personal statement describing your work and the direction you'd like to take while at Penland, why you want a residency at Penland, and how you plan to support yourself while you are there. Include an adequate SASE for return of your materials.

Deadline

October 28. Notification by January 15.

Approximate Cost of Program

$250 per month, $25 application fee, transportation, meals, materials, and incidentals.

THE SEASIDE INSTITUTE, INC.   FL

Escape to Create, P.O. Box 4730, Seaside Branch, 30 Smolian Cr., Second Floor,
    Santa Rosa Beach, Florida 32459
Attention: Karen Howell
Phone: (850) 231-2421; fax: (850) 231-1884
Web site: www.theseasideinstitute.org
Email: institute2@seasidefl.com

Type of Facility/Award

Residency.

Who Can Apply

Visual artists, musicians, and writers.

Provisos

Escape to Create is available only to emerging artists whose work-in-progress or proposed residency project represents a potential breakthrough in his or her career. Applicants, while not yet "established" in their fields, must demonstrate a modest but promising track record and must be actively producing work in their fields.

Dates of Operation

January.

Location

Santa Rosa Beach is approximately forty minutes from both Panama City and Fort Walton Beach.

History

A nonprofit educational and cultural organization, the Seaside Institute supports the restoration of civic life. The institute was founded on the belief that communities are enhanced by a rich cultural life. It sponsors residency programs for artists and scholars and presents concerts, exhibits, and literary events.

What They Offer

Artists are expected to live and work in Seaside for the full residency period. Residents receive work space and accommodations provided through the generosity of Seaside homeowners. Family and friends are allowed one brief visit during the residency—usually the weekend of presentations. The directors must be notified in advance, but housing arrangements are the responsibility of the artist or the guests.

Facility Description

None provided.

How to Apply

Rolling application process. Contact the program directly.

Deadline

June 30.

Approximate Cost of a Program

Transportation, materials, and incidentals.

SHENANDOAH INTERNATIONAL PLAYWRIGHTS RETREAT   VA

ShenanArts, Inc., Rt. 5, Box 167-F, Staunton, VA 24401
Attention: Robert Graham Small, Artistic Director
Phone: (540) 248-1868; fax: (540) 248-7728
Email: shenarts@cfw.com

Type of Facility/Award

Residency.

Who Can Apply

Playwrights and screenwriters.

Provisos

None listed.

Dates of Operation

July through September.

Location

Virginia's Shenandoah Valley.

History

Shenandoah was created in order to provide young and established writers a safe, stimulating environment and a place free from external pressures in which to test and develop new work. Residents come from around the United States and the world to collaborate and create new work.

What They Offer

Playwrights are selected each year to work and live in fellowship with a multicultural company of theatre and film artists. Room, board, and transportation are provided. Writers work in close and intense collaboration with their company of dramaturges, directors, and actors. "What occurs is a simultaneous 'on-the-feet/on-the-page' exploration of each play, culminating in a staged reading before an audience of invited professionals and advocates."

Facility Description

The Pennyroyal Farm was built in 1808. It is the headquarters of ShenanArts and the home of the Shenandoah International Playwrights Retreat. The farm has been a gathering place for theatre performance and fellowship for nearly fifty years.

How to Apply

Send an SASE for a brochure and guidelines. Submit two copies of a completed draft of a script to be worked on at the retreat, a personal statement of your background as a writer, an adequate SASE for return of materials, and an SASP for acknowledgment of receipt.

Deadline

February 1. Notification after June 10.

Approximate Cost of Program

Materials and incidentals.

THEATER AT LIME KILN   VA   **DISCONTINUED**

14 South Randolph Street, Lexington, Virginia 24450
Phone: (540) 463-7088
Web site: www.cfw.com/limekiln

> *Notice: Their contest for playwrights has been dissolved. Theater at Lime Kiln currently hosts artists-in-residence by invitation only.*

VIRGINIA CENTER FOR THE CREATIVE ARTS   VA

Admissions Committee, Box VCCA, Sweet Briar, Virginia 24595
Attention: Sheila Gulley Pleasants
Phone: (804) 946-7236; fax: (804) 946-7239
Web site: www.vcca.com
Email: vcca@vcca.com

Type of Facility/Award
Residency.

Who Can Apply
Visual artists, writers, composers, and new genre artists (including those working in video, film, installation, performance, conceptual art, interactive multimedia, etc.).

Provisos
Admission to the Virginia Center is based on professional achievement or promise of achievement. Admission criteria are competitive and selective. Craftspeople or writers of scholarly theses are not eligible.

Dates of Operation
Open year-round.

Location
VCCA is located at Mt. San Angelo, a 450-acre estate in Amherst County, approximately 160 miles southwest of Washington, D.C.

History
"The VCCA was founded in 1971 and operated for five years in the Charlottesville area. In 1977 Sweet Briar College leased the buildings and grounds of its adjacent Mt. San Angelo estate to the VCCA. It has continued to flourish in this location in Virginia's Blue Ridge Mountain Foothills."

What They Offer
Residencies of two weeks to two months are offered to twelve writers, nine visual artists, and three composers (twenty-four artists are in residence at a time). Breakfast and dinner are served in the dining room of the fellows' residence and lunches are

delivered to the studios. Everyone who can is expected to pay his or her fair share. The actual cost of a residency is over $75 per day—the center suggests a daily fee of $30 per resident. Abatements of the $30 fee may be granted when true need is indicated. Families cannot be accommodated.

Facility Description
VCCA fellows are provided with private bedrooms in a modern, comfortable residential building. Each has a separate studio in the studio/barn complex. There is a darkroom available for the use of photographers. Facilities at the residence include a library, dining room, living room, laundry facilities, a game room, and an outdoor pool.

How to Apply
Send SASE for an application form. Return two complete sets of the following: the completed application form, a current résumé, a short paragraph highlighting your professional achievements (two hundred words maximum), and samples of your work. Appropriate work samples follow. Writers: a book, six to ten poems, up to two short stories, the first chapter or twenty pages of a book, or a complete script. Visual artists: up to six color slides of recent work labeled as specified and a corresponding sheet. Composers: up to two scores (include dates completed) and, if available, a corresponding cassette or CD of the work labeled as specified. New genre artists: a video cassette (VHS, standard American format NTSC only), slides or print materials labeled as specified (whichever is most appropriate), or a Web site URL. Include a $20 nonrefundable application fee (checks payable to the VCCA) and an adequate SASE for return of your materials. Collaborators must submit separate applications and fees.

Applications will not be accepted by fax.

Deadline
May 15 for residencies between October and January. September 15 for residencies between February and May. January 15 for residencies between June and September.

Approximate Cost of Program
Artists are accepted at the VCCA without regard for their ability to pay residency fees. The cost of a residency at the Virginia Center is $75 per day per fellow. Any reduction in fees must be subsidized by the limited financial resources of the center. Subsidies are available for some residencies. The minimum suggested subsidized daily fee is $30. Any further reduction in fees must be specifically requested. Residents are additionally responsible for the $20 application fee, transportation, materials, and incidentals.

WEYMOUTH CENTER

NC

P.O. Box 939, 555 East Connecticut Ave., Southern Pines, North Carolina 28388
Attention: Brenda Bouser
Phone: (910) 692-6261; fax: (910) 692-1815
Web site: www.sandhills.org/tainment/weymouthcenter

Type of Facility/Award
Residency.

Who Can Apply
Writers.

Provisos
Writers must be natives or residents of North Carolina.

Dates of Operation
Open year-round.

Location
Located in the Sandhills area of North Carolina, the center is one hour south of Raleigh and two hours east of Charlotte.

History
The Weymouth Center was the home of author James Boyd (1888–1944) and is operated by the nonprofit organization Friends of Weymouth.

What They Offer
Residencies last from four days to two weeks. Writers are provided with a bedroom and writing area during their stay. There is currently no stipend available.

Facility Description
None provided.

How To Apply
Rolling application process. Send an SASE for current specifications.

Deadlines
Rolling deadline.

Approximate Cost of Program
Transportation, materials, meals, and incidentals.

WOLF-PEN WOMEN WRITERS COLONY   KY   **DISCONTINUED**

YUCATEC FARM   VA   **DISCONTINUED**

NEW ENGLAND COLONIES

Connecticut
Maine
Massachusetts
New Hampshire
Rhode Island
Vermont

ACADIA NATIONAL PARK

Artist-in-Residence Program, P.O. Box 177, Bar Harbor, Maine 04609
Attention: Coordinator
Phone: (207) 288-5459; fax: (207) 288-5507

Type of Facility/Award
Artist-in-residence program.

Who Can Apply
Professional writers, musicians, composers, dancers, and visual and performing artists.

Provisos
None listed.

Dates of Operation
Spring and fall.

Location
Bar Harbor, Maine.

History
"In the mid 1800's, landscape painters, including Thomas Cole and Frederic Church, came to Mount Desert Island and captured its beauty on canvas. Their work inspired writers, composers, naturalists, and folks from far away to seek the natural splendor of the island. Those who followed were known as rusticators because they ate and lived with the local fishermen and farmers during their summer stay. The rusticators returned each summer to delight in the tranquillity of Mount Desert Island, and for some, to practice their craft. Villagers' cottages and fishermen's huts soon overflowed and by 1880, thirty hotels competed for vacationers' dollars. Ballet, opera, musical festivals, and readings flourished each summer on Mount Desert Island. Over the years accommodations have increased, but the heart of what first drew people here remains Acadia National Park."

What They Offer
Acadia provides housing, with no stipend for living expenses, to artists for two-week periods of time in the spring and the fall. In return, artists are asked to donate a piece of work to the park's collection. Works will be displayed or shared with the public through appropriate means. Artists are also asked to share an offering with the public in the form of a demonstration of skills, a talk, an exploratory hike, or a performance requiring only a few hours of the artists' time.

Facility Description
Acadia National Park offers a perfect setting for artists to practice and pursue their craft. With its dramatic cliffs stretching to the sea, its balsam-scented forests, and

spring warbler serenades, the area offers artists the age-old inspiration of nature. No description of artist's housing was provided.

How to Apply

Send an SASE for a brochure. Submit six copies each of a one- to two-page résumé with a summary of your creative works and a one-page statement describing what you hope to achieve while in residency at the park. Submit an appropriate sample of your recent work and an adequate SASE for its return. Visual artists: Send six slides. Musicians and composers: Send a cassette recording. Dancers and performing artists: Send a $^1/_2$" VHS video tape. Writers and poets: Send a brief manuscript excerpt, a short story, an article, or some poems (maximum six pages).

Deadline

Applications are accepted from November 1 until January 1.
Notification by March 1.

Approximate Cost of Program

Transportation, meals, materials, and incidentals.

THE ADAMANT PROGRAM   VT   **DISCONTINUED**

AS220   RI

115 Empire Street, Providence, Rhode Island 02903
Attention: Geoff Griffin
Phone: (401) 831-9327; fax: (401) 454-7445
Web site: www.as220.org
Email: geoff@as220.org

Type of Facility/Award

Residency.

Who Can Apply

Musicians, writers, visual artists, and videographers.

Provisos

All established artists are welcome to apply. Interested artists should create a proposal that considers AS220's inclusive, community spirit.

Dates of Operation

Open year-round.

Location

Providence, Rhode Island.

History

"AS220 has functioned as an open forum for Rhode Island artists since 1985. At its current location, AS220 provides an unjuried and uncensored venue for creation and exhibition of original art."

What They Offer

Three- to six-month residencies include a single-occupancy studio and access to a shared kitchen.

Facility Description

AS220 is a 22,000-square-foot building that includes a cafe and performance space, computer lab, black-and-white darkroom, screenprinting studio, video editing suite, ten working studios, four gallery spaces, and twelve living/working studios. Residents share common facilities. Each resident has weekly cleaning obligations and monthly volunteer obligations to the organization. Pets are not allowed.

How to Apply

Send an SASE or visit the Web site for an application and brochure.

Deadline

None provided.

Approximate Cost of Program

Transportation, meals, materials, and incidentals.

BREAD LOAF WRITERS' CONFERENCE   VT

Middlebury College, Middlebury, Vermont 05753
Attention: Carol Knauss
Phone: (802) 443-5286; fax: (802) 443-2087
Web site: www.middlebury.edu/~blwc
Email: blwc@middlebury.edu

> *Notice: Though not an ordinary retreat, Bread Loaf Writers' Conference has been included because of the fellowship opportunities it offers for its program. Financial help is available. See "What They Offer" below for guidelines.*

Type of Facility/Award

Retreat.

Who Can Apply

Writers.

Provisos

Both published writers and those in the early stages of a promising career are invited to apply.

Dates of Operation

August.

Location

Middlebury College is located at the edge of the Green Mountain Forest in Ripton, Vermont. Burlington, Vermont, is the closest town with airport service.

History

"Bread Loaf is the oldest writers' conference in America. Since 1926, a generation before 'creative writing' became a course of study in educational settings, Bread Loaf has convened in mid-August at the Bread Loaf campus of Middlebury College". The idea to establish the writers conferences "came initially from Robert Frost, who loved the inspiring setting. Willa Cather, Katherine Lee Bates, and Louis Untermeyer, all of whom taught at the School of English in 1922, also suggested that the campus be used for a writers' conference when it was vacant at the end of each August."

What They Offer

The conference involves eleven days of workshops in fiction, poetry, and nonfiction. Readings, lectures, critiques, and time for writing help participants focus on their art. Tuition costs $1160; room and board are $620. Three types of financial aid are offered and must be used in the year they are awarded: fellowships, tuition scholarships, and work study scholarships. Fellowship applicants should have already published one book (but not more than two) within the last four years in the genre in which they are applying. Fellowships cover full tuition, room, and board at the conference ($1780). Tuition scholarships are awarded to writers who are actively publishing original work in distinguished magazines and literary periodicals. The tuition scholarship covers the cost of tuition at the conference ($1160). Work study scholarships are awarded to applicants whose writing shows exceptional promise. Work study scholars earn their room and board, and the scholarship covers all but $200 of the tuition fee.

Facility Description

"Bread Loafers" are housed in the Bread Loaf Inn and its cluster of cottages and buildings. Most rooms are doubles and share a bath. All buildings are within walking distance of the center of the campus. The library at Bread Loaf hosts a collection of literature, reference books, and reserve shelves. A full-featured computer room (both Macintosh- and IBM-equipped) is available with printers and Internet connections for writing, research, and email. Middlebury also provides a multitude of activities and facilities, including country auctions, antique shops, a state crafts center, museum, movie theater, and riding and golfing facilities.

How to Apply

Send an SASE for an application and guidelines. Then submit your unstapled manuscript of an unpublished work (twenty-five pages maximum of fiction or nonfiction, or ten pages maximum of poetry). Include your name on each page and include a short synopsis if your manuscript is excerpted from a longer project. Children's or young adult literature, newspaper journalism, and academic writing will not be accepted. Include an adequate SASE for return of materials. Apply as early as possible—workshops fill up quickly.

Deadline

April 15 (received). Notification by May 15. Later applications are considered on a rolling basis. Financial aid applications must be postmarked by March 15.

Approximate Cost of Program

$1780 plus transportation and incidentals. Combinations of tuition, room, and board are provided for financial aid recipients. See "What They Offer".

CARINA HOUSE: A MONHEGAN RESIDENCY   ME

William A. Farnsworth Library and Art Museum, P.O. Box 466, Rockland, Maine
    04841
Attention: Director
Phone: (207) 596-6457
Web site: www.monhegan.com

Type of Facility/Award

Residency.

Who Can Apply

Painters, drawers, printmakers, sculptors, and photographers.

Provisos

Applicants must be at least twenty-five years old and legal residents of the state of Maine. Students currently enrolled in a degree program are not eligible. The program is aimed at serious artists who have not yet won wide recognition for their work and whose financial resources would otherwise not allow them an extended stay on Monhegan.

Dates of Operation

Session A: June 1 through July 10. Session B: July 25 through August 28.

Location

Monhegan Island, Maine.

History

Because of its unparalleled natural beauty, Monhegan Island has attracted artists for over one hundred years. "The Monhegan residency is designed to give back to Maine artists part of their heritage and tradition, including a tradition of creative experimentation and exploration." The residency is funded by the contributions of anonymous individual donors and the William A. Farnsworth Library and Art Museum.

What They Offer

Two artists will each be awarded a five-week residency and a $500 stipend. The cottage is only big enough for one person, so family, friends, guests, and pets are not allowed. Residents must provide their own transportation to the island.

Facility Description

The Carina House is a small, simply furnished artist's cottage.

How to Apply

Send an SASE for a brochure.

Deadline

Variable. Contact the Carina House for current deadlines.

Approximate Cost of Program

Transportation, meals, materials, and incidentals—offset by $500 stipend.

CARVING STUDIO & SCULPTURE CENTER   VT

P.O. Box 495, West Rutland, Vermont 05777
Attention: Carol Driscoll
Phone: (802) 438-2097; fax: (802) 438-2097
Web site: www.vermontel.net/~carving
Email: carving@vermontel.com

Type of Facility/Award

Residency.

Who Can Apply

Carvers and sculptors (primarily stone).

Provisos

Open to established artists, emerging artists, and students.

Dates of Operation

May through September.

Location

CSSC is located in West Rutland on the edge of Vermont's first marble quarry.

History

The studio was patterned after the Carrara Studio in Italy. After suffering years of neglect, the old company store was turned into studios that offer various courses on carving (from granite to wood to soapstone) as well as workshops on casting bronze and working with power tools.

What They Offer

Residents are provided with room and board, use of equipment, and a small stipend for residencies of variable lengths. CSSC encourages experimentation and exploration of new media, large- or small-scale work, and work that combines several media. Residents are expected to assist with stone-moving, kitchen detail, and studio maintenance. There are courses available and artists may choose to participate, to work independently, or to do a combination of both.

Facility Description

The Carving Studio is made up entirely of marble blocks. There is a residence space for artists within walking distance of the studio.

How to Apply

Contact CSSC directly for an application.

Deadline

Rolling application process.

Approximate Cost of Program

Transportation, housing, meals, materials, and incidentals—offset by stipend.

THE CLEAVELAND HOUSE B&B   MA

P.O. Box 3041, West Tisbury, Massachusetts 02575
Attention: Cynthia Riggs, Manager
Phone: (508) 693-9352
Email: criggs@vineyard.net

Type of Facility/Award

Retreat.

Who Can Apply

Caters specifically to poets, writers, and artists, but welcomes all guests.

Provisos

None listed.

Dates of Operation

Open year-round.

Location

Located at the center of Martha's Vineyard Island in Massachusetts, the house is three miles from the airport, six and a half miles from the Vineyard Haven ferry dock, and nine and a half miles from Oak Bluffs.

History

The Cleaveland House has been in the family of poet Dionis Coffin Riggs for ten generations. Built in 1750, it is one of the oldest houses on Martha's Vineyard.

What They Offer

This is a bed and breakfast that caters to poets and writers. "It is a pleasant place to stay if you want to be around books and people who write, or if you want some quiet time to yourself." Mrs. Riggs holds a poetry workshop on alternate Wednesday afternoons. Guests are invited to bring their poems to read, join in the critique session, or simply listen.

Facility Description

The classic, gray-shingled house has large airy rooms (some with fireplaces), antique furniture, shared baths, small closets, and no televisions. Smoking is not permitted inside the house.

How to Apply

Send an SASE for a brochure. Then call or write for reservations, which are made on a first-come, first-served basis. There is no application process. One-night reservations for Friday and Saturday nights are not accepted between May 1 and October 15. Advance reservations between May 1 and October 15 require a $100 deposit.

Deadline

None.

Approximate Cost of Program

The upstairs guest rooms, which share one bath, are the East Chamber Room (double bed and fireplace) at $85 per night or $510 per week and the South Bedroom (single bed) at $70 per night or $420 per week. Both rooms together as a suite cost $145 per night or $865 per week. There is one guest room downstairs with twin beds and a fireplace at $85 per night or $510 per week. Access to the downstairs shared bathroom is through the kitchen. Continental breakfast is included, but guests are responsible for the costs of transportation, other meals, and incidentals.

CONTEMPORARY ARTISTS CENTER

MA

Historic Beaver Mill, 189 Beaver Street, North Adams, Massachusetts 01247
Attention: Janan Compitello
Phone: (413) 663-9555; fax: (413) 663-9555, ext 51
Web site: www.cacart.org
Email: cacarts@together.net

Type of Facility/Award

Artist-in-residence program.

Who Can Apply

Visual artists, all mediums.

Provisos

None listed.

Dates of Operation

May 15 through August 31.

Location

A former mill town in the Berkshire Mountains, North Adams is about three hours from New York City, two and a half hours from Boston, and one hour from Albany. It is accessible by bus or train.

History

In 1990 multimedia artist Eric Rudd and sculptor Martin Hatcher launched the center's artist-in-residence program, which has grown to include five galleries, weekly events, and community workshops—all stemming out of the center's dedication to the production and exhibition of contemporary artwork.

What They Offer

Work space includes a large studio that is accessible around the clock, a darkroom, and printmaking facilities. Residents have access to five galleries, outdoor sites, workshops, weekly lectures, readings, music events, and downtown installations. Housing is available for one or two occupants per space.

Facility Description

The center is located in a 130,000-square-foot historic mill on twenty-seven acres of woodland adjoining Natural Bridge State Park. Only a short distance away are Mass Moca, Williams College Museum of Art, and Clark Art Institute. The industrial loft, common-space studios have high ceilings, big windows, and ample room for projects of all types including large-scale and site-specific installations. The center also has a wood shop, a basic black-and-white darkroom, and printmaking facilities. CAC has hydraulic presses, a monster press (image size 4' x 8'), and a vulcanizing (heated) press. Many other industrial tools and materials are available. Residents can use (or learn to use) the monumental monoprinting press, air brush equipment, or the industrial foam-spraying equipment.

How to Apply

Send an SASE for an application and brochure. Return the completed application with one sheet of slides and your current résumé. Enclose an adequate SASE for return of your slides.

Deadline

No deadline. CAC reviews applications year-round.

Approximate Cost of Program

Rates, rent, materials, transportation, food, and incidentals. The residency costs $200 per week ($50 additional for printmaking studio use). Housing costs vary; consult CAC for more information. Workshops are available at varied costs.

CUMMINGTON COMMUNITY OF THE ARTS   MA   **DISCONTINUED**

DORSET COLONY HOUSE   VT

P.O. Box 510, Dorset, Vermont 05251
Attention: John Nassivera, Director
Phone: (802) 867-2223; fax: (802) 867-0144
Web site: www.theatredirectories.com
Email: theatre@sover.net

Type of Facility/Award

Residency.

Who Can Apply

Playwrights, writers, composers, directors, designers, visual artists, and collaborators.

Provisos

Facilities are only suitable for visual artists working on a small scale. There are no specialized studios and the quality of natural light varies.

Dates of Operation

October 1 through June 1.

Location

Dorset, a small village on the National Register of Historic Places, is near the Green Mountains of southern Vermont, four and a half hours by car from New York City.

History

The three-story farmhouse, now referred to as the Colony House, was built in the early 1800s. Victorian features were added later in the century. The Sheldon family carried out the most recent remodeling in the 1920s when the house was completely renovated and more than doubled in size. From 1960 to 1978, it was rented to Dorset's professional theater company as summer housing for the actors. In 1979, Dr. and Mrs. John Nassivera purchased the house with the assistance of the Clarence Geiger Trust in order to ensure that it would remain the home for the Dorset Theatre Festival. The house is now available for use by writers, particularly playwrights, and other artists as a workspace and retreat during the months of the year when the acting company is not in residence. The colony has hosted new writers, Pulitzer Prize winners, and Academy Award winners. Most residents have been playwrights and writers from New York City.

What They Offer

The house can accommodate up to eight writers at a time. Periods of residency are flexible—from one week to several months depending upon the artist's requirements. First-time residencies, however, are granted for periods of up to one month. The house can also accommodate groups when scheduling allows. The purpose of the residency is to give artists the opportunity to work intensively without unnecessary distraction, while also providing opportunities for interaction with other artists and access to village life.

Facility Description

The house is a large three-story structure with eight private rooms (some with fireplaces), three public areas (where conversation and fellowship are encouraged) including the kitchen, a wood-paneled library/sitting room with a fireplace, and a large dining room, also with a fireplace, that can accommodate up to twenty people. The house was fully winterized in 1979 and is well suited for efficient year-round operation. The kitchen is fully equipped and capable of serving large groups; it is open at all times and is stocked with utensils, paper goods, coffee, etc. Food services are not provided for individuals, although they are available for groups and special occasions. The Dorset Colony House is set on three acres of lawn surrounded by tall maple, oak, and pine trees that seclude it from the street and from the rest of the village. Dorset village is within walking distance, as are open fields and streams, a pond, mountain trails for hiking, cross-country ski trails, and the Dorset Marble Quarry, a favorite swimming area.

How to Apply

Send an SASE for a brochure. Submit a letter with your requested residency dates, a description of your intended project, and a résumé of publications, readings, and/or productions. After the materials have been reviewed, you will be asked to submit samples of your work with an outline of the work you hope to accomplish during your residency. The admissions policy is "based on the demonstration of a serious commitment to the discipline."

Deadline

Rolling application process.

Approximate Cost of Program

The residency fee is $120 per week, which is less than 50% of the actual cost of operation. Partial weeks are prorated at $20 per night. The minimum fee is $75. Depending upon the length of stay, the total cost of a residency can fall anywhere from $75 to $1440 plus transportation, meals, materials, and incidentals.

FINE ARTS WORK CENTER MA

24 Pearl Street, Provincetown, Massachusetts 02657
Attention: Director
Phone: (508) 487-9960; fax: (508) 487-8873
Web site: www.CapeCodAccess.com/FineArtsWorkCenter
Email: fawc@capecod.net

Type of Facility/Award
Fellowships.

Who Can Apply
Creative writers, poets, and visual artists whose careers would benefit from a seven-month residency fellowship.

Provisos
Fellows must be residents of Provincetown during their fellowships.

Dates of Operation
October 1 through May 1.

Location
Provincetown, Massachusetts, is located at the very end of Cape Cod. FAWC is surrounded by miles of dunes and national seashore beaches.

History
The program was initiated in 1968 by writers and visual artists such as Stanley Kunitz, Hans Hoffman, and Robert Motherwell and has awarded more than seven hundred fellowships over the years.

What They Offer
A seven-month fellowship includes a furnished apartment and a studio with approximately four hundred square feet of working space. Fellows are responsible for their own meals but are provided with a monthly stipend currently set at $450. Writing fellows are housed in two- and three-room apartments. FAWC also has facilities that are handicapped-accessible, including living and working space.

Facility Description
The center supports a basic woodshop, a print shop with an etching press, and a darkroom with basic equipment. If a visual artist needs other equipment that the Fine Arts Work Center (FAWC) does not provide, the artist must supply the equipment.

How to Apply
Send an SASE (in a number ten business size envelope with first-class postage) for an application and brochure. Be sure to state whether you are a visual artist or a writer. Send a check for a $35 nonrefundable application fee. Visual artists must also include

a 9" x 12" slide sheet with no more than ten 35 mm slides, a list describing the slides (complete with title, medium, size, and date), an SASP for notification of receipt of slides, an SASE for notification of results, and an SASE for return of the slides.

Deadline

December 1 for writers; February 1 for visual artists. Notifications by May 15.

Approximate Cost of Program

$35 plus transportation, meals, and incidentals—offset by monthly stipend of $450.

HARVARD SCHOOL OF PUBLIC HEALTH   MA   **DISCONTINUED**

HARVARD UNIVERSITY   MA
Nieman Foundation

Walter Lippmann House, One Francis Avenue, Cambridge, Massachusetts 02138
Attention: Program Officer, Nieman Fellowships for Journalists
Phone: (617) 495-2237; fax: (617) 495-8976

Type of Facility/Award

Fellowship.

Who Can Apply

Journalists.

Provisos

Journalists from all countries and of all ages are invited to apply. There are no educational prerequisites. The foundation looks for working mid-career journalists of particular accomplishment and promise. International journalists must be fluent in spoken and written English. International and U.S. journalists must be full-time staff or freelance journalists working for the news or editorial department of newspapers, news services, radio, television, or magazines of general public interest; must have at least three years of professional work in the media (most successful applicants have had five to ten years of experience); and must obtain their employer's consent for a leave of absence for the academic year.

Dates of Operation

Academic year (September through June).

Location

Harvard University, Cambridge, Massachusetts.

History

The Nieman Foundation's objective is "to promote and elevate the standards of journalism in the United States and educate persons deemed specially qualified for journalism." The money was bequeathed by Agnes Wahl Nieman in memory of her husband, Lucius Nieman, founder and publisher of the *Milwaukee Journal.*

What They Offer

Approximately twelve U.S. and ten to twelve international journalists are selected each year. U. S. journalists receive a stipend of $40,000 for the academic year. Funding for international journalists is not generally provided by the Nieman Foundation; those applicants must seek funding through other sources, although the Nieman Foundation has access to a few restricted grants. Journalists are allowed to design their own study plans but do not receive course credit or a degree for work done. Tuition, classroom, and library fees are covered. Most Fellows choose two to four audited courses (one per semester is required). Fellows with children receive a modest monthly allowance for childcare. Weekly "informal beer and cheese" seminars with selected faculty members, noted newspeople, and politicians are part of the tradition. Fellows must agree to return to their employer at the end of the sabbatical year, refrain from professional work during the fellowship term, complete all the work in their academic courses (one in fall, one in spring semester), and remain in the Cambridge area during the term of their fellowships while classes are in session.

Facility Description

Fellows are housed in the Walter Lippmann House, which was built in 1836 by Ebenezer Francis. The house has been "a school for 'young ladies,' a private residence, and the manse of a local church. In January 1978, the building was renovated and restored to become the Walter Lippmann House of the Nieman Foundation and home for Nieman Fellows."

How to Apply

Contact the program officer for an application form, sheet of instructions, and brochure. Return the completed application form (which asks for education, employment, professional, and award information), along with a statement describing your journalistic experience, career plans and aims, a statement discussing your proposed field of study at Harvard, and some samples of your recent professional work according to guidelines received with your application form.

Deadline

January 31 (postmarked) for U.S. journalists. Interviews in spring. Announcements in May. March 1 (received) for international journalists.

Approximate Cost of Program

Transportation, meals, and incidentals offset by stipend. (Grants to international journalists vary and may include transportation.)

JACOB'S PILLOW   MA

P.O. Box 287, Lee, Massachusetts 01238-0287
Attention: Residency Group
Phone: (413) 637-1322; fax: (413) 243-4744
Web site: www.jacobspillow.org
Email: jacobspillow@taconic.net

Type of Facility/Award
Residency.

Who Can Apply
Dance artists.

Provisos
None listed.

Dates of Operation
June through August

Location
Lee, Massachusetts.

History
Jacob's Pillow is a theater company for dance artists.

What They Offer
Jacob's Pillow presents a twelve-week performance season (June through August) in
the studio/theatre and a ten-week performance season in the Ted Shawn Theatre.
Audience size ranges from 150 to 750. There are four types of residency programs.

In-season residencies: These last from two to three weeks in June, July, and August.
Artists are provided studio space, housing, meals, and a modest stipend. In exchange,
they are expected to open up their processes to the community through workshops,
off-site outreach programs, or several informal presentations each week (open rehearsals, showings of nearly completed work) as part of the Pillow's Inside/Out series. These
free-to-the-public, outdoor presentations are scheduled an hour and a half before Ted
Shawn Theatre performances. Afterward, the audience may ask questions or offer feedback. These activities require 8–10 hours per week of the artists' time.

In-school residencies: These residencies are for one to four weeks and are usually
scheduled for spring or fall. They require a commitment to the education of students
in kindergarten through grade twelve. Artists are provided with room and board,
transportation, and a small stipend. Studio space is provided at Jacob's Pillow when
the artist is not in the schools. While in the schools, artists may teach classes, lead
workshops, lecture, or give demonstrations or informal performances for the benefit

of the children. These activities take up three full school days per week.

Creation residencies: Usually scheduled for spring or fall, these provide room, board, and studio space, but no transportation or other compensation. Artists are expected to give appropriate credit to the Pillow in any printed material referring to the work made while in residence. Use of theatrical lighting and technical support staff may occasionally be available at cost to these residents. In exchange, a portion of the artist's rehearsal process must be made open to the community.

Performance residencies: These are for performers in the Ted Shawn Theatre and the studio/theatre who "usually stay off-campus, but occasionally are placed in residence for some period of time leading up to their performances." The artist is given room, board, studio and theatre space, and a stipend. In exchange, artists may be required to participate (on a limited basis) in the Inside/Out series, teach classes, give workshops, hold open rehearsals, or participate in community outreach activities.

Facility Description
None provided.

How to Apply
Send an SASE for application guidelines. Then send a letter of interest with support materials to the residency group.

Deadline
Rolling application process. Note months of residency terms.

Approximate Cost of Program
Materials and incidentals—offset by stipend—for in-season and in-school residencies. Transportation, materials, and incidentals for creation residencies. Transportation, materials, and incidentals—offset by stipend—for performance residencies.

THE MACDOWELL COLONY   NH
100 High Street, Peterborough, New Hampshire 03458
Attention: Admissions Coordinator
Phone: (603) 924-3886 or (212) 966-4860; fax: (603) 924-9142
Email: info@macdowellcolony.org
Web site: www.macdowellcolony.org

Type of Facility/Award
Residency.

Who Can Apply
Writers, composers, visual artists, photographers, printmakers, architects, filmmakers, video artists, dramatists, and interdisciplinary artists.

Provisos

Applicants should be established in their fields, although emerging artists with promising talent are encouraged to apply. The facility is wheelchair accessible. Collaborators must apply separately, but may submit a joint project description. Couples must apply (and will be considered) separately.

Dates of Operation

Open year-round.

Location

Peterborough, New Hampshire.

History

Composer Edward MacDowell bought the Peterborough's farm in 1896 and found he tripled his creative activity after moving there. Mrs. MacDowell later founded the colony, attracting early applicants such as Edwin Arlington Robinson and later residents James Baldwin, Stephen Vincent Benet, Leonard Bernstein, Willa Cather, Aaron Copland, Frances Fitzgerald, Max Frankel, Arthur Kopit, Sara Teasdale, Studs Terkel, Virgil Thompson, and Thornton Wilder. Many colonists have been Guggenheim, Prix de Rome, or Pulitzer Prize winners, as well as Fulbright and MacArthur Fellows.

What They Offer

MacDowell offers stays of no more than eight weeks. Residents receive room, board, and individual studio space. A few studios also serve as the artists' living quarters. Breakfast and dinner are served in the colony hall; lunches are brought to the studios. The colony hosts thirty-one artists in the summer and twenty-two in the other seasons. The average stay lasts six weeks. There are no accommodations for families or spouses, and pets are not allowed. There are no medical facilities at the colony and service in Peterborough is limited. Some financial travel assistance is available.

Facility Description

"Spread out over the Colony's 450 acres of woodlands and fields are thirty-two artist studios. Almost no studio is within sight of another and each is simply but comfortably furnished with the artists' needs in mind; all have electricity and heat." All main buildings have barrier-free access as do some studios. "There are no telephones. Messages are delivered in emergencies. While most colonists sleep in a residence apart from their studio, a few studios include sleeping quarters. Composers' studios include a piano and, like the writers' space, natural northern light and full spectrum lighting. Two fully equipped darkrooms are available for the photographers in residence. Filmmakers with an editing project can request the exclusive use of a 16mm editing suite. Printmakers will find their studio equipped with lithography and plate presses, aquatint equipment and ample ventilation. A library with an extensive collection of works by colonists is available for reference purposes." The historic Lower House, the center of colony life in 1907, is currently being renovated to include new living quarters for artists-in-residence, and an adjacent structure will be built as a studio for artists in interdisciplinary fields and new genres.

How to Apply

Send an SASE for an application and brochure. Return the application with a $20 non-refundable processing fee, a description of your proposed project, a list of any special studio requirements, a list of your five most important professional achievements (vita, performances, recordings, exhibitions, filmography, videography, or published works), the names and addresses of two references, a list of any professional training, and a recent (within the last four years) sample of your work. If you want your sample returned, enclose an adequate SASE. Appropriate samples vary by discipline. Architecture/landscape architecture: If you plan to do written work, submit five sets of a published article or a ten-page sample of your writing (as closely related to the type of work you proposed as possible). If you plan to do design work, submit five sets of images (slides, photographs, photocopies) or drawings of your finished projects with a descriptive sheet. Music composition: Send two clearly reproduced scores with a separate cassette tape of each work. Label cassettes according to instructions. One piece should be in large form (a string quartet, a sonata, or an orchestral piece). Film/video arts: Send two films (16 mm or Super 8) or videos (¾" or ½" VHS video tapes), slides, or other documentation of your work. Film or video scriptwriters: Send three copies of a script. Interdisciplinary arts: Send two videos (½" VHS video tape), slides, or other documentation of your work. Visual arts: Send five color slides packaged and labeled according to instructions. Literature and drama: Work samples should be in the same genre in which you intend to work at the colony. If you submit a work-in-progress, you must also submit a finished work. If you are submitting a book, send one book and five sets of photocopies of up to twelve pages of a chapter. Playwrights: Send three copies of a complete script. Poets: Send six copies of a book or six to ten poems. Fiction: Send six copies of a book or an excerpt from a novel (if still in manuscript form). Nonfiction: Send six copies of a book or two or three essays. Call the admissions coordinator to discuss appropriate samples if your project does not fall clearly into one of the above categories. Couples must apply individually. Previous residents must wait a year before reapplying.

Deadline

January 15 (received) for stays in May, June, July, and August. April 15 (received) for September, October, November, and December. September 15 (received) for January, February, March, and April. Notification within eight weeks after deadline.

Approximate Cost of Program

$20 processing fee, daily contribution (based on ability to pay), transportation, materials, and incidentals.

MAINE RETREAT   **ME**   ****DISCONTINUED****

MEDICINE WHEEL ARTISTS RETREAT   **MA**   ****DISCONTINUED****

NANTUCKET ISLAND SCHOOL OF DESIGN & THE ARTS   **MA**
23 Wauwinet Road, P.O. Box 958, Nantucket, Massachusetts 02554
Attention: Fresh A.I.R. Program
Phone: (508) 228-9248 or (508) 228-2451
Web site: www.nantucket.net/art/nisda/

Type of Facility/Award
Residency.

Who Can Apply
Photographers, painters, sculptors, ceramists, textile artists, multimedia artists, writers, musicians, performance artists, and others.

Provisos
None listed.

Dates of Operation
Open year-round.

Location
Nantucket Island is thirty miles off the coast of Cape Cod. The Harbor Cottages are just five minutes from the center of town across from the Nantucket Harbor. The Sea View Farm Barn Studios are eight miles away in Wauwinet. The island is accessible by boat or plane.

History
"The Nantucket Island School of Design and The Arts (NISDA), a year-round cultural and Arts Education Resource Center (AERC), is dedicated to exploring the interdependence of the arts, sciences, humanities, and environment, and to enhancing education through community and the quality of life through the arts." NISDA also hosts a lecture series and a summer program.

What They Offer
There are eight cottages of three different sizes at NISDA's Bar Harbor Cottages Artist Colony. They have small studio cottages; medium cottages with small, separate bedrooms and living areas; and large cottages with larger living areas and storage lofts. All of the freshly renovated and winterized cottages have private kitchens and bathrooms. All sleep at least two people. NISDA doesn't mind if you bring a spouse, a friend, a partner, or a collaborator to share the cost of the cottage. NISDA will also

attempt to pair applicants who may be interested in sharing living space. Artists with families are welcome. You may work in your room, outside, or at the Sea View Farm Barn Studios, which are eight miles from the cottages. Studios are accessible twenty-four hours a day.

From October to June, per person rates (which include your cottage and optional use of a Sea View Farm Barn studio) are as follows. Small cottages: $600 per month. Medium cottages: $750 per month. Large cottages: $850 per month. The fee includes $100 of utilities per month. Cottage security deposit fees (for utilities after $100) are as follows. One month residency: $150. Two month residency: $275. Three month residency: $375. For $100 more per month, residents can share their cottages with friends or family members. Rates for July, August, and September are somewhat higher. Inquire about special discounted rates for six- to eight-month residencies, October through May. Each cottage (and school studio) has its own meter; billing will be adjusted according to your use. Residents must provide their own meals, materials, and incidentals. If for some reason you must cancel your residency, you will receive a refund, less a $20 handling fee, only if NISDA was able to fill your space. Otherwise, they will issue you a credit to be used within one year. NISDA has a work-exchange program for fee-reduced residencies. You can save up to twenty percent of the cost of your cottage (not utilities) by teaching, caretaking, working in the office, or otherwise helping with school maintenance.

Facility Description

Nantucket Island is seven miles wide and fourteen miles long, sporting eighty miles of sandy beaches, heath-covered moors, and small pine forests. Some of the town's homes date back to the 1600s when Nantucket was the center of America's whaling industry. The Sea View Farm Barn Studios have a large, open 2D or 3D studio (partitioned off into several work spaces), a ceramics studio (with a skutt electric kiln, an electric wheel, equipment for pit firing, and a large outdoor deck), and darkrooms. The facility also has a large community room, a library, and a kitchen for shared use.

How to Apply

Send an SASE for an application and brochure. Return your completed application with a $20 nonrefundable processing fee, résumé, statement of intent, three professional references, SASP for notification, and a sample of your work. Appropriate work samples are ten to twenty slides, black-and-white prints, sketches, demo tapes, videos, and/or writing samples such as poems, short stories, or excerpts from a novel. Enclose an adequate SASE if you want your samples returned. If you are applying for financial aid, list any writing, computer, administrative, or office skills you may have.

Deadline

Rolling application process. Cottages are assigned on a first-come, first-served basis.

Approximate Cost of Program

$20 processing fee, cost of accommodations ($600–$850 a month), utilities, transportation, meals, materials, and incidentals.

NATIONAL MUSIC THEATER CONFERENCE   CT
Eugene O'Neill Theater Center

305 Great Neck Road, Waterford, Connecticut 06385-3825
Phone: (203) 443-5378; fax: (203) 443-9653

Administration/Applications/Winter Address:

234 West 44th Street, Suite 901, New York, New York 10036-3909
Attention: Paulette Haupt, Artistic Director
Phone: (212) 382-2790; fax: (212) 921-5538
Web Site: www.eugeneoneill.org
Email: oneillctr@aol.com

Type of Facility/Award

Residency.

Who Can Apply

Playwrights, librettists, lyricists, writers, and composers.

Provisos

All applicants must be permanent residents (with visas) of the United States or U.S. citizens. All forms and styles of music theater and opera are accepted, as long as singing plays a dominant role in the play. Any works that have received a fully staged professional production are not eligible. Original and adapted works are eligible. (You must submit proof of rights with your application if adapted work is not in the public domain.) Works under option are eligible as long as this is stated in the application. Works of any length, except musical revues, are eligible. Works previously submitted are eligible if they have been revised or if they have one or more new collaborators. If you are selected, you must be in residence for the duration of the conference. New, emerging, and established creative talents are welcome.

Dates of Operation

August.

Location

Waterford, Connecticut.

History

"The O'Neill Theater Center is solely a developmental theater. We support creative artists by providing an empty stage in which they can explore their visions, take risks not possible with production deadlines, and discuss their work with other professionals in the field of music theater."

What They Offer

Selected applicants receive round-trip transportation from New York to Connecticut for the conference, room, board, and a modest stipend. The residency is between two and four weeks. In addition, residents benefit from use of and exposure to the O'Neill Center's personnel, facilities, and artistic processes. The center provides panel discussions with theater professionals and on-going discussions of works-in-progress among residents, the artistic director, directors, and musical directors. There are public and private rehearsals and readings by a group of equity actors and singers (script in hand) on an empty stage with only a piano as accompaniment. The center does not encumber any work by creative artists but asks for acknowledgment in printed programs and publicity materials for works developed during the residency.

Facility Description

None provided.

How to Apply

Send an SASE for an application and brochure. Return your application between November and March 1 with the following: a $15 nonrefundable application fee; a bound, covered, typewritten draft of the script; two audio cassettes with at least six diverse selections in chronological order to the script (include a sheet that tells where the selections are located in the script); one piano/vocal score or piano/vocal lead sheet for each selection on the tape; a one-page description of the work; a typewritten biography or résumé for each creative artist; a separate cast list including brief character and vocal descriptions; proof of rights if the work is an adaptation not in the public domain; and an SASP or SASE for notification of receipt of application materials. Include an adequate SASE if you want your materials returned, or pick up your materials at the New York office after adjudication. Additional support materials may be requested during the selection process.

Deadline

March 1 (postmarked). Notification in May.

Approximate Cost of Program

$15 application fee, transportation, and incidentals. Room and board are provided, and a modest stipend is awarded.

NATIONAL PLAYWRIGHTS CONFERENCE CT
Eugene O'Neill Theater Center
234 West 44th Street, Suite 901, New York, New York 10036-3909
Attention: James Houghton, Artistic Director
Web Site: www.eugeneoneill.org
Email: oneillctr@aol.com
Phone: (212) 382-2790; fax: (212) 921-5538

Type of Facility/Award
Opportunity for playwrights.

Who Can Apply
Playwrights, screenwriters, and scriptwriters.

Provisos
Applicants must be American citizens or permanent residents of the United States. Collaborations are eligible. All full-length plays are eligible. "A long one-act is acceptable, as is a series of short, thematically interrelated one-acts (although the Conference may choose not to work on them all)." No adaptations. All submissions must be previously unproduced and not currently under option, although scripts that have been radically rewritten (spine of the play has been changed) may be considered. Emerging and established talented writers are invited to apply. See details in the brochure or contact the office in New York for clarification on production/developmental issues.

Dates of Operation
July.

Location
Waterford, Connecticut.

History
"The National Playwrights Conference is concerned with the growth of talented writers (whether emerging or established) and exercises this commitment by offering them the opportunity to work on their plays together with other talented professional theater and media artists in a noncompetitive atmosphere."

What They Offer
Each playwright accepted (they choose ten to fifteen each year) receives a $1,000 stipend, room, board, and transportation to the conference and pre-conference. No provisions (room, board, travel) are made for the playwright's family. Families are not permitted to attend the pre-conference. The stipend is paid at the end of the conference and payment is predicated on attendance throughout. All work presented at the conference will be under option by the conference from the time

of acceptance until six weeks after the end of the conference.

Each writer is assigned a dramaturge or story editor who assists and advises during the development of the work. At the pre-conference, each playwright reads his or her work aloud to the others. Afterward, they discuss the nature of the work to be done at the conference. After a short, intensive rehearsal period (at the conference), stage plays are given two staged readings in front of an audience. "Actors work with script in hand and performances have limited production values: modular sets, minimal lights, essential props, and no costumes. Media playwrights are acquainted with the effects of the camera on their scripts; their material is developed, and the works are read to the assembled conference and invited observers by a company of actors."

Facility Description
None provided.

How to Apply
Send an SASE for information and application guidelines. Submit one copy of a typed, bound, covered script (and an adequate SASE for its return) with a $15 nonrefundable application fee (for each script). Include as part of the script the number of acts or scenes, time and place, and a list of characters. For each script, you must complete and return one set of catalog cards (two sets are sent to you when you request application guidelines). Be sure to circle the category in which you are submitting. Enclose a one-page (not attached to script) biography, including information about other plays, teleplays, and films you have written, or other literary forms in which you have worked. Also include a number ten SASE for notification of their decision. If you wish acknowledgment that your script was received, include an SASP.

Deadline
November 1 (Scripts are accepted between August 15 and November 1). Notification by May.

Approximate Cost of Program
$15 application fee, incidentals—offset by $1,000 stipend.

PHILLIPS EXETER ACADEMY   NH
George Bennett Fellowship
Phillips Exeter Academy, 20 Main Street, Exeter, New Hampshire 03833
Attention: Charlie Pratt
Phone: (603) 772-4311; fax: (603) 778-9563
Web site: www.exeter.edu

Type of Facility/Award
Fellowship.

Who Can Apply

Writers, with preference given to fiction writers. Nonfiction writers will be considered only if their work is intended for a general audience in expectation of a career as a professional writer.

Provisos

The writer must have a writing project in the works that he or she needs time to complete. Encouragement from a publisher is not a requirement. The fellowship is meant to free the writer from the obligations of accepting a publisher's advance with its inevitable restrictions. Quality and originality of the work are the main considerations.

Dates of Operation

Academic year (September through June).

Location

Exeter, New Hampshire.

History

"The manuscripts are the primary basis for the selection of the Fellow, and each manuscript will receive the careful attention of the selection committee, made up of members of the Academy English Department. We are genuine in our desire to select the most promising candidate, and we are always conscious that the Fellowship is for a writer at the beginning of his or her career and that much of the material we receive is necessarily unfinished."

What They Offer

The George Bennett Fellowship provides housing (furnished, if necessary), meals (at the Academy's dining hall) for the writer and his or her family (while school is in session), and a stipend of $6,000. The term of the residency is one academic year (September to June). Only one fellowship is awarded annually. The writer must live in Exeter and make his or her self and talents available in an "informal and unofficial way" to students interested in writing, students in English classes, and members of student literary organizations. The writer will not be required to teach any classes, will not be asked to coach athletics, dramatics, or debating, and will not be an adviser to any Academy organization. This is not a faculty position. The nature of the association between the writer and the Academy will be determined by the writer's own interests and good will, not by Academy demand. It is the hope of the Academy that the partially completed manuscript will be completed during the tenure of the fellowship and subsequently submitted to a publisher.

Facility Description

This is a private school campus, but on-campus housing is not provided. Writers choose their own housing within Academy guidelines.

How to Apply

Send an SASE for an application and guidelines. Return the completed application with a statement that addresses why the fellowship would be appropriate to your situation, a description of your partially completed project and your plan for its completion, a sample of the work (fifty typed pages of prose or at least twenty poems), and a $5 application fee. The two references listed on the application will only be contacted if you make it to the final stage of the competition.

Deadline

December 1 (postmarked). Notification on or about March 15.

Approximate Cost of Program

$5 application fee, transportation, materials, and incidentals—offset by $6,000 stipend.

THE POTATO EYES FOUNDATION   ME   **DISCONTINUED**

c/o Nightshade Press, P.O. Box 76, Troy, Maine 04987
Attention: Ray Zarucchi or Carolyn Page
Phone: (719) 684-0953
Email: potatoeyes@uninets.net

> Notice: "Due to a death in the family and a difference in our focus as a nonprofit foundation, we are on hiatus in terms of the retreat."

RADCLIFFE COLLEGE   MA
Mary Ingraham Bunting Fellowship

34 Concord Avenue, Cambridge, Massachusetts 02138
Attention: Administrator—Bunting Fellowship Program
Phone: (617) 495-8212
Web Site: www.radcliffe.edu/bunting
Email: bunting_fellowships@radcliffe.harvard.edu

Type of Facility/Award

Fellowship.

Who Can Apply

Women scholars, creative writers, and visual or performing artists.

Provisos

The institute seeks applications from women scholars in any field who have held a doctorate or appropriate final degree at least two years prior to appointment. Fiction and nonfiction applicants must have a contract for publication of a book-length manuscript or at least three published short works. For a fellowship in poetry, applicants must have a published book of poetry or at least twenty poems published in the last five years, and be in the process of completing a manuscript. Bunting Fellows may not simultaneously hold another major fellowship providing more than $20,000.

Dates of Operation

Mid-September through mid-August (specific dates vary each year).

Location

Boston area.

History

The Mary Ingraham Bunting Institute of Radcliffe College was founded in 1960. It is a multidisciplinary research center with programs designed to support women of exceptional promise and demonstrated accomplishment who wish to pursue independent work in academic studies, professional fields, and the creative arts.

What They Offer

The Mary Ingraham Bunting Institute annually grants six to ten awards of $40,000 each. Office or studio space, auditing privileges, and access to libraries and most other resources of Radcliffe College and Harvard University are provided. Fellows are expected to present their works-in-progress at public colloquia, performances, or exhibitions.

The Affiliation Program offers ten to twenty women office space and the same resources as the Bunting Fellowship Program, but without stipend. (Women holding or seeking other funded awards are invited to apply.) Appointments can be made for the fall or spring semesters or for both.

Facility Description

Radcliffe College campus, including access to libraries and most other resources of Radcliffe College and Harvard University.

How to Apply

After June 1, send an SASE for an application and brochure. Return your completed application and other specified materials before the deadline.

Deadline

October 15 (postmarked) for Affiliate Program. October 15 (postmarked) for Bunting Fellowship Program. November 15 (postmarked) for visual arts applications for both programs.

Approximate Cost of Program

Transportation, housing, meals, materials, and incidentals—offset by $40,000 stipend. No stipend for Affiliate Program.

REAL ART WAYS   **CT**   ****DISCONTINUED****

MILDRED I. REID WRITERS COLONY   NH   **DISCONTINUED**

SKOWHEGAN SCHOOL OF PAINTING AND SCULPTURE   ME
Skowhegan, Maine
Phone: (207) 474-9345

Information/applications/brochures:
200 Park Avenue South, Suite 1116, New York, New York 10003-1503
Phone: (212) 529-0505

Type of Facility/Award
Residency.

Who Can Apply
Advanced visual artists (painting, sculpture, fresco, installation, performance, video, photography, etc.). Art students are welcome to apply.

Provisos
Artists may attend Skowhegan only once. Applicants must be at least nineteen years of age. International students will be considered only if they are proficient in English and can secure the appropriate visas.

Dates of Operation
Mid-June through mid-August. Artists must attend the full nine-week session.

Location
Skowhegan is located in the heavily forested lake district of central Maine.

History
"Skowhegan was founded in 1946 by artists for artists. The residency is not a 're-treat'; rather, the intensive nine-week summer program allows sixty-five artists to produce art in a communal, rural environment of great natural beauty. The program does not offer structured classes; instead, it provides an extended and concentrated period of independent work, done with the critical assistance and camaraderie of a faculty of resident and visiting artists. The faculty changes every year."

What They Offer
Nine-week summer sessions include weekly one-on-one critiques from a rotating faculty of professional artists. Structured workshops are not offered (with the exception of fresco); instead, ample time is provided to work without limitations. Residents have access to lectures and an archive of slides and tapes. Full and partial fellowships are available based on financial need. The Matching School Fellowship Program offers full tuition fellowships to students enrolled in participating schools who are accepted to Skowhegan.

Facility Description

"Set on 3,000 heavily forested acres, Skowhegan is comprised of studios, set among rolling pastures, and dormitory-style living quarters on the edge of a large lake. Each artist usually shares a room with one or two others. Bath facilities are also shared. The Robert Lehman Library has a collection of 15,000 art books, catalogs, and bound magazines. All facilities, including the Common House, are open 24 hours a day. No pets are allowed." A sculpture shop provides basic equipment for working with wood, metal, and clay, and residents have access to a darkroom for basic black-and-white and color photography. There is a small art supply store on campus. Most artists, however, mail-order or bring supplies with them.

How to Apply

Contact the New York office for an application bulletin. You will be required to submit twelve 35 mm slides or a video tape, labeled and arranged according to the instructions. Include a $35 application fee, which covers the cost of returning your materials.

Deadline

February 1 (postmarked) for general application and financial aid application. February 26 (postmarked) for evidence of financial need. Notification by early April.

Approximate Cost of Program

$5,200 tuition fee for nine-week session, $25 activity fee, $35 application fee, transportation, and materials. Financial assistance is available for those who qualify.

VERMONT STUDIO CENTER   VT

P.O. Box 613, 80 Pearl Street, Johnson, Vermont 05656
Attention: VSC Writing Program
Phone: (802) 635-2727; fax: (802) 635-2730
Web site: www.vermontstudiocenter.com
Email: vscvt@pwshift.com

Type of Facility/Award

Residencies.

Who Can Apply

Writers and visual artists working in painting, mixed media, sculpture, printmaking, photography, and drawing.

Provisos

None listed.

Dates of Operation

Open year-round.

Location

The center is located on the banks of the Gihon River in Johnson (pop. 2,500), a traditional Vermont village in the heart of the Green Mountains. Johnson is six and a half hours from New York City, three and a half hours from Boston, and two hours from Montreal. Transportation to and from Burlington, Vermont, (a one hour drive) is provided on arrival and departure days if advance notice is given. Transportation to Burlington is available by plane or Greyhound bus, and to Waterbury by Amtrak.

A Painter on the River at the Vermont Studio Center

History

VSC was founded by artists in 1984. "The purpose of a VSC Residency is to foster independent work; in addition, VSC provides Residents access to a large, thriving, and varied community of working and professional writers and artists from across the United States and abroad." It is the country's largest artists' community, operating year-round to offer four- to twelve-week residencies (with a limited number of two-week residencies) for fifty writers and artists per month—twelve writers, twenty-three painters, twelve sculptors, two printmakers, and one photographer.

What They Offer

All VSC residents receive private studio space available round-the-clock, accommodations, and meals, as well as access to readings, open studio evenings, and slide showings. VSC also provides a monthly roster of prominent visiting writers and artists (two writers, three painters, and two sculptors) who offer readings and slide talks and are available for conferences and studio visits. "Whether these conferences are seen as a conversation between colleagues or an encounter with a mentor, or something in between, depends on each resident's needs and response." Applicants can apply for full fellowships, partial fellowships, or work-exchange grants.

Facility Description

VSC is comprised of twenty-two historic buildings which house a conference room, lecture hall, dining hall, gallery, art supply store, lounge, libraries, studios, residences, and offices. A small building has been set aside for meditation and reflection. Single and double-occupancy accommodations are available, with a supplemental fee to secure a single room. Houses are simply furnished and a linen service is provided. All meals are prepared by a gourmet chef. Special diets cannot be accommodated.

Nearby Johnson State College has a library, racquetball and tennis courts, a swimming pool, weight and aerobic rooms, and cross country ski and hiking trails, all of which are available for use by VSC residents. The center is partially handicapped-accessible and is working to make the facilities entirely handicapped-accessible.

Writing residents are housed in private rooms furnished with a large desk, reading lamp, comfortable chair, power strip, and a dictionary/thesaurus. Writers are free to use the VSC print/copy station, which includes a coin-operated copier, PC computer and printer, and a Macintosh printer.

Painting/mixed-media residents receive a private studio of approximately 300 square feet, well-lit with natural and artificial light and equipped with an easel, table, stool, rolling work cart, and ample wall space.

Sculpture/mixed-media residents are provided with private studios, a communal shop area with hand and power tools, an outdoor work yard, and the opportunity for nonpermanent site-specific pieces in the immediate environment. VSC's staff sculptor is available during the week for technical support.

Vermont Studio Center and Roswell Artist-in-Residence Program
Sculpture

Jerry Bleem

The two residency programs in which I have participated differed in several ways. Though the constant sun of New Mexico contrasted sharply with the snow and cold of Vermont in February, when trying to describe their distinctive atmospheres, I am reminded not of the climate, but of the number of people involved and the length of time I spent in each program.

Photo credit: Cathy Nelson © 2000

Located in the austere landscape of southeastern New Mexico, the Roswell Artist-in-Residence Program provided me with a full year to focus on art-making. Before I arrived in Roswell, and during my residency, I was conscious that my time was so ample that I needed to celebrate it in a particular way. I needed to waste it. When faced with this amazing luxury, I remembered all the things that I promised to do when I "had time." At the top of this list was exploring different materials (amassed for years and unusable in what had been my usual body of work), and the seemingly unrelated ideas that had been floating around in my mind for just as long.

So I packed boxes of books and read an amazing number of them, wrote long letters to astonished friends, and found the courage to fail. The length of this residency gave me the opportunity to experiment, to leave a path I had struggled to clear to consider other possibilities. Often I was uncomfortable and confused as I tried to give physical form to ideas that had, up to this point, existed as some kind of ghosts. Some nights I went to bed convinced my art-making skills had deserted me—if they had really existed in the first place. Happily, taking the chance to fail and waste my time produced results that were worth the effort.

By contrast, I arrived in Johnson, Vermont at the end of January for four weeks that kept looking shorter and shorter. As I tried to remember why coming to Vermont in February had struck me as a good idea, I also remembered the good advice of a friend: "Four weeks to make art is four weeks to make art." At the Vermont Studio Center, I unpacked prepared materials as I refined plans for a sculpture. On the first day of the residency, I started making this piece, using a familiar way of working, because of the sensation I carried with me that there was no time to waste. Yes, four weeks is shorter than a year, and my friend was right. At the end of my time, the snow was melting and I left with completed sculptures: a different kind of success.

Luckily I went to the Vermont Studio Center with my artistic life (and production) planned. My improvisation skills were taxed by something I had not anticipated—people. For the sake of round numbers, let's just say there were about 60 or 70 resident and visiting artists and staff members. By nature, I am strongly introverted; indeed, I have been accused of having eremitical tendencies to which I plead "guilty." Roswell suited me perfectly. I lived in my own house, cooked my own meals, and could, if I chose to, avoid everyone else. The program accommodates five artists. Though each can bring his or her family, the population of the "compound" (local dialect) is rarely more than a dozen or so, and that includes the director and his family.

This can also be a dangerous situation. With so few people, any division or disagreement has the potential to polarize the group and color one's time there. Of course, the experience I had is also possible. A year with a small group of people gave me the opportunity to get to know them at a reasonable pace. With months upon months to share our work and our lives, there was no rushed intimacy, but one that developed at a more natural pace. Any invitation declined simply left room for the next time. We respected each other's work habits, got art made, had parties large and small, shared sightseeing discoveries: we created our own kind of community. There are days when I still miss it.

There was no hiding at the Vermont Studio Center. Though each person is assigned her/his own studio, the walls of the studio do not always reach the ceiling: visual privacy with eavesdropping enforced. I requested and received a private bedroom, but some were shared, as were the bathrooms. The wonderful meals (after a day or two I dismissed any ideas of eating sensible portions) were served in the common dining room: 20 every week. For someone on the shy side, this translates into a neon sign that flashes DANGER! DANGER! MORE UNAVOIDABLE SOCIAL CONTACT! The first week was the worst. Obviously J survived, but it took a great deal of energy.

Lest J appear as a misanthrope, J must admit that J enjoyed having all those people around. Not all of them and not all at once, of course, but they gave a singular shape to this residency. Beyond the bonds of friendship that were formed, J particularly enjoyed having writers around. They approach the artistic enterprise in their own distinctive way which J found fascinating and illuminating. But, best of all, they read from their works. Wow! Though J live in a large urban center and have the opportunity to attend similar events, J don't. (My excuse is the usual one of lacking time.) At the Vermont Studio Center, all J had to do was go into that same threatening dining room on certain assigned nights to enjoy the unexpected pleasure of writers reading.

Pressed to give advice to those considering a residency program, J would simply say: "Know yourself and know the program." One's happiness at any program will be in direct proportion to how that program's qualities mesh with one's personal characteristics and expectations. J didn't do that, but it sounds like good counsel. J applied to programs that fit my schedule rather than my psychological profile. Jn this case, remember to pack your flexibility, patience and social skills. No one benefits from residencies being turned into battlegrounds. Moreover, challenging situations can also teach us things we never expected to learn.

Printmaking residents work in a shared print shop run by VSC's Tamarind Master Printer who is available for informal support (though residents should have prior printing experience and plan to work independently). Printers should contact VSC for equipment details.

Life models are available weekdays for drawing residents.

Photography residents should contact VSC for equipment details.

How to Apply

Contact VSC to request an application and brochure. Return the completed application with a $25 nonrefundable application fee, résumé, the names and addresses of three references who are familiar with you and your work, and a sample of your work. Writers: Send five pages of poetry or ten pages of prose or script.

Visual artists: Send twenty labeled, dated slides. Include an adequate SASE for return of your materials. If you apply for financial aid, include a copy of your tax form. You can apply for full fellowships, partial fellowships, or work exchange grants.

Deadline

February 15, June 15, or September 30 if applying for a full fellowship. Rolling application process for paid and work-exchange residencies.

Approximate Cost of Program

Anywhere from $1,000 to $3,000 (approximate costs) plus $25 application fee, transportation, materials, and incidentals. A limited number of full fellowships are available, based on merit only. Financial assistance is also available. Note: "Two-thirds of the writers and artists who participate at VSC each year receive some form of financial assistance, so do not assume that you are ineligible. Apply early so your eligibility can be determined."

WATERSHED CENTER FOR THE CERAMIC ARTS   ME

19 Brick Hill Road, Newcastle, Maine 04553
Attention: Lynn Thompson
Phone: (207) 882-6075; fax: (207) 882-6075 (please call before sending a fax)
Email: h2oshed@midcoast.com

Type of Facility/Award

Residency.

Who Can Apply

Any serious artist or student may apply. The studio focuses on ceramic arts, but any artist may attend.

Provisos

Serious artists from all countries are invited to apply.

Dates of Operation

Two-week sessions run June through August. Nine-month residencies run September through May.

Location

Watershed is located one hour from Portland, Maine, and three hours from Boston. The center is set on thirty-two rural acres, both open and wooded, with gently rolling hills. It is surrounded by a neighboring farm, Nature Conservancy land, and the Sheepscot River. There are several lakes in the vicinity, and the ocean is just a short drive away.

History

The Watershed Center was originally a waterstruck brick factory. High production costs and insufficient demand caused the factory to close. Margaret Griggs joined forces with artist George Mason to organize a pilot project to utilize the brick factory site in a new way. The program was a great success. In 1986, the center became incorporated as a nonprofit organization. Watershed provides residents with a peaceful environment, an informal atmosphere, and undisturbed time to concentrate on their work. Exchange of ideas, collaboration, experimentation, exploration, and self-inquiry are encouraged. "The mission of Watershed Center for the Ceramic Arts is to provide serious artists with time and space to create in clay."

What They Offer

Fourteen artists per session work, eat, and live in the center's intimate community setting. Watershed can also accommodate "AIA" groups (up to eleven artists working together). Four residents per summer—one per session—are fully funded and provided with room, board, and studio space. Eight additional residents are partially funded. Winter residents are provided with housing, meals, studio space, materials, and use of the kilns for nine months. Summer assistantships are awarded to applicants in need of financial aid—the residency fee is reduced in exchange for fifteen hours of work per week in the house or the studio. Watershed brick clay is free to residents; other clay and glaze materials are sold by weight at reasonable prices.

Facility Description

The studio is housed in a spacious old brick building. There is plenty of flexible studio space with 16,000 square feet on two floors. Equipment includes two 60-cubic-foot low-fire propane car kilns, a 30-cubic-foot high-fire propane kiln, a 15-cubic-foot wood kiln, various low- and high-fire electric kilns, potters' wheels, a Soldner clay mixer, and a Walker pug mill. A hillside of local earthenware brick clay is free and abundant. Other stand clay and glaze materials are available for purchase. Studio technicians manage and maintain the studio.

A separate 4,000-square-foot residence building provides dorm housing for residents. A central living area and dining room are the sites for conversation and superb, healthy meals prepared by staff artists.

How to Apply

Send an SASE for an application and brochure. Submit your completed application with a $20 nonrefundable application fee. If applying for a nine-month winter residency, also send six slides of recent work (and an adequate SASE for their return), your résumé, and the addresses and telephone numbers of two references. Inquire about specific procedures for assistantship applications; you should be able to demonstrate that you have the appropriate work skills for the assistantship.

Deadline

April 1 for summer residency. July 30 for winter residency.

Approximate Cost of Program

$20 application fee, transportation, materials, firing fees, and incidentals, plus going residency fees (unless funded).

WISDOM HOUSE RETREAT AND CONFERENCE CENTER   CT

229 East Litchfield Road, Litchfield, Connecticut 06759-3002
Attention: Ruthann Williams, OP or Registrar
Phone: (860) 567-3163; fax: (860) 567-3166
Web site: www.wisdomhouse.org
Email: info@wisdomhouse.org

Type of Facility/Award

Retreat.

Who Can Apply

Artists and writers.

Provisos

None listed.

Dates of Operation

Open year-round, but space is based on availability.

Location

The center is located in northwest Connecticut, in the foothills of the Berkshires, just three miles from the colonial town of Litchfield.

History

Formally a convent for the Daughters of Wisdom, Wisdom House has traditionally been a place for spirituality, education, the arts, and service to humanity. It now serves as an interfaith retreat and conference center.

What They Offer

The *New York Times* referred to Wisdom House as "a resort for the spirit." The staff, location, and facilities all aim to provide an environment of reflection and spirituality for artists and writers. Residents receive access to the center's varied facilities. Room and board are available for $45 to $55 per day.

Facility Description

Situated on fifty-four acres of forest land in the Berkshires, Wisdom House is surrounded by meadows, trees, and peace and quiet. Facilities include an outdoor labyrinth, swimming pool, art gallery, chapel, sun porches, and twelve meeting rooms for use by guests of residents. Rooms are available either with a bathroom or near a bathroom. Communications ports for residents' PCs are available.

How To Apply
Send an SASE for an application and specify that you wish to book an artist retreat.

Deadline
Applications should be submitted at least two weeks before expected arrival date.

Approximate Cost of Program
$45–$55 per day plus transportation, materials, and incidentals.

THE YARD: A COLONY FOR PERFORMING ARTISTS   MA
P.O. Box 405, Chilmark, Massachusetts 02535
Attention: Ernest W. Lannaccone
Phone: (508) 645-9662; fax: (508) 645-3176
Web site: www.tiac.net/users/theyard
Email: theyard@tiac.net

Type of Facility/Award
Artist-in-residence programs.

Who Can Apply
Choreographers and dancers.

Provisos
There are various application requirements for each program. Artist-in-the-Schools Program: Choreography candidates for this residency are expected to be performing at a level that would merit a creative residency; teaching experience in a school situation is a plus. Company Residency: Choreographers must have formed a company, performed professionally for a minimum of three years, and performed full-length programs of their own work. Bessie Schönberg Choreographers and Dancers Residency: Choreographers must have had their work performed professionally for a minimum of three years. Dancers must have completed an undergraduate degree at the time of residency or have a minimum of three years professional experience. Technical residencies: Inquire directly.

Dates of Operation
Various dates during the summer.

Location
The Yard is nestled between hills and meadows in Chilmark, on the island of Martha's Vineyard. The colony is a five-hour drive from New York City and a two-hour drive

from Boston. Located near the center of town, The Yard is an easy walk to the bank, post office, library, and general store. The island is accessible by car, bus, ferry, and plane. Between rehearsals, dancers can escape to the beach or the nearby fishing village of Menemsha.

History

A public, nonprofit organization, The Yard was founded in 1973 by Patricia N. Nanon. Since its founding, over 650 artists have collaborated on more than 160 new works, producing annual performances in New York City, presenting special performances for Martha's Vineyard students and senior citizens, and providing and supporting artist-in-the-school and multicultural programs in the Martha's Vineyard public schools, along with community dance classes and special events at The Yard.

What They Offer

Summer residencies take place at a theater and housing complex in Chilmark. Choreographers and dancers receive housing, stipends, rehearsal space, technical and administrative staff, an artistic advisor, and the gift of time for concentrated work. There are several different programs available.

Artist-in-the-Schools Program: One teacher or choreographer will be selected for a four-week residency to teach dance and movement in the Martha's Vineyard public schools. The choreographer may bring up to three dancers who may serve as teaching assistants. The Yard provides housing and the use of a studio for the artist to develop his or her own work. This program also requires thirty-six hours of teaching from each resident. In addition to housing, residents receive a $1,300 stipend, and up to three assistants will each receive a stipend of $100 per week. Final candidates must be interviewed by The Yard's selection committee.

Company Residency: Two choreographers and their companies will be selected for this four-week session devoted to the creation, rehearsal, and performance of a new piece by each choreographer and his or her company. Choreographers receive a critique of their new work by an outstanding practitioner in the field, and the new pieces will be premiered at The Yard's theater. Companies chosen for this session receive shared housing, studio space, and a stipend of $4,500 per company. (Total number of participants from both companies is twelve.) Finalists will audition live for the selection committee in New York City.

Bessie Schönberg Choreographers and Dancers Residency: Four choreographers and eight dancers will be selected for this five-week residency session to create, rehearse, and perform new works. Choreographers are given the opportunity to work with a company of professional dancers for an extended period of time. Choreographers will receive a critique of their new work by outstanding practitioners in the field and the new pieces will be premiered at The Yard's theatre. In addition, this residency includes a program of works from the choreographers' and dancers' repertory, special events, and outreach programs for children and senior citizens. Each artist is provided with a stipend of $1,200, and each choreographer is granted a production budget of up to $400.

Technical residencies: Positions are sometimes available for lighting directors, carpenters, technical directors, etc. Contact The Yard for current openings.

Facility Description

The Yard complex includes two houses, the "Front Yard" and the "Side Yard," which are available to accommodate up to thirteen people. The houses include full kitchens, living and dining areas, laundry facilities, and an outdoor deck and yard. The theater is a fully equipped facility featuring a 35' x 28' sprung dance floor. The theater seats approximately 110 people on folding chairs and benches and is handicapped-accessible.

How to Apply

Send an SASE for a brochure. Submit a cover letter indicating session(s) for which you are applying; a typed résumé that includes academic and professional training, choreographic, performing, and teaching experience, as well as experience in related fields; one letter of recommendation and the names, addresses, and telephone numbers of two additional references (qualified dance professionals familiar with your work); information about upcoming performances that selection committee members may attend; a sample of your work (video tape); and an SASP for acknowledgment of receipt. Enclose an adequate SASE if you want your video returned. For the Artist-in-the-Schools Program, also include a detailed description of your teaching experience, a discussion of goals for the proposed curriculum, a choreographer project proposal, and a 1/2" VHS video tape of your most recent work. For technical residencies, submit a cover letter, a typed résumé, recommendations, and visual materials.

Deadline

December 10 (received) for all residencies.

Approximate Cost of Program

Meals and incidentals—offset by stipend. Varies by program.

PACIFIC COAST COLONIES

Alaska
California
Hawaii
Oregon
Washington

ACADEMY OF MOTION PICTURE ARTS & SCIENCES   CA
The Nicholl Fellowships

Academy Foundation, The Nicholl Fellowships in Screenwriting, 8949 Wilshire
  Boulevard, Beverly Hills, California 90211-1972
Attention: Gale Anne Hurd, Chair
Phone: (310) 247-3035
Web site: www.oscars.org/nicholl

Type of Facility/Award
Fellowship.

Who Can Apply
Screenwriters.

Provisos
Screenwriters who have not earned money or other consideration as a screenwriter
for theatrical films or television, or for the sale of (or sale of an option to) any original
story, treatment, screenplay, or teleplay for more than $5,000 are eligible. Applicants
may not have received a screenwriting fellowship that includes a "first look" clause,
an option, or any other quid pro quo involving their work. Members and employees
of the Academy of Motion Picture Arts and Sciences and their immediate families
are not eligible, nor are competition judges and their immediate families. Nicholl
Fellowships may not be held concurrently with other fellowships or similar awards
or while completing a formal course of study. The fellowship year may be deferred to
allow a student winner to complete his or her education.

Dates of Operation
Fellowship year begins in mid-November.

Location
This is a nonresidential fellowship.

History
The Don and Gee Nicholl Fellowships in Screenwriting Program, established in
1985, is made possible by a gift to the academy from Mrs. Gee Nicholl. The program, established with the intent of identifying and encouraging new writers, has
come to be regarded as the nation's most prestigious competition for aspiring screenwriters. In the past decade, fifty-eight fellows have been selected from over 37,000
entries. The awards allow fellows to concentrate on their writing for a year without
having to worry too much about their financial situations.

What They Offer
Up to five awards of $25,000 each, payable in five installments over a one-year period,

may be awarded each year. Winners are expected to complete at least one original screenplay (100–130 pages in length) during the fellowship year. Installment payments are made quarterly, subject to the committee's satisfaction with the recipient's progress and work. The schedule and nature of the fellow's progress will be established at the time of the initial fellowship payment. Each fellow furnishes the academy with a copy of the work completed during the fellowship year. The academy does not acquire any rights to the work or entry screenplay and will not participate in its marketing or any other aspects of its commercial future.

Facility Description
This is a nonresidential fellowship.

How to Apply
Send an SASE or see their Web site for an application and brochure. Submit the completed application, a $30 entry fee (checks made payable to the Academy Foundation), and a single copy of your original screenplay (in standard U.S. screenplay format). "Submissions must be the original work of the applicant and may not be based, in whole or in part, on any other fictional or nonfictional material, published or unpublished, produced or unproduced. Entries may, however, be adapted from the applicant's original work, which should be noted in the application form." Screenplays must have been originally written in English. They do not accept translations or collaborative works. Scripts will not be returned. Those who make it to the final judging round will be asked to submit to the Nicholl Committee a letter giving some idea of the writer's personal and professional interests as they relate to the fellowship should he or she receive one. Substitutions of either corrected pages or new drafts will not be accepted under any circumstances.

Deadline
May 1 (postmarked). Notification in mid-October.

Approximate Cost of Program
$30 application fee, transportation, housing, meals, materials, and incidentals—offset by stipend.

CENTRUM CREATIVE RESIDENCY PROGRAM   WA
P.O. Box 1158, Port Townsend, Washington 98368
Attention: Marlene Bennett, Program Facilitator
Phone: (360) 385-3102; fax: (360) 385-2470
Web site: www.centrum.org
Email: marlene@centrum.org

Type of Facility/Award
Residency.

Who Can Apply
Writers, visual artists, printmakers, composers, and choreographers.

Provisos
None listed. Previous residents may reapply.

Dates of Operation
January through May and September through December.

Location
Fort Worden State Park is near Port Townsend, Washington, on the northeastern tip of Washington's Olympic Peninsula. The nearest major airport is Seattle-Tacoma.

History
Centrum is a nonprofit arts and education organization that also sponsors workshops, festivals, performances, and conferences. Two hundred writers, visual artists, architects, actors, dancers, and musicians have benefited from the residency program since its inception in 1978.

What They Offer
Between forty and fifty artists are selected each year for residencies, which include housing and studio space (where applicable). Former residents are eligible for residencies of up to two months, but they must cover the cost of their own housing and studio rental. Linens and bedding are supplied. No residencies will be scheduled in June, July, or August.

Facilities
Artists stay in individual cabins on the grounds of historic Fort Worden State Park, a 440-acre former military fort on the Strait of Juan de Fuca. Cabins are on a grassy knoll overlooking the water. Each contains a living room, two or three bedrooms, a bathroom, and a kitchen equipped with basic cooking and eating utensils. Cabins are simply furnished and have no phone, television, or radio. There is a laundromat on campus.

How to Apply
Send an SASE for an application and brochure. Return your completed application with a nonrefundable $10 application fee, a description of your proposed project, a current résumé, and examples of your recent work as follows. Writers: five poems or ten pages of prose. Visual artists: five to ten slides. Composers: an audiocassette sampling of your recent work (written transcription encouraged). Choreographers: a videocassette with at least one complete choreographic work. Samples

of three other pieces may be included as well. Include an adequate SASE for return of your materials.

Deadline
September 29 for new applicants. Former residents may apply at any time.

Approximate Cost of Program
$10 application fee, transportation, meals, materials, and incidentals.

CHESTERFIELD FILM COMPANY   CA
PMB 544, 1158 26th St., Santa Monica, California 90403
Attention: Writer's Film Project
Phone: (213) 683-3977
Web site: www.chesterfield-co.com
Email: info@chesterfield-co.com:

Type of Facility/Award
Fellowship.

Who Can Apply
Fiction, theater, and film writers.

Provisos
There are no age or academic requirements. Acceptance is based solely upon story-telling talent—regardless of the genre or form of the submission.

Dates of Operation
Open year-round.

Location
CFC is located in Santa Monica in a complex of film production companies which include the Kennedy/Marshall Company, Bedford Falls, and Zucker Bros., among others.

History
CFC is an independent production company originated in 1990. The Writer's Film Project (WFP) was developed with generous support from Steven Spielberg's Amblin Entertainment and Universal Pictures. Each year, fiction, theater, and film writers are chosen to participate in the program. Some have been affiliated with university writing programs and some have not. Selected writers form a screenwriting work-shop, using their storytelling skills to begin a career in film. Many program graduates have been signed by major literary agencies. Some have been hired by major studios for writing assignments and some have had their scripts acquired by various studios and production companies.

What They Offer

Up to five writers may be chosen to participate in the twelve-month program. Each will receive a $20,000 stipend to cover living expenses. The program requires participants to live in the Los Angeles area for the year. Fellows form a workshop that meets three to five times a week to consider story ideas, script outlines, and first and second drafts of each screenplay. Throughout the year, selected film professionals will meet with the writers to share their opinions and experience. Each writer is paired with a professional screenwriter and a studio executive mentor. By the end of the fellowship year, each writer will have created two original feature-length screenplays, which she or he can use as talent samples within the film industry. WFP writers are introduced to a number of literary agents and agencies.

Facility Description

Group meetings are currently held in a conference room at Amblin Entertainment.

How to Apply

Send an SASE for an application and brochure. Return two copies of the completed application with a $39.50 nonrefundable application fee, writing samples, an SASE, and an SASP (to acknowledge receipt of materials). You may submit writing samples in one or more of the categories that follow (indicating which samples are most representative of your work). Fiction: two or more short stories and/or one novel or novel-in-progress. Plays: one or two plays, including a one-paragraph synopsis of each play, no more than three or four sentences in length, attached to the front of the play. Screenplays: one or two screenplays, including a one-paragraph synopsis of each screenplay, no more than three to four sentences in length, attached to the front of the script. Bind each screenplay with white paper and standard brads.

Deadline

June 1. Notification by December 15.

Approximate Cost of Program

$39.50 application fee, transportation, housing, meals, materials, and incidentals—offset by $20,000 stipend.

WALT DISNEY PICTURES & TELEVISION FELLOWSHIP   CA

500 South Buena Vista Street, Burbank, California 91521-1735
Attention: Fellowship Program Director
Phone: (818) 560-6894
Web site: www.disney.com

Type of Facility/Award

Fellowship.

Who Can Apply
Writers.

Provisos
The program is meant to seek out and employ culturally and ethnically diverse new writers. Writers with WGA credits are eligible and should apply through the Guild's Employment Access Department at (213) 782-4648.

Dates of Operation
One-year period beginning in mid-October.

Location
Los Angeles, California.

History
The program is in its twelfth year.

What They Offer
Up to ten writers may be chosen. Each will be provided with a $33,000 salary for a one-year period. Fellows from outside the Los Angeles area will be provided with round-trip airfare and one month's accommodations. Housing and work space are not included.

Facility Description
Major motion picture offices and film studios.

How to Apply
Send an SASE or check the Web site for application materials, which include an application form, a fellowship program letter agreement, a standard letter agreement, and an Exhibit "A" form. Return completed application materials with a writing sample and a one-page résumé. Partner submissions are only acceptable if both writers submit separate applications under one cover. Application materials should be clipped to the front, rather than bound within the script. You may only submit a single script; no subsequent revisions will be accepted. Send materials by certified return receipt mail for submission acknowledgment. No faxed applications will be accepted.

Deadline
April 19 (postmarked). Applications are only accepted between April 1 and April 19. Notification in mid-August.

Approximate Cost of Program
Housing, meals, materials, and incidentals—offset by $33,000 salary.

DJERASSI RESIDENT ARTISTS PROGRAM   CA

2325 Bear Gulch Road, Woodside, California 94062-4405
Attention: ADMISSIONS (plus year for which you are applying)
Phone: (650) 747-1250; fax: (650) 747-0105
Web site: www.djerassi.org
Email: drap@djerassi.org

Type of Facility/Award

Residency.

Who Can Apply

Choreographers, writers, composers, painters, sculptors, installation artists, photographers, filmmakers, video artists, performance artists, experimental theater artists, and sound and radio artists.

Provisos

Both emerging and established artists are welcome to apply. Students are not eligible. Applications from artists of varied cultural and ethnic backgrounds are encouraged.

Dates of Operation

Late-March through mid-November.

Location

Djerassi is located in the Santa Cruz Mountains overlooking the Pacific Ocean, forty miles south of San Francisco and fifteen miles west of Palo Alto. Although there is no public transportation available from the ranch, staff members provide weekly rides to Palo Alto.

History

"The Mission of the Djerassi Resident Artists Program is to support and enhance the creativity of artists by providing uninterrupted time for work, reflection, and collegial interaction in a setting of great natural beauty, and to preserve the land upon which the Program is located."

What They Offer

Sixty artists per year are provided with housing, studio space, and all meals for four- to five-week sessions. Choreographers may request to bring up to two dancers with them who will share one additional room. Additional dancers are welcome to work in the studio by special arrangement. Transportation to and from the Bay Area airports is also provided.

Facility Description

Grounds include six hundred acres of rangeland, redwood forest, and hiking trails. "Residents work and are housed in two buildings on the ranch according to artistic discipline and creative project. Living quarters and studio space consist of a four-bed-room house and a unique, remodeled twelve-sided barn. The rooms in the Artists' House are set up to accommodate writers, each with a large desk, work space, and outdoor deck. The Artists' House also contains the main kitchen, living and dining area, a library, laundry facilities, shared bathrooms, and a large deck. The Artists' Barn contains three visual art studios, a large dance studio, a darkroom, and a music compo-sition studio with a baby grand and electric piano. The studios are rustic with wood burning stoves and modest sleeping lofts. There are also a kitchen, a large common area, shared bathrooms, and laundry facilities in the Barn. The Program employs a chef who prepares communal dinners Monday through Friday, and provisions both kitch-ens. Residents are expected to prepare their own breakfasts, lunches, and weekend dinners using ingredients supplied by the Program. Vegetarian meals are available."

Equipment available for use on projects includes a slide projector and screen, video camera, television, VCR, a limited number of PC and Macintosh computers for word processing, two Internet stations, printers, and standard power tools. Smoking is only allowed in designated outdoor areas. Accommodations are limited to selected indi-viduals only (no housing is available for spouses, mates, or children, and overnight guests are not allowed—although day guests are welcome to stay for dinner).

How to Apply

Send an SASE or check the Web site for an application form. Collaborators and couples must apply separately. Alumni must wait three years before reapplying. Return com-pleted application form (printed or typewritten in English), a $25 nonrefundable appli-cation fee, your current résumé, a collaborative proposal (if applicable), and documenta-tion of recent creative work. Dancers/choreographers: Send a cued VHS video tape (la-beled with name, date, and titles) of two examples of choreography not more than ten minutes total with an accompanying descriptive sheet. Writers: Send either a set of six to ten poems, one script, or a maximum of twenty-five pages of fiction or literary nonfic-tion (all labeled with name, title, date, and publication information, if applicable, though unpublished material is welcome). Securely clip or bind all pages. Composers: Send two full compositions on cued audio cassette, CD, or DAT, and include a brief descriptive statement about your work. If submitting cassettes, send each composition on a separate tape. Scores are optional. (Composers should also check the Web site for information on the Oshita Fellowship). Visual artists: Send at least six, but no more than twenty, quality slides with standard mount for use in a Kodak Carousel projector. Numbers 1–6 will be projected. Number each slide in the top right corner, identify each with your name and title of work at the bottom, write "Top" at the top of each slide, and place a dot in the lower left corner. Include a separate slide list or descriptive sheet, and do not send previ-ously submitted slides. Media and new genre artists: Submit either a labeled VHS video, CD (for Macintosh or audio player), or slides (following instructions for visual artists), and an accompanying descriptive sheet. Enclose an adequate SASE for return of your sample(s). Samples will not be returned if you are accepted. Also return the notification postcard sent with your application packet.

Deadline
February 15. Notification by August 15.

Approximate Cost of Program
$25 application fee plus additional travel expenses, materials, and incidentals. The program supplies room, board, and studio space.

DORLAND MOUNTAIN ARTS COLONY   CA
Box 6, Temecula, California 92593
Attention: Admissions
Phone: (909) 302-3837
Web site: www.ez2.net/Dorland
Email: dorland@ez2.net

Type of Facility/Award
Residency.

Who Can Apply
All artists in music, literature, and the visual arts.

Provisos
Dorland has no electricity. If your work requires electrical apparatus (computers, tools, etc.), this is not the place for you. Spouses and collaborators may be in residence at the same time, but they must apply and will be considered separately.

Dates of Operation
Open year-round.

Location
Dorland is approximately one hundred miles from Los Angeles, about sixty miles from San Diego, and about eight miles from the town of Temecula. The closest airport is in San Diego. A private van will take you from the airport to the colony for a fee.

History
An internationally recognized haven for artists, writers, and composers, Dorland grew from the dream of Ellen Babcock Dorland, a world famous concert pianist, and her friend Barbara Horton, an environmentalist. "Between 1974 and 1988, Dorland was under the stewardship of the Nature Conservancy, an international land preservation group. The Conservancy designated Dorland as a nature preserve to protect its unique plants and wildlife. Dorland is also recognized as an Indian burial ground

and considered sacred by neighboring Indian tribes. In July 1988, the Conservancy deeded the property back to the Dorland board of directors with the restriction that the land be protected from development in perpetuity." The lack of electricity at Dorland has become "a symbol of our separateness from the modern-day world."

What They Offer

Dorland offers residencies of two to six weeks in length. Individual cottages house each artist. Kitchen utensils, linens, and housewares are provided. Residents are responsible for their meals. Weekly trips into town provide opportunities for shopping, banking, and laundry. A cottage fee of $5 per day is requested to cover the cost of firewood, wicks, and fuel. (Propane is used to fuel stoves and water heaters.) Residents communicate by placing notes in each other's mail boxes so as not to disturb one another's privacy. There is a pay phone for residents' use. Occasionally, residents organize potluck dinners or impromptu open studios. There is an eclectic library. Dorland is serious about privacy: no overnight guests are allowed without prior staff approval. Children may not stay overnight. Day visitors may be allowed with prior staff approval. No pets are allowed. Wheelchair accessibility is possible, but difficult.

Facility Description

Cottages include a kitchen, bathroom, and living and working areas. The cottages are heated by woodstoves. Kerosene or Coleman lamps are used to provide light. There are miles of natural trails on the grounds for those who like to walk or hike. There's also a spring-fed pond for cooling off.

How to Apply

Send an SASE for an application and brochure. Return the original application and three copies with a brief description of your proposed project and reasons for wanting a Dorland residency, three copies of your educational and professional experience, two references in your field, and a sample of recent work. Composers: Send three copies of two tapes or scores (no records, please). Poets: Send three copies of at least six poems. Visual artists: Send three sets of six slides in plastic sleeves. Writers: Send three copies of three works (short manuscripts or chapters). You may include other items to help the selection committee evaluate your work. Accepted artists have two years in which to schedule residencies, which are on a first-come, first-served basis, so plan ahead. Within ten days after scheduling, you are required to send a $50 nonrefundable processing fee (to hold your dates).

Deadline

March 1; notification May 15. September 1; notification November 15.

Approximate Cost of Program

$300 a month, $50 processing fee, transportation, meals, materials, and incidentals.

THE WILLARD R. ESPY LITERARY FOUNDATION   WA
Writers Residency Program
P.O. Box 614, Oysterville, Washington 98641
Attention: Polly Friedlander, President
Phone: (360) 665-5220; fax: (360) 665-5220

Type of Facility/Award
Residency.

Who Can Apply
Writers.

Provisos
Each applicant must be connected with the Pacific Northwest in at least one of the following ways: the applicant is a current Pacific Northwest resident; the applicant grew up in the Pacific Northwest; the applicant has spent considerable time living in the Pacific Northwest; or the applicant's proposed project deals with subject matter that specifically and substantially reflects the Pacific Northwest. Emerging and established writers who have demonstrated talent and commitment to their work are encouraged to apply. Espy Foundation board members, advisory board members, staff, consultants, and immediate family members of the aforementioned may not apply.

Dates of Operation
Months of the program are determined annually, so dates may vary.

Location
The village of Oysterville is located near the northern tip of the Long Beach Peninsula in southwestern Washington State between the Pacific Ocean and Willapa Bay. It is approximately 180 miles from Seattle and 120 miles from Portland, Oregon.

History
"Launched in the fall of 1997, the Willard R. Espy Foundation is a nonprofit organization based in Oysterville, Washington, and dedicated to advancing and encouraging the literary and linguistic arts. The Foundation has been named for Oysterville native Willard R. Espy, a wordsmith and memoirist whose prolific career celebrated language, word play, light verse, and what Henry James once called the 'visitable past': the events in the history of a time and place that can be recovered and preserved by the reach of a long memory and a gifted imagination."

What They Offer
The program is designed to provide residents with an environment in which they can pursue their writing without interruption or distraction. One-month residencies are available for several writers during various months of the year and include cottage accommodations and a substantial food stipend.

Facility Description

Residencies include a private writing space in shared bay-front cottages with kitchens. Bedroom linens and towels are provided, and laundry equipment is available. Residents must provide their own computer equipment, writing materials, and transportation (residents are encouraged to bring their own cars). Just a few miles from Oysterville is Leadbetter Point, home to Willapa Bay National Wildlife Refuge, where residents have access to bayside, woodland, and ocean hiking trails, as well as bird-watching opportunities.

How to Apply

Send an SASE for current information regarding application procedures, deadlines, manuscript requirements, and references. A nonrefundable $20 fee applies for each application.

Deadline

Variable.

Approximate Cost of Program

$20 application fee plus transportation, materials, and incidentals. A substantial food stipend is included.

THE WILLARD R. ESPY LITERARY FOUNDATION   WA
Willard R. Espy Award

P.O. Box 614, Oysterville, Washington 98641
Phone: (360) 665-5220; fax: (360) 665-5220

For Application and Information

Department of English, The University of Washington, Box 354330, Seattle,
   Washington 98195-4330
Attention: Shawn Wong

Type of Facility/Award

Cash award.

Who Can Apply

Emerging writers.

Provisos

Work must be set in the Pacific Northwest. Writers who have published a book are not eligible, but applicants may have published stories, excerpts, or chapters in magazines, literary journals, or newspapers. Applicants' works may be simultaneously submitted to other awards programs, contests, or publications. Officers, trustees, and immediate family members of the Willard R. Espy Literary Foundation may not apply. Faculty, students, or employees of the University of Washington are likewise not eligible.

Dates of Operation

The Espy Award is given annually.

Location

Not applicable in this listing.

History

"Launched in the fall of 1997, the Willard R. Espy Foundation is a nonprofit organization based in Oysterville, Washington, and dedicated to advancing and encouraging the literary and linguistic arts. The Foundation has been named for Oysterville native Willard R. Espy, a wordsmith and memoirist whose prolific career celebrated language, word play, light verse, and what Henry James once called the 'visitable past': the events in the history of a time and place that can be recovered and preserved by the reach of a long memory and a gifted imagination."

What They Offer

"The selected author of a work-in-progress set in the Pacific Northwest receives a monetary award, currently set at $1,000. The winner is announced to the public through the Foundation's newsletter and other regional media. The award will be given for a different literary genre each year, to be announced in January."

Facility Description

Not applicable in this listing.

How To Apply

Send an SASE to Shawn Wong at the University of Washington for application information. Submit three copies of up to twenty-five pages (no more than 9,000 words) of your manuscript and a one-page synopsis of the remainder of the project. On the title page of each entry include the title, word count, and number of pages submitted, as well as your name, mailing address, and phone number. Include your last name and the page number at the top of all subsequent pages. All manuscripts must be double-spaced, clearly printed or typed, unpublished, and an original work written in English (no translations). Include a $15 nonrefundable application fee, payable by check or money order to the Willard R. Espy Literary Foundation.

Deadline

May 15, though deadlines are subject to change.

Approximate Cost of Program

$15 application fee. Otherwise not applicable in this listing.

THE EXPLORATORIUM   CA

3601 Lyon Street, San Francisco, California 94123
Attention: Pamela Winfrey or Donna Wong
Phone: (415) 563-7337 or (415) 353-0482; fax: (415) 561-0370
Web site: www.exploratorium.edu
Email: art@exploratorium.edu

Type of Facility/Award
Residency and artist-in-residence program.

Who Can Apply
Visual and performance artists, writers, and storytellers.

Provisos
Artists whose interests are relevant to the thematic concerns of the museum are invited
to send informal proposals. (See "How to Apply" below.) The museum's central theme
is human perception. The Exploratorium is looking for interesting exhibits (using any
form of artistic media) that will work, will last, and will stand up to interactive use by the
museum's visitors. As the Exploratorium is an interactive science museum, successful
candidates will be those artists who like to experiment, who invite challenge, and who
like the idea of working with an enlightened and exploratory scientific community.

Dates of Operation
Open year-round.

Location
San Francisco's Marina District, near the Presidio and the Golden Gate Bridge.

History
"The Exploratorium, San Francisco's museum of science, art, and human perception, was founded in 1969 by Dr. Frank Oppenheimer, a noted physicist and teacher.
From the beginning, the museum has used the observations made by artists as means
of developing a clearer understanding of nature among our visitors.... Though the
Exploratorium is best known as a science museum, the museum has used the percep-
tions of both artists and scientists to establish notions of how we see, know, and
understand the world around us. Artists' works illustrate the reoccurrence of natural
processes in a multiplicity of contexts, and they thus convey a sense of the unity
between nature and culture which encompasses both art and science."

What They Offer
Experimental residencies generally lasts between one and two weeks and are intended
to introduce the artist's work to the museum and to promote communication between
the artist and museum staff. This is a process-oriented residency. "There is no expecta-

tion that the artist will develop a physical exhibit or installation during his or her stay."
An experimental residency may serve as the preliminary experimental phase that precedes the more formal artist-in-residence program, which lasts between one and six months. Like the experimental residency, the AIR program is fundamentally experimental. Artists-in-residence, however, do focus on the production of a specific piece of work. Past projects have included interactive installation pieces, visual pieces, and performances. The AIR program is usually divided into two phases: the experimental phase and the implementation phase. During the implementation phase, the artist works closely with the museum staff to complete the project that he or she developed during the experimental phase. Experimental residencies cover round-trip travel expenses, living expenses, and a small stipend. Artists-in-residence must negotiate contracts with the museum individually. The museum covers expenses for the project.

Facility Description

The Exploratorium, located in San Francisco's cavernous Palace of Fine Arts building, is a center of cultural investigation. The artists have use of a sophisticated electronics and machine shop and the technical problem-solving skills of a staff fascinated by aesthetics. The Palace of Fine Arts building itself is a work of art and a famous San Francisco landmark.

How to Apply

"Submit a letter of interest that describes, in general terms, what you would like to do and, if appropriate, which type of residency you would like to be considered for. Include background information, slides, and other supporting materials. If you would like your materials returned, please enclose an SASE." The directors stress that applicants should be familiar with the museum's goals. If possible, applicants should visit the museum before submitting an application. The museum is especially interested in proposals that relate to the five major thematic concerns of the museum: seeing, living, matter and the world, mind and learning, and hearing. If an applicant is accepted into the AIR program, he or she must submit a specific proposal for the project after completing the experimental phase of the residency. Proposals may be rejected at that time if, after a review process, they are deemed inappropriate for the museum.

Deadline

There is no formal deadline for applications. However, annual curating occurs in October and November, so many residencies are awarded in the winter when the museum is planning for the coming year.

Approximate Cost of Program

Experimental Residency: housing, meals, materials, and incidentals—offset by living expenses and a small stipend. AIR program: artists must negotiate a contract with the museum individually.

FRANCISCAN CANTICLE, INC.   **CA**   ****DISCONTINUED****
Canticle Arts Center

GLENESSENCE   **CA**   ****DISCONTINUED****

HEADLANDS CENTER FOR THE ARTS   CA
944 Fort Barry, Sausalito, California 94965
Attention: Holly Blake, Residency Manager
Phone: (415) 331-2787 or (415) 331-2887; fax: (415) 331-3857
Web site: www.headlands.org
Email: staff@headlands.org

Type of Facility/Award
Residency.

Who Can Apply
Visual artists, media artists, performing artists, and writers.

Provisos
Applicants must be residents of California, Ohio, or North Carolina. (Residence restrictions may change as funding sources change—check with the center.) North Carolina and California artists pursuing undergraduate or graduate degrees may not apply while enrolled in a degree-granting program. See "How to Apply" below for specific artists' eligibility. Bay Area artists may apply for the Affiliate Artists program wherein they can rent studio space at Rodeo Beach for up to three years.

Dates of Operation
Open year-round.

Location
The Marin Headlands is the area just north of the Golden Gate Bridge and west of the town of Sausalito.

History
On the northern edge of San Francisco Bay, the Marin Headlands, once the home of the coastal Miwok tribe, is now a national park. Headlands Center for the Arts is housed in historic Fort Barry, which was built in 1907 and occupied by the Army until 1972 when the Anti-Ballistic Missile Treaty was signed. The National Park Service entered into an arrangement with Headlands Center for the Arts (and other nonprofit groups) to let them occupy the buildings in exchange for their renovation. Headlands Center for the Arts was incorporated in 1982 and the artist-in-residence program began in 1987. Up to thirty artists each year come from all over the world to live and work on-site.

What They Offer

Offerings vary by state of residence since funding sources vary. Generally, three artists from Ohio and three artists from North Carolina are awarded three-month residencies each year. In addition to shared living space (a four-bedroom house shared with other resident artists), each artist is provided with either studio space or work space ranging from 200 to 2,000 square feet, a stipend of $500 per month, round trip airfare, use of the center's car for local trips, and dinner five nights each week. The same is provided for Bay Area residents, except for the airfare. In addition, Bay Area residents may qualify for an eleven-month live-out residency program wherein they receive a stipend of $2,500, dinner two nights a week, and studio or work space ranging from 200 to 2,000 square feet. All AIRs attend dinner and discussions and take part in the center's tri-annual open houses. Traditionally, AIRs participate in a "show and tell" evening, sharing and discussing work that is of interest to them. Please be sure to call the center for updated offerings. All information is subject to change.

Facility Description

The center is situated in nine historic army buildings amidst 12,000 acres of coastal open space. Seven of the buildings have been renovated, some by internationally renowned American artists.

How to Apply

Send an SASE for a brochure. Along with your résumé, submit a letter (two pages maximum) indicating your interest in working with Headlands Center for the Arts that discusses how the residency will affect your work and what you can contribute to the community of the Headlands. California residents only: Please state the category and the residency period (one, two, three, or eleven months) for which you are applying and indicate the dates you are available to be interviewed. In addition to the items listed above, each state requires various support materials to be submitted, as well as an SASE adequate for their return. Support materials required for each state are as follows. California and Ohio: visual artists submit no more than fifteen 35 mm slides (labeled according to instructions) or up to ten minutes of $1/_2$" video or audio tape; choreographers/dancers/performance/cross-disciplinary artists submit slides, photographs, scripts, video documentation, and other materials that adequately describe your work; writers submit one copy of no more than twenty pages of poems, thirty pages of prose, or three one-act plays; musicians/composers/radio/audio artists submit up to thirty minutes of audio (cassette or CD) or $1/_2$" video tape of recent work cued for primary review; and film/video artists submit up to thirty minutes of 8 mm or 16 mm film, or $1/_2$" video tape, cued for primary review.

California: Arts professionals (critics, art administrators) submit sufficient material to evidence the breadth of your work and interests.

North Carolina: Visual artists submit no more than fifteen 35 mm slides (labeled according to instructions), or up to ten minutes of $1/2$" video or audio tape. Writers submit one manuscript copy of no more than twenty pages of poems or thirty pages of prose.

Deadline
June 2.

Approximate Cost of Program
Some meals, materials, transportation, and incidentals—offset by stipend.

HEDGEBROOK   WA
2197 East Millman Road, Langley, Washington 98260
Attention: Writer's Residency Program
Phone: (360) 321-4786

Type of Facility/Award
Residency.

Who Can Apply
Writers.

Provisos
Women writers of all levels of experience, all ages, from all nations, of all racial, ethnic, and cultural groups who work in a variety of genres are invited to apply. Hedgebrook is handicapped-accessible.

Dates of Operation
For the year 2000: January 9 through May 31 and June 21 through December 8. Dates vary from year to year. Please send a business size SASE to above address.

Location
Hedgebrook is located on Whidbey Island, a twenty minute ferry ride from the town of Mukilteo, which is about an hour's drive north of the Seattle-Tacoma International Airport.

History
Cottages at Hedgebrook were established as a not-for-profit organization in 1988 by Nancy Skinner Nordhoff to provide a natural place to work for women writers, published or not, of all ages, and from all cultural backgrounds.

What They Offer
Hedgebrook offers one-week to two-month residencies to six writers at a time. Breakfast materials are supplied, lunch is brought to your cottage, and dinner is served at

the farmhouse. Many meals are made from the bounty of the farm's award-winning vegetable garden. All necessities (and many nonnecessities) are provided. All the writer needs to bring is writing equipment, clothes, a bath towel, and a flashlight. Typewriters and computers may be rented from a nearby shop. Limited travel scholarships and application fee waivers (based on need) may be available.

Facilities

Hedgebrook is situated on a woodsy thirty-acre farm on Whidbey Island in Puget Sound. The grounds include natural trails, a waterfall, ponds, a fire pit, and areas for horseshoes, volleyball, and croquet. Each writer has her own private, handcrafted cottage with a writing space, a reading chair, bookshelves, a window seat, a small kitchen, a toilet, and a sleeping loft with stained glass windows. Cottages are fully furnished, including appliances, utensils, cleaning supplies, bed linens, a radio, a dictionary, and a thesaurus. All cottages have electricity and one is wheelchair accessible. Each has a wood stove for heat. (Wood is provided.) A bathhouse (with laundry facilities) serves all six cottages. The main farmhouse has a small library, a dining room, a living room, a telephone for residents' use, and the colony offices. Another telephone, located in the pumphouse near the cottages, is also available for writers' use. There are no phones or televisions in the cottages. No overnight guests or pets are allowed. The utmost care is taken to give writers uninterrupted time to concentrate on their work.

How to Apply

Send an SASE (#10 business size) for an application and brochure. Return the completed application with a $15 nonrefundable application fee and five copies each of the following: a description of the project you would work on at Hedgebrook, a statement about why a stay at Hedgebrook would be important to your work, and a sample of your writing (ten pages maximum). Put your name on the application form only.

Deadline

October 1 (postmarked) for stay between mid-January and mid-June; April 1 (postmarked) for stay between July and mid-December.

Approximate Cost of Program

$15 application fee and transportation. Limited travel scholarships and application fee waivers are available.

RICHARD HUGO HOUSE

WA

1634 11th Avenue, Seattle, Washington 98122
Attention: Writer-in-Residence Program
Phone: (206) 322-7030; fax: (206) 320-8767

Type of Facility/Award
Artist-in-residence program.

Who Can Apply
Writers.

Provisos
Applicants must be published.

Dates of Operation
Open year-round.

Location
Seattle, Washington.

History
"The Richard Hugo House was started as a place for writers, readers, and audiences to blend academic and activist strategies to reach out with words to connect schools, families, individuals and other civic institutions through writing and reading."

What They Offer
For a minimum of nine months, writers are each provided with their own office space in the Richard Hugo House and a monthly stipend of $500. Housing is not provided. Residents have three responsibilities during their stay: they must teach a class, develop a public program for the Seattle community, and hold office hours at the Richard Hugo House to meet with the public.

Facility Description
The house serves as a community center in the downtown Seattle area.

How To Apply
Variable. Call or write for current application procedures.

Deadline
Deadline not provided.

Approximate Cost of Program
Transportation, housing, meals, materials, and incidentals—offset by monthly stipend of $500.

INTERSECTION FOR THE ARTS

CA

446 Valencia Street, San Francisco, California 94103
Attention: Kevin Chen
Phone: (415) 626-2787; fax: (415) 626-1636
Web site: www.theintersection.org
Email: intrsect@wenet.net

Type of Facility/Award
Cash awards.

Who Can Apply
Writers.

Provisos
Awards are meant to encourage young, unpublished writers to continue to write. Applicants must be between twenty and thirty-five years of age on January 31 of the application year. Applicants for the Joseph Henry Jackson Award must be residents of Northern California or the state of Nevada for three consecutive years prior to January 31 (of the year of application). Applicants for the James Duval Phelan Award must have been born in the state of California, but need not be current residents. Previous winners are ineligible to receive the same award again. Proof of birth, age, and residence may be required and must be furnished within ten days if requested.

Dates of Operation
Not applicable in this listing.

Location
Not applicable in this listing.

History
"The awards are made annually under the terms of the Joseph Henry Jackson Fund and the James D. Phelan Trust, housed at the San Francisco Foundation. A special fund, established by the author Mary Tanenbaum in memory of Joseph Henry Jackson, makes a third $1,000 award available to encourage nonfiction writing."

What They Offer
Awards are $2,000 each for the Joseph Henry Jackson and James Duval Phelan awards, and $1,000 for the Mary Tanenbaum Award. Award-winning manuscripts become the property of the San Francisco Foundation and part of its permanent archives. Authors retain full rights for the publication and distribution of their works.

Facility Description
Not applicable in this listing.

How to Apply

Send an SASE for an application and brochure. Return your completed (official) application signed by you (you may use one application and one work sample to apply for all three awards) with a brief description of the work submitted. For the Phelan Award, the unpublished work-in-progress submitted may be fiction, nonfictional prose, poetry, or drama. For the Jackson Award, the unpublished work-in-progress may be fiction (novel or short stories), nonfictional prose, or poetry. Nonfiction writers who apply for either the Jackson or Phelan award, but are not selected as winners, are considered for the $1,000 Mary Tanenbaum Award for Nonfictional Prose. No separate application for this award is required. No candidate may win more than one award. Manuscripts must be no longer than 100 pages, 8 ¹/₂" x 11", typed, and double-spaced. Each manuscript must have a title page with the title of the work, author's name, and address. No handwritten or illegible manuscripts.

Deadline

January 31. Notification on or about June 15.

Approximate Cost of Program

Not applicable in this listing.

KALA INSTITUTE   CA

1060 Heinz Avenue, Berkeley, California 94710
Attention: Don Parcella, Program Director
Phone: (510) 549-2977; fax: (510) 540-6914
Web site: www.kala.org
Email: kala@kala.org

Type of Facility/Award

Artist-in-residence program.

Who Can Apply

Visual artists.

Provisos

None listed. Artists from all countries are invited to apply.

Dates of Operation

Open year-round.

Location

Kala is in a light industrial area in the Oakland, Emeryville, Berkeley corridor.

History

Now in its twentieth year, Kala was founded by artists for artists, to provide them with access to technical equipment and assistance twenty-four hours a day, 365 days a year. Kala subsidizes eighty percent of the cost of maintaining a world-class intaglio and lithography studio. Proceeds from gallery sales go to support Kala's other nonprofit programs, including lectures, demonstrations, and performances.

What They Offer

The artist-in-residence program provides inexpensive studio space to selected artists for a fee. Artists work on a contract. The average length of a residency is six months at $125 per month. Some fellowships are available, depending on funding. Call Kala for specific details. Discounts are available for previous residents, or for new residents in exchange for work. Inquire about senior rates, limited-use rates, single-day-use rates, media-lab-use rates, and various other rate categories. Kala averages fifty to eighty AIRs per year. Half of these are international artists.

Facility Description

Kala's gallery, graphic arts workshop, art archive, consignment sales department, office, and media lab occupy 8,000 square feet. The equipment includes: two American French Tool etching presses—48" x 78" and 40" x 70"; three Griffin etching presses—54" x 32 $1/2$", 44" x 21 $1/2$", and 32" x 18"; KB etching press—26" x 47"; Takach-Garfield motorized litho press—56" x 32"; Bumpodo litho press—45" x 34"; Vandercook letterpress—(SP-20); cylinder proof press; Nu Arc Plate Maker (Arc-lamp); aquatint box; and darkroom. In addition to its intaglio and lithography equipment, Kala provides facilities for silkscreen, letterpress, and an electronic media laboratory for digital imaging, video editing, and multimedia productions. Media lab equipment includes seven Macintosh systems (each system has a 200 mb Syquest drive and a CD-ROM), a 600 dpi flatbed opaque/transparency, 2700 dpi slide scanner, 100 mb Zip drive, and a 600 dpi Hewlett-Packard laser printer. The most powerful system includes video and sound production and editing capabilities, in addition to a CD-recorder. Software includes: Aldus Photoshop, Illustrator, Painter, PageMaker, MacroMind Director, Premier, HyperCard, and QuickTime.

How to Apply

Send an SASE for information and guidelines. Then, if you live nearby, make an appointment with the director for a review of your portfolio. If you are applying by mail, send a résumé and some slides of your work. Include an SASE.

Deadline

Rolling application process.

Approximate Cost of Program

$125 per month plus transportation, housing, meals, materials, and incidentals.

KALANI HONUA

Kalani Oceanside Eco-Resort, Institute for Cultural Studies, R.R. 2, Box 4500,
    Pahoa- Beach Road, Hawaii 96778-9724
Attention: Richard Koob, Artistic Director
Phone: (808) 965-7828 or (800) 800-6886; fax: (808) 965-0527
Web site: www.kalani.com
Email: kalani@kalani.com

Type of Facility/Award
Retreat and artist-in-residence program.

Who Can Apply
Visual, media, performing, folk, literary, and humanities artists.

Photo by Richard Koob

Provisos
The main consideration is the professionalism of the artist and his or her ability to complete the proposed project.

Dates of Operation
Open year-round.

Location
Kalani is situated near Kalapana on the big island of Hawaii, forty-five minutes from the city of Hilo and one hour from Hawaii Volcanoes National Park. From Honolulu, book inter-island service on Hawaiian Air or Aloha Airlines to Hilo. Rent a car in advance or reserve a taxi. Transfer fee is $60 per person. Advance reservations are required.

Kalani Honua Resident Roger Montoya

History
The center was established in 1980 as an intercultural retreat, conference center, and retreat for professional artists by dance artists Richard Koob and Earnest Morgan. Kalani Honua means "the harmony of heaven and earth" in Hawaiian. The annual

calendar of events includes several week-long workshops including a hula festival, men's and women's conferences, tai-chi, a Hawaiian intercultural dance festival, and several yoga programs. Other workshops are available on an ongoing basis, including yoga, olelo Hawaii, hula, qigong, life drawing, fitness training, massage, watsu, and spa therapies.

What They Offer

Artists are welcome year-round at regular rates. Stipends for reductions in lodging fees are available by application—more are available during the periods of May through July and September through December than at other times. Stipends provide fifty percent of the lodging costs; they may not be applied to dorm lodging, camping, or a reduction in food or transportation costs. Standard fees are $75–$120 per night for a single with private bath, $95–$145 per night for a double with private bath, $65–$75 per night for a single with shared bath, and $75–$95 per night for a double with shared bath. An additional fee may be required if a private studio or work space is needed. A ten percent lodging discount is available on stays of seven or more nights. Group rates are available. Children under three stay for free; rates are $10–$15 per night for children ages three to twelve. Breakfast, lunch, and dinner are served buffet style and consist of mostly vegetarian cuisine. Priced individually, all three meals together run about $27 per day. Children ages three to twelve are half price. There are refrigerators in each of the lodges. A residency at Kalani Honua provides the artist with the impetus to complete works in progress, strike out in new directions, or simply exchange ideas with other resident artists from many disciplines, ethnic backgrounds, and cultures.

Facility Description

The site is located on twenty acres of secluded forest and dramatic coastline within Hawaii's largest conservation area. "Unlike virtual 'destinations,' Kalani treats you to real, healthful cuisine, thermal springs, a dolphin beach, spectacular Volcano National Park, and traditional culture." Four two-story wooden lodges and four private cottages provide simple but comfortable accommodations. Each lodge offers private rooms, has a 500- to 1,000-square-foot multipurpose studio space with an ocean view on the upper level, common kitchen facilities, and shared or private bath options. Visual artists and dancers use the studio spaces as needed. Writers generally work in their rooms, outdoors, or in the reading lounge or cafe. Every effort is made to protect the artists' privacy during working hours. Studio visits without prior arrangement are discouraged. Telephone messages are delivered only in an emergency.

Activities available on-site include a pool, spa, volleyball, tennis, track, ping-pong, basketball, fitness room, and a massage/meditation lanai. Nearby, you'll find snorkeling, warm springs and steam bathing, and sea cliff meditation.

How to Apply

Send an SASE for an application and brochure if you are requesting a fee reduction. Otherwise, just call the 800-number for reservations. Return the completed application (preferably at least one month in advance of your intended residency) with a $10 nonrefundable processing fee, a description of your proposed project, a list of your professional achievements, a current résumé, two photos of you or your work for publicity and documentation purposes, two references (authorities in your field who have been informed about your application and are familiar with your work), and samples of your recent work (with an adequate SASE for their return). Visual artists: Send ten 35 mm color slides (packaged and labeled according to instructions) and an accompanying descriptive sheet. Performing artists: Send one copy of performance reviews, news articles, or other documentation, and one copy of a video (VHS format) of work in rehearsal or performance. Writers: Send one copy of your writing samples with your name on each piece (ten poems, two short stories, two chapters of a novel, or one act of a play) and a synopsis. Photographers: Send ten photographs.

For retreat reservations only, call toll-free: (800) 800-6886. For information, call the main number listed above. A deposit (one night's lodging cost) is required at the time of reservation confirmation. If you cancel your reservation no less than two weeks prior to arrival, your deposit, less $20, will be refunded. No refunds will be given if the reservation is canceled less than two weeks prior to arrival date.

Deadline

Applications are reviewed monthly. Space is awarded based on availability. (To date, over 80% of the applications for fee reductions have been approved.)

Approximate Cost of Program

50% of above lodging fees, $10 processing fee, transportation, meals, materials, and incidentals.

THE LORD LEEBRICK THEATRE COMPANY   OR

540 Charnelton Street, Eugene, Oregon 97401
Attention: Northwest Playwrights Series
Phone: (503) 465-1506
On 12/13/99 Randy Lord, Artistic Director, wrote:

> "The Northwest Playwrights Series was a wonderful program that LLTC did from 1993–1996. Unfortunately, it became too big for the theatre to manage properly, and local support was less than enthusiastic. We certainly hope to revive it once we're sure of better organization, but until then the NWPS is on hiatus. Wish I could be more optimistic. For what it's worth, we do make our theatre available to independents to produce their own work (for a modest fee), and we're always happy to host a reading for free."

THE MESA REFUGE

c/o Common Counsel Foundation, 1221 Preservation Park Way, Suite 101,
 Oakland, California 94612
Attention: Elizabeth Wilcox, Executive Director
Phone: (510) 834-2995; fax: (510) 834-2998
Web site: www.commoncounsel.org
Email: ccounsel@igc.org

Type of Facility/Award

Residency.

Who Can Apply

Essayists, journalists, economists, naturalists, poets, playwrights, memoirists, fiction
writers, and nonfiction writers.

Provisos

"Writers and visionaries interested in restructuring the economy and its relationship
to people and the environment" are encouraged to apply. "The Mesa Refuge welcomes both experienced writers and accomplished individuals new to writing. The
focus of the Refuge is on the human economy, the environment and social equity.
We encourage applicants from diverse backgrounds and disciplines."

Dates of Operation

Spring/summer residencies run between April 1 and July 21. Summer/fall residencies run between July 22 and November 10.

Location

Located near the seashore of Point Reyes, California, one hour north of San Francisco, the refuge sits atop the San Andreas fault on a bluff overlooking both Tomales
Bay and a dairy ranch soon to be restored to wetlands.

History

Cofounders Peter Barnes and Leyna Bernstein opened the site in July of 1998 as a
means of sharing the inspirational force of beautiful Point Reyes. The refuge has proved
to be a unique sanctuary since its foundation, visited by over seventy writers and over-
seen by a distinguished advisory board, including accomplished members such as writers Bill McKibben, Deirdre English, and Urban Habitat's Carl Anthony.

What They Offer

"The Refuge is misty bluffs, hummingbirds and herons, winding paths of lavender
and sage, daisies and dairy cows, solitude, the company of other writers, and the
blissful absence of noise, demands and daily chores." The residency offers participants the opportunity to develop ideas and projects involving issues of the human

economy, the environment, and social equity. A two- or four-week residency includes housing and most meals for up to three writers at a time. There are no formal requirements except that fellow artists respect each other's needs for quiet and privacy. Beyond that, artists may enjoy uninterrupted time devoted to their work. If necessary, staff members are available to assist participants with transportation to and from the San Francisco International Airport.

Facility Description

"Each of the three residents at the Mesa Refuge enjoys a private room in a spacious shared house. A printer is available for common use. However, residents need to bring their own computers and writing supplies. The kitchen is stocked with breakfast and lunch makings for residents to prepare. Dinners are provided five nights a week by Tomales Bay Foods, which specializes in fresh local organic food. Since this is a shared living arrangement, it is important that residents are quiet, considerate and respectful of the privacy of others. There is no smoking in the Refuge buildings. The Mesa Refuge is not set up to accommodate residents' partners or spouses overnight."

How to Apply

Send an SASE or check the Web site for an application and brochure. Your application packet must include five double-sided copies of the following items: a completed application form, your current résumé, a statement regarding your project proposal that includes a description of how the project will fit into the refuge's goals (not to exceed two pages), and a writing sample (which may include essays, articles, poems, or book/script excerpts, not to exceed fifteen pages). Three people will be selected for each residency period.

Deadline

Spring/summer residencies: February 15. Summer/fall residencies: June 15.

Approximate Cost of Program

Transportation, materials, and incidentals. Transportation to and from the airport is available if needed.

OCEAN HAVEN (FORMERLY GULL HAVEN LODGE)   OR

94770 Highway 101 North, Yachats, Oregon 97498
Attention: Christine DeMoll or Bill James
Phone: (541) 547-3583; fax: (541) 547-3583
Web site: www.oceanhaven.com
Email: office@oceanhaven.com

Type of Facility/Award

Retreat.

Who Can Apply
Anyone.

Provisos
None listed.

Dates of Operation
Open year-round.

Location
Ocean Haven is eight miles south of Yachats and eighteen miles north of Florence on the Oregon coast. The lodge sits atop a bluff overlooking the Pacific Ocean and borders the Siuslaw National Forest.

History
The old Gull Haven Lodge was bought by its current owners in February 1997 and they have since dedicated their efforts to restoring the natural surroundings.

What They Offer
Writers and artists are attracted to Ocean Haven for the pure enjoyment of its magical natural surroundings. The lodge contains seven peaceful rooms. Established quiet hours, no televisions, and bedrooms free of telephones (even cell phones don't work well here) ensure an environment for uninterrupted work. Regular guests include bird illustrators, ornithologists, marine-mammal researchers, *National Geographic* journalists, hiking guide authors, renowned poets, and published novelists. Ocean Haven provides binoculars and a lending library of nature, marine, and hiking guides, as well as books written by past guests.

Facility Description
A quiet hideaway perched atop a bluff overlooking the sea, Ocean Haven offers a variety of cedar-paneled rooms with paintings, prints, and photographs by Oregon artists. All units have unobstructed views of the sea and sky. Most include living rooms, equipped kitchens, and modern tiled bathrooms. Some have small libraries of books and magazines. Units are unique and are therefore available at variable rates. All rooms at Ocean Haven are smoke-free and no pets are allowed.

Surrounding areas are just as inspiring as Yachats itself. Just to the south of Ocean Haven are the Sea Lion Caves, Heceta Head Lighthouse, and the Oregon Dunes. To the north are Neptune Beach, Cape Perpetua, the Devil's Churn, the charming town of Yachats, and Oregon Coast Aquarium.

How to Apply
Call for reservations. A fifty percent deposit is required prior to arrival. Payment in full is due upon arrival. Call for current rates. Gull Haven offers a discount from regular rates to those who mention this listing.

Deadline

Based upon availability.

Approximate Cost of Program

Room rental (varies by room, but ranges from $65 per night to $85 per night for two people), plus transportation, meals, materials, and incidentals.

ON THE BOARDS   WA

100 West Roy Street, Seattle, Washington 98119
Attention: Artists Project Grants
Phone: (206) 217-9886 or (206) 217-9888; fax: (206) 217-9887
Web site: www.ontheboards.org

Type of Facility/Award

Fellowships/grants.

Who Can Apply

Contemporary dancers, theater performers, musicians, and multimedia artists.

Provisos

Applicants cannot be full-time students or members of the staff or board of directors of On the Boards. Collaborative artists (not organizations) who have been residents of Alaska, Oregon, or Washington for at least one year may apply to the Northwest New Works Festival. All other programs are open to all artists.

Dates of Operation

Open year-round.

Location

Lower Queen Anne Hill in Seattle, Washington.

History

"On the Boards was founded in 1978 by a group of young artists who came together to test the boundaries of the performing arts discipline. They found a home for themselves in Washington Hall, a 1908 building which was originally a center for Seattle's Danish community. By leasing the charming, intimate ballroom space, the organization's cofounders established a development venue for local artists and began to host informal showings of dance, theater, and music works-in-progress which drew audiences primarily from Seattle's artist community."

What They Offer

On the Boards administers Artists Projects: Regional Initiatives, a regranting program funded by the National Endowment for the Arts, the Rockefeller Foundation, and the Andy Warhol Foundation for the Visual Arts. Award amounts are not specified, but have ranged in the past from $1,000 to $5,000 in support of the creation of innovative works that challenge traditional artistic disciplines. OTB also hosts five major programs dedicated to exposing Northwest audiences to contemporary performance and supporting Northwest artists in developing their art. Some of the programs offer performance and rehearsal space, technical aide, and a modest honorarium. Contact OTB directly for specific information about all of these programs: the New Performance Series, the Northwest New Works Festival, 12 Minutes Max, the Artists Access Program, and Special Events and Educational Programming.

Facility Description

In October 1998, after six years of planning, research, and a two-and-a-half-year campaign, OTB completed its renovation of the 1912 building, formerly owned by A Contemporary Theatre, and opened a new permanent home called the Behnke Center for Contemporary Performance. The renovated facility boasts a 340-seat mainstage theater with a 42' x 65' staging area, a 99-seat "black box" studio theater, and a 1,000-square-foot rehearsal studio. In addition, the new facility offers dressing rooms and showers, kitchen and lounge facilities for performers, efficiently designed administrative offices, and a community resource room. Two of four ground-floor commercial spaces have also been developed and rented—one space to the Crane Gallery, which specializes in Asian artifacts, and one to the Sitting Room, a European-style cafe.

How to Apply

Send an SASE for an application and brochure.

Deadline

Variable.

Approximate Cost of Program

Not applicable in this category.

OREGON COLLEGE OF ART & CRAFT   OR

8245 Southwest Barnes Road, Portland, Oregon 97225
Attention: Junior Residency Program
Phone: (503) 297-5544; fax: (503) 297-3155
Web site: www.ocac.edu

Type of Facility/Award

Artist-in-residence program.

Who Can Apply

Artists working in book arts, ceramics, drawing, metalsmithing/jewelry, photography (in combination with other media), and furniture-making.

Provisos

Applicants must be U.S. citizens or permanent residents. Preferred applicants will have an M.F.A. or three to five years as a working artist. Minority applicants are encouraged to apply.

Dates of Operation

September through December for fall residency. January through May for spring residency.

Location

Portland, Oregon.

History

Oregon College of Art and Craft traces its origins to 1907 when Julia Hoffman founded the Arts and Crafts Society to educate the public about the value of arts and crafts in daily life through art classes and exhibitions featuring the best examples of American crafts. Today, Oregon College of Art and Craft is an accredited independent art college offering studio classes in book arts, ceramics, drawing, fibers, metal, photography, and wood. Students can pursue a B.F.A., a three-year certificate in crafts, or enroll in the college's extension series of Studio School classes.

What They Offer

Residents receive a stipend, some travel reimbursement to and from the college, campus housing, studio space, money to cover the cost of supplies, and part of the cost of shipping their completed work. Workshops may be provided based on availability. Residents' work will be exhibited on campus in the Hoffman Gallery.

Facility Description

Book arts residents have the use of two etching presses (27" x 48" and 27" x 48" Griffin), two Vandercook presses, platen and proofing presses, and a large collection of type for printing. Book binding equipment includes a forty-foot board sheet, French standing press, drymount press, and miscellaneous sewing, punching, and backing equipment. During summer workshops, residents may use a Hollander beater, miscellaneous moulds, and equipment for papermaking.

The ceramics department has sixteen built-in electric/kick potter's wheels, three electric wheels, a spray booth, sandblasters, a fully-stocked glaze lab, fifty- and sixty-cubic-foot downdraft kilns, five electric kilns, three computer kiln controllers, a salt kiln, a wood kiln, an Alpine updraft kiln, and an experimental firing area.

Drawing residents have access to a large open studio with a two-story window facing the courtyard, easels, drawing boards, a tool bench, hand and power tools, a human skeleton, and a large supply of still-life props.

Fiber facilities include weaving studios that provide twenty-eight floor looms (including jack looms and a sixteen-harness avl dobby loom), fifteen vertical tapestry looms (including a twelve-foot shannock loom), computers for drafting, and an extensive yarn room. The construction studio houses large work tables, drum carders, rug tufting tools, a pleater, and eight sewing stations that each include a Bernina 1280 and two sergers. Residents also have access to padded print tables, equipment and materials for painting, block printing, screen printing, and batik, as well as a fully equipped dye studio for synthetic and natural dye processes for surface design.

Metalworking equipment includes drill presses, rolling mills, a hydraulic press, horizontal and vertical band saws, a metal lathe, a chop saw, an arc welder, a wax injector, a vulcanizer, a sandblaster, jump and beverly shears, a steam cleaner, sanders, grinders, a box break, and a scroll saw. There is also equipment for centrifugal and vacuum casting, soldering, annealing, raising, forming, plating, enameling, stonecutting, lapidary, oxyacetylene welding, and tumbling.

Photography residents may use the photo lab, which has both black-and-white and color capability, enlarging capacity from 35 mm to 4" x 5", camera and lighting equipment, process camera and non-silver capabilities, and access to digital workstations.

Wood facilities include a bench room and machine room. The bench room provides chisels, saws, planes, layout and forming tools, finishing and belt sanders, drills, routers, and grinders. The machine room is equipped with twenty- and fourteen-inch band saws, a twelve-inch radial arm saw, a ten-inch compound power, a miter saw, three forty-inch lathes, twenty- and fifteen-inch planers, eight- and sixteen-inch joiners, a horizontal slot mortiser, an oscillating spindle sander, a twelve-inch disc sander, a six-inch belt sander, a two-stage compressor, and a spray booth with HVLP and conventional spray guns.

The Hoffman Gallery schedules monthly exhibitions ranging from traditional to contemporary art and craft.

How to Apply

Send an SASE for an application form and guidelines. Return the completed application form with your résumé, a brief statement, a description of your proposed project, ten slides of your work (packaged and labeled according to instructions), an accompanying slide inventory, and two letters of reference. Include an adequate SASE for return of your work samples.

Deadline

April 1. Notification by June 1.

Approximate Cost of Program

Meals and incidentals—offset by stipend.

OREGON WRITERS COLONY

Colonyhouse

Rockaway Beach, Oregon

Administration:

Oregon Writers Colony, P.O. Box 15200, Portland, Oregon 97293-5200
Attention: Martha Miller, President
Phone: (503) 827-8072; fax: (503) 286-7952
Web site: www.teleport.com/~witch/owc/owc.htm
Email: mattie@inetarena.com

Type of Facility/Award

Residency.

Who Can Apply

Writers and other artists.

Provisos

Applicants must be members or become members of the Oregon Writers Colony and must reside in Oregon. Writing groups receive special consideration.

Dates of Operation

Open year-round.

Location

Rockaway Beach on the Oregon coast.

History

The Oregon Writers Colony was founded in 1981 by a group of five writers who wanted to develop a place on the coast for writing. In 1988, after seven years of plans and dreams, OWC established Colonyhouse, a haven by the sea for Northwest writers.

What They Offer

For a modest usage fee, members of the OWC may use the house on a space-available basis. Members must supply their own food, bed linens, pillows, blankets, and wood for the fireplace. Premises must be left as clean as they were found. There are four bedrooms, two baths, a kitchen, and a gallery. One week a month at the house is designated "writers only." At other times, the house may be rented out for workshops, conferences, vacations, and getaways.

Membership in the OWC comes in four categories: regular at $35 per year, patron at $50 per year, member-plus at $70 per year, and angel at $1,000 per year. Colonyhouse usage fees barely cover the cost of maintaining the property. For a list of current usage fees, you must become a member of the group.

Facility Description

"Designed by one of the architects of Oregon's celebrated Timberline Lodge, Colonyhouse amenities include a panoramic view of the Pacific to the west, and wooded Lake Lytte to the east; a spacious living room with a twenty-foot high riverstone fireplace; four large bedrooms, and a modern, fully-equipped kitchen. The rustic interior of hand-hewn logs, carved door handles and hammered iron fixtures, combined with the western sweep of terraced slopes delight the eye and add to the seaside ambiance. The house can sleep up to twelve people."

How to Apply

Send an SASE for information about becoming a member and current usage rates. Space must be reserved in advance and is based on availability, so include at least two alternative dates. Current rates were not specified, but past rates were $150 for a weekend or $350 for a week (October through April) and $275 for a weekend or $500 for a week (May through September).

Deadline

Reservation requests should be made three to five months in advance.

Approximate Cost of Program

Annual membership fee, transportation, rental, meals, materials, and incidentals.

PILCHUCK GLASS SCHOOL   WA

Stanwood campus: (May through September)

1201 316th Street N.W., Stanwood, Washington 98292-9600
Phone: (360) 445-3111; fax: (360) 445-5515

Seattle office: (September to May)

315 Second Avenue South, Seattle, Washington 98104-2618
Attention: Artist-in-Residence Program
Phone: (206) 621-8422; fax: (206) 621-0713

Type of Facility/Award

Residency.

Who Can Apply

Glass and other visual artists.

Provisos

Applicants should have prior achievement in glass and other visual arts media.

Dates of Operation

Mid-September through mid-November.

Location

Stanwood, Washington, is one hour north of Seattle.

History

In 1971, artist Dale Chihuly and patrons Anne Gould Hauberg and John H. Hauberg founded the school. Pilchuck is now a leading model of education in the visual arts. Both glass blowing as a studio art and the broader contemporary interest in glass as a medium have evolved in part because of Pilchuck. Pilchuck supports experimentation, investigation, team work, and personal growth. Pilchuck also "nurtures artists at all stages of their careers; the school values artistic pursuits and the people who engage in them, and rejoices in international friendships."

What They Offer

The Emerging Artists-in-Residence Program is an eight-week program for five or six artists at a time that includes living accommodations on campus, studio space, and a $1,000 stipend. Pilchuck also has a Professional Artists-in-Residence Program with the same application requirements as the Emerging AIR program. The durations of these residencies vary, lasting a few days to a week or more. The program is designed for experienced professional artists seeking to extend their education through creative experimentation. Two or three artists will be invited to participate in this program and will be responsible for funding their own projects.

Facility Description

Artists have access to many Pilchuck studios and equipment including: the glass plate printmaking shop; plaster studios; fusing, slumping, and pâte-de-verre kilns; and such cold working equipment as sandblasters, Vibralaps, lathes, and saws. Residents have limited access to the flat shop and two hot shops.

Pilchuck is nestled in the hillside meadows overlooking Puget Sound. The 50-acre wooded site is set in the middle of a 15,000-acre tree farm, providing isolation from the influence of commerce and urban centers and allowing a community of artists to focus on art. The lodge, with its massive wood posts, great stone hearth, and three levels of decks overlooking the islands of the Puget Sound, is a prominent example of the award-winning architecture found at the school. It is located at the heart of the campus and houses the library, projection equipment, and printmaking studio. Residents have access to a kitchen in which they can prepare their own meals. The campus gallery is a showcase for exhibitions and installations.

How to Apply

Send an SASE for an application and brochure. Return your completed application and a $25 nonrefundable application fee with the following support materials: ten slides and two slide scripts (at least five slides should show your work in glass); a brief proposal describing your objectives and intentions for the residency in aesthetic, technical, and conceptual terms; a current résumé; two recommendations from persons familiar with your work and character; and an SASE for return of your slides.

Deadline
April 1.

Approximate Cost of Program
$25 application fee, transportation, materials, and incidentals—offset by $1,000 stipend.

SITKA CENTER FOR ART AND ECOLOGY   OR
Neskowin Coast Foundation, P.O. Box 65, Otis, Oregon 97368
Attention: Sitka Residency Program
Phone: (541) 994-5485; fax: (541) 994-8024
Web site: www.teleport.com/~aac/sitka.html
Email: sitka@orednet.org

Type of Facility/Award
Artist-in-residence program.

Who Can Apply
Visual artists, writers, musicians, dancers, performers, architects, designers, naturalists, scholars, and others.

Provisos
This program is designed for artists and naturalists who have earned a B.A., B.S., B.F.A., M.A., M.S., M.F.A., or Ph.D., or for those who have equivalent professional experience. If you have had a residency at a nonprofit arts institution within the last two years, you are not eligible to apply. Preference is given to those doing research on the Oregon coast environment.

Dates of Operation
October 1 through January 21 or February 1 through May 21.

Location
Otis lies just north of Lincoln City on the Oregon coast. Located at Cascade Head Ranch, which is part of the Cascade Head National Science Research Area, the center borders a Nature Conservancy preserve and the Siuslaw National Experimental Forest and overlooks both the Salmon River Estuary and Pacific Ocean. The center is situated within a national scenic research area and a United Nations biosphere reserve.

History
Founded in 1970, the Neskowin Coast Foundation strives "to promote interest in and opportunity to study various forms of art and music and the ecology of the

central Oregon coast." The center was built in 1971, and the residency program was established ten years later.

What They Offer

Residencies are provided for three categories of artists: emerging artist/naturalist, mid-career artist/naturalist, and artist/naturalist on sabbatical. Residencies are for four months during autumn or spring. Shorter residencies may be available by arrangement. There is no stipend except for the recipient of the Founders' Series Award, which includes $500 to be given to one of the four artists-in-residence each year.

The center provides living accommodations, studio space, and equipment in exchange for twenty hours per month of community service on behalf of Sitka and some maintenance responsibilities. Residents are encouraged to present workshops or hold open studios or community outreach programs at Sitka one day per month during residencies. In January and May, Sitka hosts an exhibition of artists' works. Sitka charges a fee of twenty percent of the sales for work produced and sold while at Sitka.

Facility Description

The center itself is semi-isolated. The 1,500-square-foot Boyden Studio is the main workspace and can be shared by two residents. Gallery Studio, which is 550 square-feet, and a newer 800-square-foot studio may be used in coordination with printmaking and ongoing workshop activities. Residents live in the Morley House or in Russ's Treehouse. Both are self-contained and equipped with a sleeping loft, kitchen, and bathroom. Residents also have access to a 36" x 72" etching press, skutt kiln, and mechanical wheel.

How to Apply

Send an SASE for an application and brochure. Return the completed application form with a description of your project, the names of three references, your résumé, two letters of recommendation, and samples of your work (with an adequate SASE for their return). Appropriate work samples may include slides, a written manuscript, a thesis, or a copy of a published work.

Deadline

June 20.

Approximate Cost of Program

Transportation, meals, materials, and incidentals.

622 SE 29th Avenue, Portland, Oregon 97214
Attention: Ruth Gundle, Director
Phone: (503) 233-3936; fax: (503) 233-0774
Web site: www.soapstone.com
Email: soapston@teleport.com

Type of Facility/Award

Residency.

Who Can Apply

Women writers working on fiction, poetry, drama, screenwriting, or other literary writing.

Provisos

Serious women writers from a wide variety of cultures and backgrounds are invited to apply.

Dates of Operation

Open year-round.

A Writer at Work in a Cabin at Soapstone

Location
Soapstone is in Oregon's Coast Range, about a ninety-minute drive from Portland.

History
Soapstone was conceived as a place for women writers to find the peace and support they need to work on their projects. Directors Judith Barrington and Ruth Gundle (also directors of the Flight of the Mind Writers' Conference) have spent years raising funds for this project so that women, whose lives generally make it impossible for them to go away and concentrate on their writing, can put their own needs above those of others in order to write. "The practical support and validation offered by an organization devoted to women's writing is essential to the creation of work that embodies the powerful truths of women's lives." Residencies at Soapstone began in 1999.

What They Offer
Two writers stay at a time, each with her own private sleeping and work space. A kitchen, sitting room, bathroom, and laundry facilities are shared. The cabin includes electricity for computers and telephones for local calls. Pillows and blankets are provided, but writers must bring their own linens. Resident are advised to bring their own vehicles, as the nearest town is nine miles away. Terms are from one week to one month. The directors hope to build additional studios to accommodate more writers.

Facility Description
A twenty-four-acre expanse of densely forested alder, hemlock, cedar, maple, and fir, Soapstone is home to a variety of wildlife, including deer, elk, and beaver. There is nearly a mile of creek running through the property. In the winter, the salmon-spawning creek swells to a thirty-foot-wide river. In the summer, it sports two fishing holes. The sound of water coursing through a series of rapids can be heard year-round from anywhere on the property. The original cabin was built by a Portland artist and architect. The interior, with its series of lofts soaring up to the treetops, is beautifully finished in white pine and topped by a cube-shaped study with bubble windows on four sides overlooking the creek. In 1992, the cabin was restored to good condition in preparation for expansion (to provide additional sleeping and work spaces).

How to Apply
Send an SASE for an application and brochure. Return the completed application along with samples of your writing and information about your proposed project. Friends or writing partners may apply, but each must submit a separate application.

Deadline
August 16 for the following year.

Approximate Cost of Program
Transportation, meals, materials, and incidentals.

SOUTHERN OREGON STATE COLLEGE
Walden Residency

Extended Campus Programs, 1250 Siskiyou Boulevard, Ashland, Oregon 97520
Attention: Brooke Friendly
Phone: (541) 552-6901; fax: (541) 552-6047
Web site: www.sou.edu/ecp
Email: friendly@sou.edu

Type of Facility/Award
Residency.

Who Can Apply
Writers (fiction, creative nonfiction, poets, playwrights, essayists, and all other creative writers).

Provisos
Applicants must be residents of Oregon and must be nonsmokers.

Dates of Operation
March through mid-April, late April through early June, and mid-June through late July. Contact the program directly for specific dates.

Location
Ten minutes from Gold Hill, Oregon, and forty minutes from Ashland.

The Garden at the Walden Residency Site in Southern Oregon

History

This award, offered since 1987, is sponsored by a private citizen.

What They Offer

There are three residencies of six weeks each. The cabin is provided with no charge for utilities. Residents are asked to bring their own computers, do their own cooking, and keep the cabin in good order. In exchange, they are asked to acknowledge the assistance of the Walden Fellowship in any publications resulting from their work at the cabin.

Facility Description

The residency provides a fully furnished cabin (suitable for one working writer) on a quiet and beautiful mountain farm in southern Oregon. The cabin sits on a meadow surrounded by forest and is equipped with a telephone.

How to Apply

Send an SASE for an application (also available on the Web site) and brochure. Return the completed application with your project proposal, a list of your recent publications (if any), your choice of dates, and three copies (original plus two) of a writing sample produced within the last five years. Appropriate samples—eight to ten poems or no more than thirty pages of prose—should be representative of the genre in which you intend to write during the residency. Enclose an adequate SASE if you want your writing sample returned and an additional SASE if you would like to be notified of the winners.

Deadline

The last working day in November. Notification by mid-January.

Approximate Cost of Program

Transportation, meals, materials, and incidentals.

STANFORD CREATIVE WRITING FELLOWSHIPS   CA
Stanford University

Creative Writing Program, Department of English, Stanford University, Stanford, California 94305-2087

Attention: Gay Pierce, Program Administrator

Phone: (650) 723-2637; fax: (650) 723-3679

Web site: www.stanford.edu/dept/english/cw

Email: gay.pierce@forsythe.stanford.edu

Type of Facility/Award

Fellowship.

Who Can Apply
Poets and fiction writers.

Provisos
No degree is required. No degree is awarded. When reviewing the writer's portfolio, the program looks for potential for growth and the ability to contribute to and benefit from the workshops. No fellowships are offered for drama, nonfiction prose, or screenwriting.

Dates of Operation
Academic year.

Location
Stanford University is located just south of San Francisco, California.

History
The program has been in existence for over forty years. Ten of the fellowships are named for Wallace Stegner, founder of the Stanford Writing Program. The other ten are named for Karen O. Brownstein, Truman Capote, Harriet Doerr, Elsie P. Ettinger, Scott Clarkson Kovas, Jean Lane, Joan Lane, Edith R. Mirrielees, Richard P. Scowcroft, and Sheila and Walter Weisman.

What They Offer
"Each year, the program awards at least twenty fellowships—ten in poetry and ten in fiction. Fellowships are awarded for two years, depending upon satisfactory performance. The terms of the fellows are staggered so that there are five new poetry fellows and five new fiction fellows each year." Fellowships include a living expense stipend of $15,000 and workshop tuition costs. Fellows must register for and participate in the writing workshop. Members read and criticize each other's work. They also participate in various events sponsored by the program and occasionally serve as judges for undergraduate writing prizes. Winners of fellowships will receive an official application form by April 1, which must be filled out and returned with all the required credentials, including college transcripts (although possession of a college degree is not a consideration in evaluating candidate's suitability for the program).

Facility Description
University campus. Brochure does not mention on-campus housing provisions.

How to Apply
Send an SASE for an application and brochure. Return the completed application with a $25 processing fee, a statement briefly explaining your writing plans, mailing labels, and a business size SASE. Be sure to fill out the request for recommendations and waiver of confidentiality on the back of your application form. Poets: Send a manuscript of poems ten to fifteen pages in length. Fiction writers: Send no

more than 9,000 words—either two stories (three if they are very short) or up to forty pages of a novel. Fiction manuscripts must be typed and double-spaced. Also complete and return the mailing labels that come with your application packet.

Deadline
Applications must be returned between September 1 and December 1. No applications will be accepted before September 1. Notification by early April.

Approximate Cost of Program
Transportation, housing, meals, materials, and incidentals—offset by $15,000 stipend. Fellowships also include the cost of tuition.

UNIVERSITY OF CALIFORNIA AT LOS ANGELES   CA
Center for 17th and 18th Century Studies
University of California at Los Angeles (UCLA)
Center for 17th and 18th Century Studies

For all fellowships contact:
310 Royce Hall, UCLA, 405 Hilgard Avenue, Los Angeles, California 90024-1404
Attention: Fellowship Coordinator
Phone: (310) 206-8552; fax: (310) 206-8577
Web site: www.humnet.ucla.edu/humnet/c1718cs
Email: c1718cs@humnet.ucla.edu

Type of Facility/Award
Fellowship.

Who Can Apply
Scholars.

Provisos
Scholars with a Ph.D. who might benefit from research in the extensive holdings of the William Andrews Clark Memorial Library are invited to apply.

Dates of Operation
Academic quarters.

Location
Los Angeles, California.

History
"The Center for the 17th and 18th Century Studies, an organized research unit of the University of California, provides a forum for the discussion of central issues in the study of the 17th and 18th centuries, facilitates research and publication, supports scholarship, and encourages the creation of interdisciplinary, cross-cultural programs

that advance the understanding of this important period. The William Andrews Clark Memorial Library, which is administered by the Center, is known for its collections on 17th and 18th century Britain, Oscar Wilde and the 1890's, the history of printing, and certain aspects of the American West."

What They Offer
The university offers various fellowship programs. The Ahmanson/Getty Postdoctoral Residential Fellowship, which is theme-based (theme changes annually), carries a stipend of $9,200 per quarter for two or three academic quarters. The Clark Short-term Fellowship is a residential award for one to three months and carries a stipend of $1,500 per month. The ASECS/Clark Fellowship carries a stipend of $1,500 for a one-month fellowship. The Predoctoral Fellowship carries a stipend of $4,500 for a three-month residential fellowship.

Facility Description
University campus library.

How to Apply
Send an SASE for an application and brochure. Respond as directed for specific fellowships.

Deadline
March 15.

Approximate Cost of Program
Transportation, housing, meals, materials, and incidentals—offset by stipend.

VILLA MONTALVO CENTER FOR THE ARTS   CA
15400 Montalvo Road, P.O. Box 158, Saratoga, California 95071-0158
Attention: Kathryn Funk, Artist Residency Coordinator
Phone: (408) 961-5818; fax: (408) 741-5592
Web site: www.villamontalvo.org
Email: kfunk@villamontalvo.org

Type of Facility/Award
Residency.

Who Can Apply
All artists and writers.

Provisos
"Anyone may apply who has completed formal training or the equivalent and is seriously engaged in the production of art." Established and emerging artists may apply. Couples must apply separately—accommodations for couples are limited.

Prior residents must wait one year before reapplying.

Dates of Operation
Spring/summer residencies: April through September. Fall/winter residencies: October through March.

Location
Villa Montalvo is in the foothills of the Santa Cruz Mountains, about an hour's drive south of San Francisco and a half-hour's drive from Santa Cruz. The small city of Saratoga is about a mile and a half from the center, and Los Gatos is about four miles away. Both have interesting specialty shops, pharmacies, restaurants, hardware stores, markets, and gas stations. The closest airport is in San Jose, about a half-hour's drive.

History
Villa Montalvo, a nineteen-room Mediterranean-style villa built in 1912 and on the National Register of Historic Places, was the home of James D. Phelan, a California politician who invited many of the era's leading writers, musicians, and artists to perform there and stay for a while as his guests. Senator Phelan's will stipulated that Montalvo be used as a public park and for the development of the arts. In 1942, the first artist residents were invited to the villa. From April through October, Montalvo hosts arts-related events that operate independently of the residency program.

What They Offer
Residencies last one to three months, operating in two seasons. Spring/summer is a very busy season and is recommended for artists who enjoy an active environment and who don't need quiet or solitude. During the fall/winter season, there are very few visitors and the grounds often close early, providing solitude for residents. This season is more appropriate for those who need more serenity. Montalvo hosts only five residents at a time. Each has a furnished, private apartment with a well-equipped kitchen, bed and bath linens, and minimal cleaning equipment. Residents are responsible for their own meals, materials, and incidentals. If you use a computer, bring a surge protector, since the villa's electrical system can't handle excessive draw. Four fellowships, based solely on merit, are awarded during the selection process. One fellowship is designated specifically for a woman artist. Artists may be invited to hold open studios or share their work with interested members of the community. Residents are provided complimentary tickets to the center's events, including plays, concerts, dance performances, readings, workshops, exhibits, and receptions. The road to the villa is steep (one mile up a mountain road) and the center may seem remote, so having a car to use while you're in residence might be helpful. Also, in the past, the center has sponsored a biennial (deadline in odd-numbered years) poetry competition. Included with the first prize is a one-month residency at Villa Montalvo.

Facility Description

The grounds are a public park maintained by Santa Clara County. The 175-acre site includes redwoods, formal gardens, and four or five miles of hiking trails. The center has two theaters, a gallery, a public arboretum, and wedding facilities. There are two studio apartments (with pianos) on the second floor of the villa. In the guest house, there are two one-bedroom apartments (with pianos) and one studio apartment with a skylit 20" x 15" artist's studio. There is an artist's barn studio near the villa. The Carriage House Theatre has a Baldwin grand piano. There is a shared laundry.

How to Apply

Send an SASE for an application and brochure. Return your completed application with a $20 nonrefundable application fee and a professional résumé (two pages maximum), three letters of recommendation (form provided with application packet), a brief project proposal, and a sample of your recent work, as follows. Composers: Send three sets of a cassette tape and a corresponding score (packaged and labeled according to instructions). Performers: Send three sets of a cassette tape (packaged and labeled according to instructions) cued to a ten minute segment. Writers: Send seven sets of a writing sample (twenty pages maximum) such as poems, chapter(s) from a novel, short stories, essays, or playscripts. Do not put your name on writing samples. Visual artists: Send five color slides of your recent work (packaged and labeled according to instructions). Enclose an adequate SASE for return of samples.

Deadline

March 1 for fall/winter residencies. September 1 for spring/summer residencies.

Approximate Cost of Program

$20 application fee, transportation, meals, materials, and incidentals.

VOLCANO WRITERS' RETREAT   CA

P.O. Box 163, Volcano, California 95689
Attention: Karin Hexberg, Director
Phone: (209) 296-7945
Web site: www.volcano.net
Email: khexberg@volcano.net

Type of Facility/Award

Retreat.

Who Can Apply

Writers at all levels.

Provisos

None listed.

Dates of Operation
April and October.

Location
The tiny town of Volcano (pop. 85) is located in Amador County, just east of highway 49 and the city of Jackson. Founded in 1848, the town was named Volcano because the valley in which it lies looks much like a volcano crater.

History
Award-winning poet and short story writer Karin Hexberg began the retreat in 1997 when she left a twenty-year career as an advertising copywriter in San Francisco. When not writing or hosting the retreat, Karin works as a reading coach at a local junior high school and teaches creative writing at Preston Youth Correctional Facility under the auspices of the Arts in the Youth Authority. She taught writing at the college level while pursuing her M.F.A. in creative writing at the University of Houston.

What They Offer
Retreats take place over three-day weekends "organized around a series of facilitated writing exercises followed by group sharing. The job of the groups, which are kept small, is to encourage and embolden one another in our work. Ample time is also built into the agenda for individual free writing, for exploring the area, or for just sitting quietly and being." The retreat includes a Friday night buffet, Saturday night dinner, and continental breakfasts. Participants are invited to read at an open-mike night to which the public is invited.

Facility Description
None provided.

How to Apply
There is no need to complete a formal application. Contact the retreat director to receive information about the retreat, including a registration form.

Deadline
Six weeks prior to scheduled retreat.

Approximate Cost of Program
All rates include participation in all sessions, Friday night reception, two continental breakfasts, and Saturday night dinner. The cost, including a two-night stay in the historic St. George Hotel is $210 (shared bath). With a two-night stay in the St. George Motel (private bath), the cost is $230. If you prefer to find your own accommodations, the cost of the program is $125. Accommodations at the St. George Hotel are limited and are available on a first-come first-served basis. A nonrefundable deposit of $50 must accompany your registration form in order to reserve your place.

YOSEMITE RENAISSANCE ARTISTS-IN-RESIDENCE   CA

Yosemite National Park, P.O. Box 100, Yosemite, California 95389
Attention: Bob Woolard
Voice and Fax: (209) 372-4024
Web site: www.yosemiteart.org

Type of Facility/Award
Artist-in-residence program.

Who Can Apply
Visual artists.

Provisos
Artists should have established reputations within the art community. Students, Sunday painters, and amateur artists are generally not considered for the artists-in-residence program but are welcome to participate in the group's annual arts competition.

Dates of Operation
Open year-round.

Location
Various locations within Yosemite National Park or directly adjacent to it are used (according to availability). Yosemite is located in the Sierra Nevada Mountains of central California. It is about a four-hour drive from San Francisco, and about two hours from Fresno.

History
In early 1994, the program was inactive because of National Park Service budget cuts. Previously administered by the curator of the Yosemite Museum, the program is now in the hands of Yosemite Renaissance, a nonprofit organization. By July of 1995, the program was fully revived. Yosemite Renaissance was founded "to encourage amateur and professional artists to reexamine Yosemite in light of twentieth century artistic developments through a series of competitive exhibits; to develop an Artists-in-Residence program to give professional artists time to become more intimately acquainted with Yosemite; and to encourage dialogue between artists through an annual seminar."

What They Offer
Six to ten artists a year will be selected for the artist-in-residence program. Free housing for up to one month is provided. No exchange of services is required, but the artist is asked to choose a piece of work resulting from the residency (in consultation with Yosemite Renaissance and the museum curator) to donate to the National Park

Service's Yosemite Museum. The Yosemite Gallery hosts an annual exhibition of works by previous artists-in-residence. Yosemite Renaissance exhibits have also traveled to numerous exhibit in the San Joaquin Valley and the San Francisco Bay Area.

Facility Description

Artists will be accommodated in a private house in the Yosemite area, usually in Wawona, Yosemite West, or El Portal. The house will be fully furnished and equipped. Yosemite Valley was carved by glaciers and is surrounded by steep walls of granite. There are many spectacular waterfalls, rock formations, and meadows to tantalize any artist and all visitors.

How to Apply

Send an SASE for application guidelines. Submit a résumé, ten to forty 35 mm slides of your recent work (packaged in plastic sleeves), and any other support materials that would be helpful to the selection committee. Include an adequate SASE for return of your slides and support materials (return may take up to four months).

Deadline

Rolling application basis.

Approximate Cost of Program

Transportation, meals, materials, and incidentals.

Studio at Yaddo (photo courtesy of Yaddo)

MIDDLE ATLANTIC COLONIES

Delaware
District of Columbia
Maryland
New Jersey
New York
Pennsylvania

THE EDWARD F. ALBEE FOUNDATION, INC.   NY
The William Flanagan Memorial Creative Persons Center
Fairview Avenue, Montauk, New York 11954
Phone: (516) 668-5435

Administration/Information/Applications
The Edward F. Albee Foundation, Inc., 14 Harrison Street, New York, New York
    10013
Attention: David Briggs, Foundation Secretary
Phone: (212) 226-2020

Type of Facility/Award
Residency.

Who Can Apply
Writers, painters, sculptors, and composers.

Provisos
The foundation encourages qualified artists of all backgrounds to apply. It is the
policy of the foundation that no one with the AIDS virus, ARC, or HIV shall be
denied admission as long as he or she is qualified. The foundation expects all those
who are accepted to work seriously and to aid fellow artists in their endeavors.

Dates of Operation
June 1 through September 30.

Location
The center is in Montauk on Long Island.

History
The foundation was established in 1968.

What They Offer
The Edward F. Albee Foundation offers one-month residencies at the William
Flanagan Memorial Creative Persons Center, which can comfortably accommodate
four or five artists at a time. Writers and composers are offered a room. Composers in
residence are requested to conduct their work with headphones. Visual artists are
offered a room and studio space. Residents are responsible for their own food, travel,
and other expenses. Residents are expected to do their share of work to maintain the
condition and peaceful atmosphere of the center.

Facility Description
The center rests on a secluded knoll, offering residents a quiet, private, and peaceful
atmosphere.

How to Apply

Send an SASE for application forms and a brochure. Submit your completed application and personal information form with a résumé, two letters of recommendation from professionals familiar with you and your work, a letter of intent (outlining your proposed project), two labels bearing your name only (last name first), and samples of your work (with an adequate SASE for their return). Painters or sculptors: Send six to twelve slides of your work. Playwrights or screenwriters: Send a manuscript. Poets: Send twelve poems. Fiction writers: Send one short story or two chapters from a novel. Nonfiction writers: Send three essays or articles. Composers: Send a recording of at least two original compositions. When you apply, you should request a specific month for residency. Please also choose two alternative months; the center is often unable to accommodate first choices. If there are months during which you will be unavailable, you should make that clear. The center also requests that you indicate whether you are applying to any other programs for the same time period.

Application materials must be sent to the Harrison Street address by regular mail only. No hand deliveries or mail deliveries that require extra postage or signed receipts will be accepted.

Deadline

Applications will only be accepted between January 1 and April 1 (postmarked) each year. Notification by May 15.

Approximate Cost of Program

Transportation, meals, materials, and incidentals.

ART AWARENESS   NY

Route 42, Box 177, Lexington, New York 12452-0177
Attention: Artists Residencies Director
Phone: (518) 989-6433; fax: (518) 989-6398

Type of Facility/Award

Residency.

Who Can Apply

Artists in the fields of dance, theater, performance art, and artists collaborating on interdisciplinary projects that include at least one of the above disciplines.

Provisos

Art Awareness is especially interested in providing a supportive environment, time, and funds for the development of new works. Students will not be considered for residencies but may inquire about summer internships.

Dates of Operation
June through August.

Location
Lexington, New York, is three hours north of New York City and an hour and a half west of Albany, New York, in the northern Catskill Mountains.

History
Art Awareness is a nonprofit, multidisciplinary development-center for visual and performing artists. The center is located on the grounds of the Lexington House Resort, a turn-of-the-century Victorian hotel, now a center for the development of new works of art and for the presentation of new and established works by contemporary professional artists.

What They Offer
Residencies offer artists between two weeks and three months to work on their projects, after which time they either mount an exhibition of their work or create an installation indoors in the galleries or outdoors on the grounds of Art Awareness. All works created belong to the artist. A stipend of up to $125 per week, a minimum travel allowance of $100, and up to $3,000 to cover fees, materials, and supplies are available. (Average amount provided is $750 for fees and supplies.) Artists-in-residence are provided a combination living/studio space (private bedroom) and use of a shared kitchen and bath. Lodging and cooking facilities are provided for groups of up to twenty artists. Additional lodging is available for larger groups at nearby facilities at prevailing rates.

Facility Description
The center has a print studio and invites sculptors, painters, and other visual artists wishing to explore the printmaking process to submit proposals for two-week residencies in the silkscreen print studio.

How to Apply
Send an SASE for their brochure. Submit a project proposal with a budget and appropriate supporting materials, including slides (at least twenty) or video/audio tapes, your résumé, and any reviews (if appropriate). Enclose an adequate SASE for return of your materials.

Deadline
May 30 (for current year). October 30 (for residencies the following year).

Approximate Cost of Program
Limited transportation costs, meals, and incidentals according to approved budget—offset by $125 weekly honorarium.

ART/OMI

55 Fifth Avenue, 15th Floor, New York, New York 10003
Attention: Director
Phone: (212) 206-6060; fax: (212) 727-0563
Email: ARTOMI55@AOL.COM

Type of Facility/Award
Residency.

Who Can Apply
Visual artists, writers, translators, and musicians.

Provisos
Artists worldwide are welcome to apply. Some artists are invited to apply because of referrals from professionals, while others are selected through the application process.

Dates of Operation
Facilities are available year-round for writers and translators, July for visual artists, and August for musicians.

Location
OMI is located in Columbia County, New York, in the Hudson River Valley.

History
In 1991, ART/OMI's first program, a three-week international visual artists' residency, was held in renovated farm buildings that now serve as the art studios near Ghent, New York. The success of this program led to the establishment of the Ledig House International Writer's Colony in a nearby farm house in 1992. Two years later, ART/OMI acquired property adjacent to the art studios, thereby consolidating facilities for ART/OMI and Ledig House into one location. Music/OMI, a residency for musicians, was begun in 1997, and a major contemporary sculpture park, The Fields, was opened to the public in the fall of 1998. Featuring the collection of New York gallerist Andre Emmerich, the park further contributes to ART/OMI's growing reputation as a major cultural attraction in the Hudson Valley.

What They Offer
ART/OMI offers between twelve and twenty intensive three-week residencies. Residents receive housing, food, and studio space. At the end of the residencies, artists exhibit their work. These exhibitions tend to attract a considerable amount of publicity and a large audience. Because ART/OMI is a nonprofit organization, each artist is asked to donate a piece of work created during the residency to the organization for inclusion in a fundraising project.

Facility Description

Residents are housed in the surrounding community. Meals and other group activities are held in a central location. A large, modern two-story barn, sitting on fifteen acres of farmland, houses the studios. Several sheds lend themselves well to large sculpture projects, while the grounds provide room for site-specific installations.

How to Apply

Send an SASE for application guidelines. Submit six 35 mm slides (packaged and labeled according to instructions) accompanied by a descriptive sheet and a curriculum vitae listing your education, exhibitions, name, address, telephone number, age, sex, and language. Include an SASE for return of your slides.

Deadline

November 31 for writers and translators. April 1 for musicians. March 1 for visual artists.

Approximate Cost of Program

Transportation, materials, and incidentals.

ASIAN AMERICAN ARTS CENTRE   NY   **DISCONTINUED**

26 Bowery, New York, New York 1003
Phone: (212) 233-2154 or (212) 766-1287

> *Notice: Although the Centre is still in operation, its artist-in-residence program has been discontinued.*

The Baltimore Clayworks

BALTIMORE CLAYWORKS   MD

Lormina Salter Fellowship, 5706 Smith Avenue, Baltimore, Maryland 21209
Attention: Leigh Taylor Mickelson, Program Director
Phone: (410) 578-1919; fax: (410) 578-0058
Web site: www.baltimoreclayworks.org
Email: clayworks@erols.com

Type of Facility/Award
Artist-in-residence program.

Who Can Apply
Anyone with clay experience who wishes to continue as a professional in the field.

Provisos
None listed.

Dates of Operation
Open year-round. Fellowships are for a full year and begin the first of September.

Location
The Clayworks is in the Mt. Washington neighborhood of northwest Baltimore.

History
"Baltimore Clayworks was founded in 1978 by nine potters and sculptors to provide both facilities and a stimulating environment for ceramic artists. Our facilities permit experimentation with a variety of clay bodies and methods of glazing and firing. Our members have many approaches to clay, from production work to sculptural pieces. Clayworks enables the artist to work in a supportive, communal environment which also facilitates his/her individual growth." The establishment became a nonprofit organization in 1980, and over the years has developed a national reputation as a high-quality ceramic arts organization.

What They Offer
Each year one person is awarded a one-year residency with a $100 monthly stipend for materials and firing, an individual work area (approximately 100 square feet), use of the common area (2000 square feet, including storage), access to telephone/trash collection, receptionist services, administration services, a consignment gallery, use of the kilns and other equipment, storage, teaching and networking opportunities, the opportunity to take various workshops, co-op purchases of supplies, and use of equipment. The resident must spend at least twenty-four hours each week on the premises working on a project and up to ten hours annually on community outreach. The resident must participate in the collective life of the studio, be willing to abide by environmental concerns, mount a solo exhibition, and have a home residence established in the Baltimore metropolitan area.

Facility Description

The facility is a renovated library, offering studio and exhibition spaces, classes, workshops, and ceramic supplies. Equipment available includes two slab rollers, an Alpine spray booth with 1hp compressor, a ball mill, and an extruder. The Clayworks provides several types of kilns: 60-cubic-foot and 45-cubic-foot downdraft natural-gas kilns, a 30-cubic-foot propane kiln, a raku propane kiln, a 30-cubic-foot wood fire kiln, six electric kilns, and an electric test kiln.

How to Apply

Send an SASE for an application and guidelines. Submit completed application with the following: a description of your formal art education and any residencies, workshops, or other school experience you may have had; a brief description of your experience with ceramics and any other artistic interests; a proposal for how a residency at the Clayworks would benefit your work as a clay artist and how your talents and abilities would benefit the collective studio environment at the Clayworks; a mention of any other residencies, fellowships, or opportunities you are applying for; and whether or not you might be interested in renting studio space from the Clayworks if you are not awarded the residency. Also include references (their affiliations and telephone numbers), a current résumé, and ten slides of your work (with a slide list and details about materials and processes used). An in-person interview is required of finalists.

Deadline

June 15 for 2000. Yearly deadline is subject to change.

Approximate Cost of Program

Housing, transportation, meals, materials, and incidentals—offset by $100 monthly stipend.

BLUE MOUNTAIN CENTER   NY

Blue Mountain Lake, New York, New York 12812-0109
Attention: Harriet Barlow, Director
Phone: (518) 352-7391

Type of Facility/Award

Residency.

Who Can Apply

Established creative and nonfiction writers as well as other artists and musicians.

Provisos

"The committee is particularly interested in fine work that evinces social and ecological concern and is aimed at general audiences." Established writers and other artists and musicians who do not require exceptional facilities are invited to apply.

Dates of Operation
Early summer through fall.

Location
Located in the heart of the Adirondack Mountains, BMC is two hours from the Albany airport and five hours from New York City.

History
Established in 1981, BMC sponsors readings and discussions by guests who choose to share their work with the local community. For six weeks prior to and following the residency period (see below), BMC hosts seminars and work groups concerned with social, economic, and environmental issues.

What They Offer
Blue Mountain Center runs four separate sessions each summer. Up to fifteen artists at a time are invited to spend four weeks in residence each session. Writers are housed in the lodge with bedrooms serving as their studies. Visual artists and composers have separate studios. Breakfast and dinner are served in the dining room. Lunch is served picnic-style to avoid interruption of work. Residents must provide their own transportation to the center. Guests are asked to contribute to a studio improvement fund, but such contributions are entirely voluntary.

Facility Description
Guests are housed in individual bedroom/studies in a turn-of-the-century Adirondack lodge surrounded by woods, lakes, and mountains. Facilities include a tennis court, lakes, boats, trails, a video and reading room, a linen and laundry room, and a photocopy machine. There is a pay phone for use by guests.

How to Apply
Send an SASE for information and guidelines. Then submit a brief biographical sketch including your professional achievements, your plan for work at the center, the names of any previous BMC residents you know, samples of your work (and an adequate SASE for their return), copies of reviews of previously published books or shows (if available), a $20 nonrefundable application fee, and your preference for an early, late summer, or fall residency. Appropriate work samples vary by discipline. Writers: ten pages. Artists: up to ten slides. Musicians/composers: call BMC for appropriate submittal instructions. Spouses must apply separately and will be evaluated independently.

Deadline
February 1. Notification by April.

Approximate Cost of Program
$20 application fee, transportation, and incidentals.

THE BRANDYWINE WORKSHOP   PA

Firehouse Art Center, 730–32 South Broad St., Philadelphia, Pennsylvania 19146
Attention: Assistant Gallery Director
Phone: (215) 546-3657 or (215) 546-2825
Web site: www.libertynet.org/brandywn/
Email: brandywn@libertynet.org

Type of Facility/Award
Residency.

Who Can Apply
Artists working in all media, including experimental forms.

Provisos
Applicants must reside in the United States and must have been out of school for at
least one full year. No graduate or undergraduate students are eligible to apply.

Dates of Operation
Open year-round.

Location
Brandywine is located on the Avenue of the Arts in Philadelphia.

History
The Brandywine Workshop, founded in 1972, is a "nonprofit, culturally diverse institution dedicated to promoting interest and talent in printmaking and other fine arts."

What They Offer
Brandywine offers three residencies:

Visiting artists receive paid travel, housing, and $30 per day for food allowances
over the period of one week.

Regional artists must live within commuting distance to Brandywine's south Philadelphia location. No honorarium, travel, or housing is provided for this one- to four-
week residency.

Young artists reside in Philadelphia, are under the age of thirty-five, and are not
currently students. They receive a one- to four-month residency and no honorarium,
travel, or housing.

Fifteen short-term fellowships are awarded each year, depending on funding. Some
partial fellowships for local artists are also available on a restricted basis. Artists produce
limited edition (one hundred or fewer) prints during their stay. The artist and Brandywine
each keep half of every print run. Artists are required to leave their mylars and separa-
tion sheets with the center to document their creative processes. All artists-in-residence
are provided studio space, supplies, equipment, and printer services for free.

Facility Description

Brandywine operates an offset lithography and screenprinting facility. Since expanding into the Firehouse Art Center, they now have galleries, classrooms, a museum shop, archives, and an expanded printmaking workshop.

How to Apply

Send an SASE for an application and brochure. Return the completed application with ten 35 mm slides of your current work (labeled according to instructions), an accompanying descriptive sheet, and a résumé.

Deadline

May 1. Notification within thirty days.

Approximate Cost of Program

Materials and incidentals for all three residencies. In some cases residents are also responsible for transportation, housing, and meals.

BUCKNELL UNIVERSITY   PA
The Bucknell Seminar for Younger Poets

Stadler Center for Poetry, Bucknell University, Lewisburg, Pennsylvania 17837
Attention: Andrew Ciotola, Assistant to the Director
Phone: (570) 577-1853
Email: ciotola@bucknell.edu

Type of Facility/Award

Fellowship.

Who Can Apply

Poets.

Provisos

Students from American colleges who have completed their sophomore, junior, or senior year may compete for eight fellowships awarded annually.

Dates of Operation

June 5 through June 30, though dates may vary.

Location

Lewisburg, Pennsylvania.

History

"A generous gift from Jack Stadler (a 1940 graduate of Bucknell) and the late Ralynn Stadler provided the major impetus for Professor John Wheatcroft to establish a Center for Poetry at Bucknell in 1981. The Center is housed in handsomely renovated Bucknell Hall, a historic campus building that contains a large auditorium for poetry readings and musical events, offices for the staff, a seminar room, and the Mildred Martin Poetry Library and Lounge. Founding director John Wheatcroft retired from Bucknell in 1996. At the time of his retirement, a Poetry Center Board was formed. In 1999, the Stadlers' original gift was used to establish a permanent fund for poetry at Bucknell."

What They Offer

The seminar provides young poets with an extended opportunity to write and to be guided by established poets. Private time for writing is balanced with disciplined learning in an atmosphere of peer support and camaraderie. Each fellow receives tuition, room, board, and private space for writing. Eight students are chosen annually. Staff poets conduct two workshops each week, offer readings of their own verse, and are available for tutorials. Interaction with Bucknell's poet-in-residence is a valuable feature of this program. Fellows may also participate in weekly readings. All academic, cultural, and recreational facilities of the University are open to fellows.

Facility Description

Poets stay in the Stadler Center for Poetry on the Bucknell campus.

How to Apply

Send an SASE for a brochure. Applications should include an academic transcript, two supporting recommendations (one must be from a poetry writing instructor), a letter of self-presentation (a brief autobiography stressing commitment to poetry writing and detailing relevent experience and publications), and a ten- to twelve-page portfolio. Include an adequate SASE if you want your portfolio returned.

Deadline

March 1. Notification April 7.

Approximate Cost of Program

Transportation, materials, and incidentals.

BUCKNELL UNIVERSITY   PA
The Philip Roth Residence in Creative Writing

Stadler Center for Poetry, Bucknell University, Lewisburg, PA 17837
Attention: Andrew Ciotola, Assistant to the Director
Phone: (570) 577-1853
Email: ciotola@bucknell.edu

Type of Facility/Award

Residency.

Who Can Apply

In alternate years the residence will be awarded to a fiction writer or a poet.

Provisos

Applicants need to be more than twenty-one years old, must be U.S. residents, and cannot be students in a college or university. Some publication history is expected. The selected resident typically uses the time to work on a first or second book.

Dates of Operation

October through mid-December.

Location

Lewisburg, Pennsylvania.

History

"A generous gift from Jack Stadler (a 1940 graduate of Bucknell) and the late Ralynn Stadler provided the major impetus for Professor John Wheatcroft to establish a Center for Poetry at Bucknell in 1981. The Center is housed in handsomely reno-vated Bucknell Hall, a historic campus building that contains a large auditorium for poetry readings and musical events, offices for the staff, a seminar room, and the Mildred Martin Poetry Library and Lounge. Founding director John Wheatcroft retired from Bucknell in 1996. At the time of his retirement, a Poetry Center Board was formed. In 1999, the Stadlers' original gift was used to establish a permanent fund for poetry at Bucknell."

What They Offer

The two-and-a-half-month residency includes a furnished two-bedroom apartment, meals in the university dining service, a studio on campus, and a $1,000 stipend. All academic, cultural, and recreational facilities of Bucknell are available to the resident.

"Although the person selected will have no university responsibilities, it is hoped that he or she will constitute a presence as a working writer on campus, talking informally from time to time with students who are interested in writing. The Philip Roth Resident is expected to offer a public reading of his or her work during the semester of residence."

Facility Description

Bucknell University campus.

How to Apply

Send an SASE for a brochure. Applications should include a curriculum vita; a self-introductory letter including a brief biography that stresses commitment to the writ-ing of poetry or fiction and that also presents a statement of intention and project proposal; two letters of recommendation, at least one of which should come from a writer or a teacher of writing who is familiar with you and your work; no more than twenty pages of your writing; and an adequate SASE for return of materials.

Deadline
March 1. Notification by April 1.

Approximate Cost of Program
Transportation, materials, and incidentals—offset by $1,000 stipend.

CENTER FOR THE ARTS AND RELIGION   DC
Wesley Theological Seminary, 4500 Massachusetts Ave. NW, Washington, DC 20016
Attention: Catherine Kapikian, Director
Phone: (202) 885-8617 or (202) 885-8660
Web site: www.wesleysem.org/car.htm
Email: ArtsandReligion@wesleysem.org

Type of Facility/Award
Fellowship.

Who Can Apply
All artists.

Provisos
The Center for the Arts and Religion (CAR) will consider applications from artists of all faiths whose work evidences concern with issues of the religious community, artists who work at the boundary between the secular and the sacred, and artists who are willing to articulate the relationship between their work and their faith.

Dates of Operation
Academic year (September through May).

Location
Washington, D.C.

History
"CAR personnel reflect a history of interactive work with churches of diverse denominations, as well as with colleges and universities nationwide. A long-standing collaboration with The Catholic University of America (CUA) sustains a CUA-sponsored liturgical artist-in-residence in our studio."

What They Offer
Residencies of one academic year, one semester, or one (concentrated) six-week period provide an artist with studio space, a stipend (amount unspecified) and/or room and board (depending upon the nature of the residency), free audit of one seminary class per semester, the opportunity to teach classes to members of the community for

a stipend, the opportunity to participate in an on-campus exhibit of his or her work, and invitations to forums, lectures, and concerts sponsored by the seminary and CAR. Artists have use of the seminary library and ongoing affiliation with other artists, faculty, and staff in an inclusive, ecumenical context. Access is provided to some of the best museums, galleries, and theaters in the nation. In return, CAR expects residents to participate in the artistic community through support, instruction, and critique of one another's work. Residents participate in community outreach (exhibits and lectures, for example, with entrepreneurial arrangements to be negotiated between the artists and the sponsoring institution) and donate one piece of work to CAR/Wesley Theological Seminary for its permanent art collection.

Facility Description

"In the museum-quality Dadian Gallery, exhibitions communicating religious themes inspire sacred values, and disclose the numinous. Forums or lectures accompany all gallery openings, whether a one-person show, group show, or collaborative exhibition with another institution. In the WTS Chapel, art installations, liturgical dance, and chancel dramas join a variety of musical expressions—such as organ, piano, choir, and instrumental music—to companion and enhance worship, enriching spiritual life." The campus also includes classrooms, administrative offices, and a library.

How to Apply

Send an SASE for information. Submit a résumé (with professional credentials and a personal statement describing your interest in working at the seminary and how your artistic process and product work in relationship to your spirituality), a portfolio of twenty slides of your recent work (labeled according to instructions), and a cover letter. A telephone or in-person interview will be arranged after review of your material.

Deadline

Rolling application process.

Approximate Cost of Program

Transportation, housing, meals, materials, and incidentals—offset by possible stipend. Room and board may be provided depending upon the nature of the residency.

CHESTER SPRINGS STUDIO   PA

P.O. Box 329, 1671 Art School Road, Chester Springs, Pennsylvania 19425
Attention: Dina Schmidt
Phone: (610) 827-7277; fax: (610) 827-7157
Email: chesstudio@aol.com

Type of Facility/Award

Residency.

Who Can Apply
Visual artists interested in working with clay.

Provisos
Applicants must be citizens or legal residents of the United States. Students enrolled in a degree program will not be considered. "The Studio is particularly interested in artists who continue to turn to the landscape as a source to develop ideas—whether they are expressed in a nontraditional or traditional form."

Dates of Operation
August 1 through July 31.

Location
Thirty miles west of Philadelphia in the historic village of Yellow Springs.

History
Chester Springs Studio is a nonprofit art center committed to the support of serious visual artists through teaching, exhibition, and residency opportunities.

What They Offer
Residents are provided with 250 square-feet of studio space, access to kilns, a solo exhibition, and a monthly stipend of $650. Clay and glaze materials are available at cost. In return, artists must help maintain the studio, which has a quarterly enrollment of approximately one hundred students, and train a small group of advanced students to carry out custodial chores. Residents may be able to teach for pay.

Facility Description
The studio is housed in a mid-eighteenth-century stone barn. Ceramic studio dimensions are 36' x 20'. There are two portable propane raku kilns, a sprung-arch downdraft wood kiln, a cross-draft two-chamber wood/salt kiln; and a Baily's gas kiln (31 $1/2$" x 36 $1/4$" ID). For two- or three-dimensional projects, a 36' x 36' x 20' H studio is available with a large northern skylight. Surrounding the facilities are 145 acres of protected land containing ruins of a Revolutionary War hospital, springhouses for spa-goers, and bog gardens.

How to Apply
Send an SASE for an application and brochure. Submit a completed application with a letter outlining your reasons for applying to the residency program. Also describe your formal art education, other post-high-school education, your experience with ceramics, and any experience you have teaching art. Include a copy of your résumé and any relevant published materials. Send up to ten slides of your work, as specified in the literature, and an adequate SASE for their return.

Deadline
April 15 (postmarked). Notification by May 7.

Approximate Cost of Program
Transportation, housing, meals, materials, and incidentals—offset by $650 monthly.

THE CLAY STUDIO PA
Evelyn Shapiro Foundation Fellowship, 139 N. 2nd Street, Philadelphia,
    Pennsylvania 19106
Phone: (215) 925-3453; fax: (215) 925-7774
Web site: www.libertynet.org/claystdo/cs.html

Type of Facility/Award
Artist-in-residence program and fellowship.

Who Can Apply
Ceramic and clay artists of all levels of interest and proficiency.

Provisos
None listed.

Dates of Operation
September 1 through August 31.

Location
Philadelphia, Pennsylvania.

History
The Clay Studio, founded in 1974, is a nonprofit educational arts organization dedicated to the ceramic arts and to the work of new clay artists through its gallery, studio space, and lecture series. The studio has experienced dramatic growth since 1995, made possible by the development and renovation of the Second Street Art Building, which provides the studio and three other artist collectives with expanded facilities.

What They Offer
The Evelyn Shapiro Foundation Fellowship provides one year of free studio space (two hundred square-feet), a monthly stipend of $500, a materials and firing allowance, access to electric and gas firing kilns, access to glaze materials, and opportunities to teach in the studio's school and to exhibit work in the studio's gallery and shop. Fellows receive a solo exhibition of their work toward the end of the residency.

The Clay Studio also hosts the Resident Artists Program, which provides studio space for up to five years (by application and competition) for a minimal fee and membership. The Associate Artists Program offers work space on a first-come, first-served basis to applicants with some clay experience for a minimal fee.

Facility Description

Facilities include a gallery, studios, classroom space, and a retail shop.

How to Apply

Send an SASE or check the Web site for an application and brochure. Submit your completed application with a résumé, a statement of your reasons for wanting to participate in the program, and ten slides of recent work. Include an adequate SASE for return of the slides. An in-person interview will be required of all finalists.

Deadline

May 31 (postmarked).

Approximate Cost of Program

Transportation, housing, meals, and incidentals—offset by stipend.

COUNCIL ON FOREIGN RELATIONS   NY
Edward R. Murrow Fellowship

Council on Foreign Relations, 58 East 68th Street, New York, New York 10021
Attention: Elise Lewis, Director of Membership and Fellowship Affairs
Phone: (212) 434-9489; fax: (212) 861-2701
Web site: www/foreignrelations.org
Email: Fellowships@cfr.org

Type of Facility/Award

Fellowship.

Who Can Apply

Journalists.

Provisos

Each applicant must be a U. S. citizen who is serving as "a correspondent, editor, or producer for radio, television, a newspaper, or a magazine widely available in the United States, and who is either currently serving abroad or, having recently served abroad, plans to return to foreign posts."

Dates of Operation

Fellowships typically begin in September and extend into May.

Location

Council of Foreign Relations offices in New York City.

History

The fellowship, made possible by a grant from the CBS Foundation, was first awarded in 1949. "The purpose of the Edward R. Murrow Fellowship is to help the Fellow increase his/her competence in reporting and interpreting events abroad and to give him/her a period of nearly a year for sustained analysis and writing free from the daily pressures that characterize journalistic life. The Fellowship is expected to promote the quality of responsible and discerning journalism that characterized the work of Edward R. Murrow during his life."

What They Offer

The council, which is a nonprofit and nonpartisan organization, has no affiliation with the U.S. government and takes no position on foreign policy. It offers the fellow, who is an "outstanding correspondent, editor, or producer, who has been living abroad and has been preoccupied with short deadlines, an opportunity to broaden his/her perspective through a coordinated program of reading, study, discussion, writing, and renewed contact with the American domestic scene." Fellows are provided office space at the council's building in New York and access to meeting rooms and the in-house library. Fellows are encouraged to participate in events sponsored by the Meetings and Studies Programs of the council and are expected to contribute to the council by leading study groups, acting as speakers or moderators at council events around the United States, and other similar activities. The fellowship stipend is roughly equivalent to the salary relinquished by the fellow during the nine-month term of residency. The amount will not exceed $60,000 per annum prorated for the nine months.

Facility Description

None provided.

How to Apply

To receive an application, a nomination letter must be submitted to the director of membership and fellowship affairs. You may be nominated by a council member, a former or current Murrow fellow, your employer, or by yourself. "The nomination letter should confirm the candidate's eligibility as well as provide a brief description of his or her background and why the nominator believes the candidate to be an appropriate prospect for the Fellowship." If you nominate yourself, also submit a copy of your most recent résumé with the letter of nomination. If you qualify, you will be asked to complete an application with full biographical details, current and previous employment information, educational information, and the names and addresses of five references who are well acquainted with your work. Also include a statement of 2,500 words or less which summarizes your experience as a foreign correspondent and explains how the fellowship would contribute to your professional development. The statement should propose an overall plan of work for the year and indicate how the plan relates to your long-term career goals. Additional materials may be submitted.

Deadline

January 5 for letters of nomination. February 23 for applications. Notification by late April. Exact dates may vary from year to year. Be sure to obtain the specific information before you submit the letter of nomination.

Approximate Cost of Program

Transportation, housing, meals, materials, and incidentals—offset by a stipend.

CREATIVE GLASS CENTER OF AMERICA   NJ

1501 Glasstown Road, Milville, New Jersey 08332
Attention: Denise Gonzalez-Dendrinos, Program Coordinator
Phone: (609) 825-2410, ext. 2733; fax: (609) 825-2410

Type of Facility/Award

Fellowship.

Who Can Apply

Glass artists.

Provisos

Glass artists must be over twenty-one years of age when fellowship commences. All applicants must have basic English language skills and basic hot glassworking skills.

Dates of Operation

January 10 through April 21. April 24 through July 21. September 11 through December 8.

Location

Wheaton Village is located in rural southern New Jersey, forty-five minutes from both Philadelphia and Atlantic City, and less than three hours from New York City and Washington D.C.

History

Established in 1983, the Creative Glass Center of America is a division of the Wheaton Cultural Alliance, Inc. CGCA provides creative artists with the time, space, and equipment to work out their creative concepts without the restrictions imposed by production costs and sales needs. This allows artists to establish a body of work regardless of their personal financial limitations.

What They Offer

Three-month fellowships provide access to the glassworking facilities at Wheaton Village, all the glass they can use, free (shared) housing in the center's four-bedroom Cape Cod house just two blocks from the campus, and a $500 monthly stipend to defray expenses for up to four fellows at one time. Fellows are responsible for their own cooking and cleaning. A studio technician is available for consultation and to familiarize artists with the equipment and its use. Fellows take turns assisting one another with glassblowing and casting, generally working in teams of two. Teams rotate throughout the session. The hot shop closes during the last week of each fellowship session to allow time for finishing work and packing. Interaction and exploration of ideas with Wheaton Inc.'s research and development people are encouraged. Fellows must work in view of the museum visitors twelve hours per week, not including assisting time. Fellows are asked to donate one of their works made during the residency for permanent inclusion in the CGCA collection in the Museum of American Glass at Wheaton Village.

Facility Description

The center sits on an eighty-eight-acre site that features the Museum of American Glass with over 7,500 objects (including over one hundred works by past fellows) and a 2,000-volume library of glass history and technology. The studio is in a recreated 1888 glasshouse. The Wheaton Village glass factory has been designed to accommodate a wide variety of glass working techniques. It has an excellent hot shop served by a glass factory, with an unlimited volume of batch and a wide range of colors. The 3,000-square-foot hot shop has two furnaces, two glory holes, eight annealers, and two benches. The hot shop is accessible round-the-clock, seven days a week. Facilities are equipped to produce both cast or kiln-formed glass, with one roller-bed casting oven and three general casting ovens for use in pate de verre, fusing, and slumping. A cold working studio is available with five grinding and polishing wheels, a large capacity sandblaster, and two reciprolaps. Each fellow is given her or his own studio within the factory.

How to Apply

Send an SASE for an application and brochure. Return eight copies of each of the following: the completed application, a current résumé, a brief statement explaining how you would use the fellowship to benefit your artistic career development, and two letters of recommendation (letters may be sent directly to CGCA who will be responsible for making multiple copies). Include ten slides of your work (labeled according to instructions) and an adequate SASE for their return. Include a paragraph about you and your work to be used for publicity purposes.

Note: Slides submitted by applicants chosen for the fellowships or as alternates become the property of the Creative Glass Center of America.

Deadline

September 15 (all sessions). Notification by early November.

Approximate Cost of Program

Transportation, meals, some materials, and incidentals—offset by $500 monthly stipend.

DUMBARTON OAKS

1703 32nd Street, N.W., Washington, DC 20007
Attention: Office of the Director
Phone: (202) 339-6490
Web site: www.doaks.org
Email: dumbartonoaks@doaks.org

Type of Facility/Award
Fellowship.

Who Can Apply
Anyone wishing to do extensive research in three areas of study: Byzantine studies (including related aspects of late Roman, early Christian, western medieval, Slavic, and Near Eastern studies), Pre-Columbian studies (of Mexico, Central America, and Andean South America), and studies in landscape architecture.

Provisos
Applicants must be able to speak and write in English.

Junior fellowships apply to students who at the time of application have fulfilled all preliminary requirements for a Ph.D., or appropriate final degree, and will be working on a dissertation or final project at Dumbarton Oaks under the direction of a faculty member at their own university. In exceptional cases, applications may be accepted from students before they have fulfilled preliminary requirements.

Fellowships apply to scholars who hold a doctorate (or appropriate final degree) or have established themselves in their field and wish to pursue their own research. Applications are also accepted from graduate students who expect to have a Ph.D. prior to taking up residence at Dumbarton Oaks. (Successful applicants will revert to the status and stipend of junior fellows if the degree has not been conferred.)

Summer fellowships are available to scholars of any level of advancement.

Dates of Operation
Fellowships are typically awarded for the academic year (September–May), but awards may also be made for a single term (September–January, or January–May). Summer fellowships are six to nine weeks, between June and August.

Location
Washington, D.C.

History
Dumbarton Oaks is administered by the trustees for Harvard University.

What They Offer
"Fellowship awards range from an equivalent of approximately $18,060 for an unmarried Junior Fellow to a maximum of $38,700 for a Fellow from abroad accompanied

by family members. Support includes a stipend of $13,545 for a Junior Fellow or $24,635 for a Fellow for the full academic year; housing (an allowance may be offered if Dumbarton Oaks is unable to provide accommodations); $1,850 (if needed) to assist with the cost of bringing and maintaining dependents here; a research expense allowance of $870 for the year; lunch on weekdays; and Dumbarton Oak's contribution to health insurance. Travel expense reimbursement for the lowest available airfare, up to a maximum of $1,300, may be provided for Fellows and Junior Fellows if support cannot be obtained from other sources (such as a Fulbright travel grant)."

Summer fellowship awards include a maintenance allowance of $185 per week, housing in a Dumbarton Oaks apartment or at the Fellows Building, weekday lunches, contribution to health insurance, and travel expense reimbursement for the lowest available airfare if other travel support cannot be obtained. No housing allowances or funds for dependents are available in the summer months.

Facility Description
None provided.

How to Apply
Send an SASE for an application and brochure. Return ten collated sets of the entire application packet: an application letter, proposal, and personal/professional data. The letter must specify your project title, the type of fellowship you prefer, your field of study, and the precise period for which the award is requested; it should additionally include names and addresses of the three scholars (two for summer fellowships) who are to send letters of recommendation directly to Dumbarton Oaks (one of the three letters for junior fellows must be from a faculty advisor). Your proposal should be no longer than 1,000 words and should describe the work you have planned for your residency; also indicate the progress already made on the project, your anticipated completion date, and your needs regarding Dumbarton facilities. Finally, provide personal and professional data, including your name, address, telephone number, family status (including names and ages of dependents who would accompany you to Dumbarton Oaks), your education and academic degrees (with dates conferred, awards, and honors), present and past positions, your publications, papers read, field research, and your proficiency in the requisite languages, which must include facility in written and spoken English. Junior fellowship applicants must have their university registrar send an official transcript of their graduate record directly to Dumbarton Oaks.

Deadline
November 1 (postmarked). November 15 (received). Awards are announced in February and must be accepted by March 15.

Approximate Cost of Program
Most meals (daily lunches provided), materials, and incidentals—offset by stipend.

EXPERIMENTAL TELEVISION CENTER

109 Lower Fairfield Road, Newark Valley, New York 13811
Attention: Sherry Miller Hocking, Assistant Director
Phone: (607) 687-4341; fax: (607) 687-4341
Web site: www.experimentaltvcenter.org
Email: etc@servtech.com

Type of Facility/Award

Artist-in-residence program.

Who Can Apply

Video and film artists, or artists interested in working with electronic media.

Provisos

Artists must have prior experience in media production. Artists working in all genres are encouraged to apply.

Dates of Operation

February through June. September through January.

Location

The center is located in the historic district of Owego, a small village centrally positioned upstate along major interstate highways. Direct air and bus transportation is available. The center is within twenty miles of Binghamton and Ithaca.

History

"The Experimental Television Center was founded in 1971, an outgrowth of a media access program established by Ralph Hocking at Binghamton University in 1969. Today the Center offers a unique concentration on electronic image-making through the Residency Program, provides administrative and support services to individual artists and projects, and a grants program open to New York State's media and film artists and organizations." The center is also active in the area of preservation, and is engaged in the Video History Project, a research effort on the Web.

What They Offer

The residency program provides an estimated $50,000 of services annually to selected artists, supporting projects that approach video as a contemporary electronic arts medium. About forty-five artists participate each year to better understand video and digital technologies and to explore their uses within documentary as well as more experimental forms. The center offers a self-directed environment, providing personalized instruction, access to facilities, and time and space for aesthetic exploration in the creation of new work. Artists reside at the center. A five-day residency costs $100. Artists provide their own transportation and meals, and have complete aesthetic and technical control over all aspects of the creative process. Though the center provides instruction and technical assistance, all equipment is operated by the artist. The center's staff does not act as a production crew. Residents retain all rights over their work but are required to donate one copy of completed work to the library. Each artist must pay a $100 residency fee.

Facility Description

"The system includes modules designed at the Center as well as commercially available tools and integrates both analog and computer-based components. The architecture of the system is designed to be flexible, multifaceted, and multipurpose. Included are analog tools such as colorizers, keyers and mixing devices as well as sound processing equipment; computer-based components include the Amiga platform with a Toaster, and a Mac platform with nonlinear digitizing and other image processing software. A complete list of equipment and software is available." The center is within walking distance from a library, post office, shops, and a large bookstore. Looking out over the Susquehanna River, the studio at the center is a large loft-like space which also houses the tape collection.

How to Apply

Send an SASE for a brochure and application guidelines. Submit a project description indicating how you would use the center's imaging system. Include a résumé with information relating to past video works and their exhibition, a clear indication of your knowledge of equipment operation, your choice of a five-day period (with alternative dates listed by priority), and, if you are a first time applicant, a $3/4$" or VHS tape of recently completed works (and an adequate SASE for return of the tape).

Deadline

December 15 for February through June residencies; July 15 for September through January residencies.

Approximate Cost of Program

$100 for five days plus transportation, meals, materials, and incidentals.

THE FABRIC WORKSHOP MUSEUM   PA

1315 Cherry Street, 5th Floor, Philadelphia, Pennsylvania 19107
Attention: Artist Advisory Committee
Phone: (215) 568-1111; fax: (215) 922-3791

Type of Facility/Award

Artist-in-residence program.

Who Can Apply

Visual artists.

Provisos

Well-known and emerging artists of various disciplines who desire to broaden their aesthetic by doing silkscreen printing on fabric are invited to apply.

Dates of Operation

Open year-round.

Location

Philadelphia, Pennsylvania.

History

"The Fabric Workshop and Museum is the only nonprofit organization in the United States devoted to experimental fabric design and printing by nationally recognized and emerging artists representing all disciplines. Founded in 1977, The Fabric Workshop has developed into a renowned institution with an Artist-in-Residence program, an extensive permanent museum collection of unique contemporary art, the Museum Sales Shop, and comprehensive educational programming including exhibitions, lectures, tours, and student apprenticeships."

What They Offer

Ten to twelve artists each year are selected for this program. Artists receive an honorarium (no amount stated in the literature), photographic documentation of finished projects, and pieces of their experimental works. All materials necessary, including screens, ink, fabric, and the labor needed to complete the project in the workshop's laboratories are provided. Technical assistance is available from the highly skilled staff.

Facility Description

Facilities include print studios, dye and pigment mixing rooms, an exhibition area, and a museum sales shop.

How to Apply

Send an SASE for a brochure. Submit ten to twenty slides, a résumé, and any other materials of interest.

Deadline

Rolling application process.

Approximate Cost of Program

Transportation, housing, meals, and incidentals—offset by honorarium.

THE FARM: AN ART COLONY FOR WOMEN NY

20 Old Overlook Road, Poughkeepsie, New York 12603
Attention: Kate Millett
Phone: (914) 473-9267

Administration/Applications/Information:
Kate Millett, 295 Bowery, New York, New York 10003
Phone: (212) 473-2846

Type of Facility/Award
Artist-in-residence program.

Who Can Apply
Any female artist, writer, or scholar.

Provisos
Women writers and women visual artists of all kinds from the United States and elsewhere are invited to apply.

Dates of Operation
May through December.

Location
Village of LaGrange near Poughkeepsie, New York. The Farm is approximately eighty miles north of New York City.

History
The Farm, established in 1979, is a self-supporting and economically independent colony for women artists. The crops, Christmas and landscape trees, help support the colony's expenses—keeping buildings in repair and providing studio space.

What They Offer
In exchange for housing, studio space, and access to facilities, residents contribute four hours of work each weekday morning. From one o'clock until eight o'clock each evening when dinner is served, residents are free to work on their art. Artists are free to do as they please on weekends. Every participant contributes $80 per week for food.

Facility Description
The Farm is a tree farm in New York. Facilities include a darkroom, woodshop with power tools, and silkscreen printing facilities.

How to Apply
Send an SASE to the administrative address for information and application guidelines. Then submit examples of your work, a description of yourself, your interest in The Farm, and your preferred dates of residency.

Deadline
Apply as early as possible for the following summer. Applications are read until May.

Approximate Cost of Program
$80 per week plus transportation, materials, and incidentals.

FRANKLIN FURNACE   NY
Franklin Furnace Archive, Inc., 45 John Street, #611, New York, New York
    10038-3706
Attention: Performance Proposals or Emerging Performance Artists Series
Phone: (212) 766-2606; fax: (212) 766-2740
Web site: www.franklinfurnace.org
Email: info@franklinfurnace.org

Type of Facility/Award
Fellowship/grant.

Who Can Apply
Performance artists.

Provisos
Emerging performance artists or performance artists developing new works are invited to apply. Artists from all areas of the world are eligible. Funded performances must take place in the state of New York. Performance artists who are interested in developing new temporal artwork for the Internet are encouraged to apply for the Emerging Performing Artists Series.

Dates of Operation
Open year-round.

Location
New York City.

History
Begun in 1985 "Franklin Furnace's Fund has boosted the careers of such emerging artists as Papo Colo, Karen Finley, John Fleck, Holly Hughes, Cathy Weis, Pamela Sneed and Murray Hill."

What They Offer
The Franklin Furnace Fund for Performance Art, supported by the Jerome Foundation and the New York State Council on the Arts, awards grants of $2,000 to $5,000 to artists for production of a major work anywhere in the state of New York. The Emerging Performance Artists Series includes an honorarium and a month-long residency for producing temporal artwork (Internet-oriented) at Parsons School of

Design's Design and Technology Department. Franklin Furnace provides the residency (artists are paired with M.F.A. design and technology students), technical equipment, technical assistance, and publicity.

Facility Description
None provided.

How to Apply
Send an SASE for an application and brochure. For either program, return the completed application with a fifty-word summary of your proposed work. Include a VHS videotape, cued for five minutes, of your proposed work or past work. You may also include your résumé, reviews of previous work, and any other supporting materials, such as a detailed project description, audio cassettes, slides, photos, CD-ROMS, Jaz, Zip, or floppy disks (PC-format). All Web-based work must be submitted on removable media. You may also include a budget for space rental, equipment costs, etc. Provide an adequate SASE for return of your materials.

Deadline
April 1 (postmarked) for either program.

Approximate Cost of Program
Not applicable in this listing.

THE FUND FOR NEW AMERICAN PLAYS   DC
The John F. Kennedy Center for the Performing Arts, 2700 F Street, N.W.,
    Washington, DC 20566
Attention: Max Woodward
Phone: (202) 416-8024 or (202) 416-8020; fax: (202) 416-8026
Web Site: www.kennedy-center.org/newwork/fnap
Email: mawoodward@kennedy-center.org

Type of Facility/Award
Playwright's offering.

Who Can Apply
Theater groups and affiliated playwrights.

Provisos
Nonprofit professional American theaters may apply. The fund encourages playwrights to write new plays and to stimulate the development of plays and plays with music. The fund does not provide support for musicals or translations of foreign plays.

Dates of Operation
Full calendar year for production.

Location
Various locations throughout the U.S.

History
The fund, founded in 1987, has awarded more than two million dollars to nonprofit theaters throughout the country to enable them to produce forty-nine new plays by fifty playwrights. Three of the plays have won Pulitzer Prizes and others have been nominated for various awards, including Tonys and Outer Circle Critics Awards. Some have been produced in New York and other U.S. cities.

What They Offer
Grants underwrite specific or extraordinary expenses relating to creative support (expenses beyond the theater's budget, and expenses allowing the playwright's choice of director or designer), actor support (costs of guest artists beyond the theater's budget and productions with larger casts than the theater can support), and production support (living and travel expenses of playwrights during rehearsal and performance in order to guarantee a minimum four-week rehearsal period and allow the author to remain at the theater for rewriting during the play's run). Funding for sets or costumes may be considered under special circumstances. No funding is offered for publicity, marketing, payroll taxes, box office, or other non-artistic aspects of production. The playwright receives an award of $10,000. A separate grant for $2,500, the Roger L. Stevens Incentive Award, is given from time to time to playwrights of exceptional promise.

Facility Description
Varies according to theater.

How to Apply
Send an SASE for information and guidelines. Submit one proposal; five copies of the play; a production budget; proof of nonprofit status; a copy of the exclusive arrangement between the playwright and the theater; a history of the play's readings, workshops, or other developmental work; disclosure of any encumbrances to the script; biographies of the playwright and any artist(s) for whom financial support is being requested; disclosure of any co-production agreements with other theaters or producers in regard to the script; and a short paragraph about the theater. Also include a short bio, two black-and-white headshots of the playwright, a short paragraph about the artistic director, and a synopsis of the play suitable for press releases.

Deadline
May 5. Announcements in fall.

Approximate Cost of Program
Not applicable in this listing.

GELL CENTER OF THE FINGER LAKES   NY

c/o Writers and Books, 740 University Avenue, Rochester, New York 14607
Attention: Kathy Pottetti, Gell Center Coordinator
Phone: (716) 473-2590; fax: (716) 442-9333
Web site: www.wab.org
Email: joef@wab.org

Type of Facility/Award

Retreat.

Who Can Apply

Writers (including, but not limited to, poets, playwrights, novelists, magazine editors, and journalists).

Provisos

None listed.

Dates of Operation

Open year-round.

Location

Naples, New York, lies at the foot of the Bristol Hills. Located at the end of Canandaigua Lake, the area is one of the world's great grape-growing regions. The Finger Lakes region is easily accessible by major highways, by rail, or via Rochester International Airport, forty-five minutes to the north. It is approximately an hour's drive from Rochester, Ithaca, Corning, and Elmira.

The Gleason Lodge at the Gell Center

History

"Writers and Books is a Literary Arts Center providing Western New York with a variety of programs supporting the creation and appreciation of contemporary literature. These programs include readings by regional and national writers, an extensive workshop series, and community outreach programs. Writers and Books is supported in part with grants from The New York State Council on the Arts and The National Endowment for the Arts, as well as by corporations, memberships, and contributions."

What They Offer

Retreats at the Gell House are available through Writers and Books. Applicants must become Writers and Books members to use the facility. The annual membership fee is $30. Additionally, residents are charged $35 per night for use of the facility. Please note: The house is equipped with two private bedrooms, each containing separate writing areas. If you choose to be alone in the house, you must pay for both bedrooms.

Facility Description

The charming Gell House is a completely furnished hillside home with a landscaped yard surrounded by twenty-three acres of woodlands and trails. The house has two bedrooms, two baths, a living room, dining area, fully-equipped kitchen, and indoor and outdoor porch areas. There are wonderful territorial views from several large windows in the house, and it is common to see deer near the spring-fed brook that falls along a terraced waterway. The setting is ideal for quiet study and reflection. The Gleason Lodge, which is handicapped-accessible, provides a space that can accommodate seventy-four people for social gatherings or fifty people for meetings, seminars, or workshops. The Lodge has a commercially equipped kitchen and a dining area which seats up to twenty-five people. Plans are underway to add a residential wing to the lodge which will house up to twenty people. Nearby are many cultural and recreational attractions, including the Bristol Valley Playhouse, Cumming Nature Center, Mees Observatory, Finger Lakes Hiking Trail, High Tor Wildlife Management Area, and the Finger Lakes Performing Arts Center. In the winter, the area is ideal for downhill and cross-country skiers—at other times, you can hike, bike, swim, sail, or simply enjoy the rolling landscape. Also nearby are many restaurants, vineyards, and wineries.

How to Apply

Call or write for an application. Reservations are taken on a first-come, first-served basis. If you write, indicate your preference of dates and desired length of stay.

Deadline

None.

Approximate Cost of Program

$245 for a one-week stay plus transportation, meals, incidentals, and $30 membership fee for those who are not already members.

HARVESTWORKS, INC.   NY

The Audio Arts Organization, 596 Broadway, Suite 602, New York, New York
   10012
Attention: Chris Anderson, Production Coordinator or Laurie Brown, Education
   Director
Phone: (212) 431-1130; fax: (212) 431-8473
Web site: www.harvestworks.org
Email: harvestw@dti.net

Type of Facility/Award

Artist-in-residence program.

Who Can Apply

Any artist who uses sound, picture, or technology as a creative medium. This includes composers, film and video makers, choreographers, and installation and multimedia artists. Emerging artists and artists of color are encouraged to apply.
Harvestworks encourages such artists to apply regardless of their technical abilities.

Provisos

No students, groups, or ensembles. Two years must pass before previous Harvestworks
artists-in-residence can reapply.

Dates of Operation

Open year-round.

Location

New York City.

History

Harvestworks was founded in 1977 as a not-for-profit organization. It provides support to artists who use sound, picture, and technology as media for creative work. Its
mission is to "foster the creation of works by emerging and mid-career artists, particularly those artists seeking to expand the vocabulary of media art forms and to
increase the audience for that work." Harvestworks obtains funding and equipment
through donations from private corporations and government agencies.

What They Offer

Artists-in-residence are awarded twenty to sixty hours of studio time to work on
their projects. Artists work with professional engineers, editors, and programmers in
newly renovated recording and multimedia production studios. Studios can also be
rented by artists on a daily or weekly basis. Rates range from $15 to $78 per hour
depending upon whether the studio is set up for sound or video editing. Members
receive discounted rates.

Facility Description

Studio PASS is equipped with a live recording room, audio-to-video synchronization, Macintosh computer-controlled music sequencing capabilities, and ProTools, a computer-based digital recording and editing program by Digidesign. This is a well-equipped, state-of-the-art facility with a digital audio workstation, a multimedia workstation, tape recorders, outboard equipment, microphones, monitor speakers, synthesizers, video, other MIDI equipment, and software. They offer (for use and sale) hardware and software from the STEIM research center in the Netherlands.

How to Apply

Send an SASE for an application and brochure. Return six copies of the completed application with a detailed project description plus one copy of a two-page résumé summarizing your experience in the field. (Do not send reviews, reference letters, program notes, or record albums.) Include a work sample. Cue a ten-minute audio or video segment for the panel's consideration or send a up to eight slides. Label all samples with your name. Formats include $1/4$" reel-to-reel audio tape, cassette, DAT, Beta, VHS, $3/4$" videotape, or slides in a clear plastic slide sheet. Do not send masters or originals. Include an adequate SASE for return of materials; you may also pick up your samples in-person at Harvestworks after December 31.

Deadline

November 15.

Approximate Cost of Program

Transportation, housing, meals, and incidentals.

THE HASTINGS CENTER   NY   **DISCONTINUED**
Journalist-in-Residence Program

HENRY STREET SETTLEMENT   NY
Abrons Art Center, 466 Grand Street, New York, New York 10002-4804
Attention: Visual Arts Program
Phone: (212) 598-0400; fax: (212) 505-8329

Type of Facility/Award

Artist-in-residence program.

Who Can Apply

Visual artists.

Provisos

Applicants must be from New York City.

Dates of Operation
Open year-round.

Location
Lower East Side section of Manhattan.

History
None provided.

What They Offer
Five artists each year are selected to work in the center's collective studio. One ceramics artist is selected to work in a separate space next to the clay classroom. The studio is available on weekdays from 9 A.M. to 8 P.M., most Saturdays, and some Sundays. It is closed on national holidays. The residency term is for one year beginning in September. Artists are asked to make use of the studio for at least twenty hours each week. Space is limited, so the center cannot accommodate large sculptures or printing equipment. In exchange, artists contribute three hours per week of "in-kind" services, such as teaching art workshops, leading gallery tours, installing exhibitions, or other special projects. Anyone accepted into the program who is of Latino, African-American, Asian, or Native American background, under the age of thirty-five, and has financial need and a demonstrated commitment to the visual arts may also be eligible for the $5,000 Van Lier Fellowship. Application forms for this fellowship are included with the forms for the artist-in-residence program.

Facility Description
This is an open-space art studio collective in the Abrons Art Center. It is suggested that artists visit the center before applying to the program.

How to Apply
Send an SASE for an application and guidelines. Return the completed application with a résumé, ten slides of your work accompanied by a slide script (form included), an SASE for return of your slides, and a short statement about your work (optional). The four-page application asks for detailed information about your work, work habits, past experience, and income. It also asks for two letters of reference and two telephone references. The Van Lier Fellowship application asks you to briefly describe how this award will make a difference in your life over the next year.

Deadline
May 31.

Approximate Cost of Program
Transportation, housing, meals, materials, and incidentals.

INSTITUTE FOR CONTEMPORARY ART

NY

P.S.1 Museum and the Clocktower Gallery, 22–25 Jackson Avenue, Long Island City, New York 11101-5324
Attention: Studio Program
Phone: (718) 784-2084 or (212) 233-1440; fax: (718) 482-9454
Web site: www.ps1.org
Email: mail@ps1.org

Type of Facility/Award

Artist-in-residence program.

Who Can Apply

Visual and performance artists.

Provisos

The applicant must be a professional artist. No high school, college, or graduate students will be considered. Applicants must be citizens or legal permanent residents of the U.S. or citizens of Northern Ireland. Other foreign artists may be able to apply through the International Studio Program—call or write for details.

Dates of Operation

The program lasts for one year—September 1 through August 31.

Location

Studios are located at the Clocktower Gallery in lower Manhattan.

History

None given.

What They Offer

The institute provides rent-free, non-living studio space in the Clocktower Gallery for a period of one year. Each artist receives individual studio space in which he or she can work within a professional, international art community. Participating artists have access from 6 A.M. to 12 midnight weekdays, and from 12 P.M. to 8 P.M. on weekends. The institute supplies light, security, and heat. A Northern Ireland studio has been added. International residents may be eligible for a stipend, which varies by country. There is no stipend for Americans. While there is no formal work-exchange program, some artists work within the institute's school program. Residents' work is sometimes shown in the annual New York Exhibition of Studio Artists.

Facility Description

Studios range in size from 375 to 530 square-feet. There are no darkroom, printing, or welding facilities. Each artist must supply his or her own materials and equipment. Under no circumstances can studio workspaces be used as living quarters.

How to Apply

Selection of the artists is made by a panel comprised of individuals active in the field (artists, critics, curators, dealers) and one member of the staff of P.S.1. Studios are allocated by the selection panel and the executive staff of the institute. International applicants must submit a video of their work in a U.S. format (VHS).

To receive details and guidelines, send an SASE in mid-January. No application forms are available before that date. Do not request applications from the Web site.

Deadline

April 15 (postmarked).

Approximate Cost of Program

Transportation, housing, meals, materials, and incidentals.

JUST BUFFALO LITERARY CENTER, INC.   NY

2495 Main Street, Suite 512, Buffalo, New York 14214
Attention: Ed Taylor, Executive Director
Phone: (716) 832-5400; fax: (716) 832-5710
Email: justbflo@aol.com

Type of Facility/Award

Fellowship/grant.

Who Can Apply

Writers.

Provisos

Applicants must have been residents of western New York for nine of the twelve months preceding the application deadline.

Dates of Operation

None provided.

Location

Buffalo, New York.

History

The 1997 winner of the New York State Governor's Award and a proud member of the Lila Wallace Reader's Digest Fund Audiences for Literature Network, Just Buffalo is one of the country's leading independent literary centers.

What They Offer

Western New York Writers-in-Residence Fellowships provide $750 to emerging writers and career support through activities such as presentations at community events and public readings.

Facility Description
None provided.

How to Apply
Contact them directly for application guidelines.

Deadline
Applications are accepted in December.

Approximate Cost of Program
Transportation, housing, meals, materials, and incidentals—offset by $750 fellowship.

LEDIG HOUSE INTERNATIONAL WRITERS COLONY NY
59 Letter S Road, Ghent, New York 12075
Attention: Executive Director
Phone: (518) 392-7656; fax: (518) 392-2848

Type of Facility/Award
Residency.

Who Can Apply
Writers.

Provisos
Professional writers from around the world are invited to apply, although proficiency in English is required. The colony welcomes writers of fiction and poetry, translators, playwrights, screenwriters, and nonfiction writers. Nominations for future residents are welcome.

Dates of Operation
April 1 through June 26. August 14 through October 31.

Location
The colony is about two and a half hours from New York City.

History
The Ledig House was named in honor of the great German publisher, H. M. Ledig-Rowohlt. The writers colony was founded in 1992. "Ledig House is sponsored by a group of international publishers, literary agents, charitable foundations, and friends. Our associations include the greater literary community, theatre, and film. Professionals from these fields are invited to meet with resident writers during each session. It is our hope to create opportunities for exchange between writers that geographical distance or political boundaries might otherwise deter."

What They Offer

Residency terms are from two to eight weeks. The colony provides each writer with a combined bedroom and work space and all meals. Breakfast and lunch supplies are provided for self-service, and dinner is prepared. Transportation to the colony is not provided; however, limited funds (based on need or economic disparity) for accepted international applicants may be available. At the end of your residency, Ledig House asks you to write a brief note about the value of the residency to your work.

Facility Description

The Ledig House is located atop a 130-acre compound overlooking the Catskill Mountains. The house, built in 1830, is a renovated farmhouse. Bedrooms are on the upstairs level, and common rooms, for dining and conversation, are located on the main level.

How to Apply

Send an SASE for application guidelines. Submit a letter of recommendation from one or more of the following: published writers, critics, editors, publishers, translators, or members of the board of directors or board of advisors of Ledig House. Also send a biographical sketch including a history of your published or performed works, one nonreturnable copy of your latest published work, and a one-page description of your proposed residency project.

Deadline

Rolling application process. Notification ninety days prior to session.

Approximate Cost of Program

Transportation and incidentals.

LIGHT WORK   NY

316 Waverly Avenue, Syracuse, New York 13244
Attention: Jeffrey Hoone, Director
Phone: (315) 443-1300; fax: (315) 443-9516
Web site: www.lightwork.org
Email: cdlight@syr.edu

Type of Facility/Award

Residency.

Who Can Apply

All artists working in photography or digital imaging.

Provisos

None listed.

Dates of Operation
Open year-round.

Location
Syracuse, New York on the Syracuse University campus.

History
For twenty-five years, Light Work has been supporting artists through publications, exhibitions, and an internationally acclaimed artist-in-residence program. Their quarterly journal, *Contact Sheet*, features Robert B. Menschel Photography Gallery exhibitions and profiles of artists who participate in the residency program.

What They Offer
Artists selected to participate in the program are invited to live in Syracuse for one month, sharing a furnished apartment with other invited guests of Light Work. They receive a $2,000 stipend, use of a private darkroom, and have twenty-four-hour access to the photo and computer lab facilities. "Participants are expected to use their month to pursue their own project, i.e., photographing, printing, book or portfolio preparation, etc. They are not obligated to teach though we hope that the artists are friendly and accessible to local artists." In return, Light Work asks each artist to leave a few examples of the work made during their residency, some of which will be featured in *Contact Sheet*.

Facility Description
Light Work's lab can accommodate almost any black-and-white process, from film processing to mural printing. The color lab features a Hope RA-4 20" color processor, and the digital computer lab features Power Macintosh computers equipped with flatbed and film scanners, a film recorder, a Kodak DS8650 dye sublimation printer, a Hewlett Packard 36" large-format color printer, a CD-ROM recorder, Adobe Photoshop, Fractal Design Painter, Quark Xpress, Adobe Illustrator, and MacroMedia Director software.

How to Apply
There are no application forms or deadlines. Send a letter of intent describing the project or type of work you wish to accomplish while in residence. Also send twenty slides of your work, your résumé, and a short statement about your work. Include an adequate SASE for return of your materials.

Deadline
Rolling application process.

Approximate Cost of Program
Transportation, meals, some materials, and incidentals—offset by $2,000 stipend.

LILA WALLACE-READER'S DIGEST FUND AWARDS   NY

Two Park Avenue, 23rd Floor, New York, New York 10016
Attention: Grants Manager
Phone: (212) 251-9800; fax: (212) 679-6990
Web site: www.wallacefunds.org

Notice: We have included information on this program because the fund supplies various types of grants, fellowships, and financial support for all aspects of the arts. It is a valuable resource for all artists. If you are interested in their programs, please write and ask for information. Specify your field of interest and they will send the appropriate booklet, detailing all the offerings available in that category.

Type of Facility/Award
Fellowships/grants/funding.

Who Can Apply
Artists and organizations involved in theater, dance, multidisciplinary arts, visual arts, literary arts, folk arts, arts education, adult literacy, urban parks, and other forms of art.

Provisos
The fund does not award grants for health care, social services, public education, research projects, historical restoration, capital campaigns, or private foundations. Other provisos are listed in the literature.

Dates of Operation
Ongoing.

Location
Variable.

History
Lila Acheson Wallace (1889–1984) and DeWitt Wallace founded *Reader's Digest* magazine. "The business success of the company provided Lila with the resources to turn her talents to philanthropy. She funded many visual and performing arts organizations such as the Metropolitan Opera, New York City Ballet and the Martha Graham Dance Company, as well as many parks and urban beautification projects. Lila's belief that the arts belong to and should be made accessible to people from diverse walks of life continues in the Fund's current grant programs."

What They Offer
The fund provides a variety of awards, grants, and fellowships. The fund approved $22,980,127 in grants for 1998. See the brochure for more specific information.

Facility Description

Variable.

How to Apply

Send an SASE with a letter requesting the brochure for your particular artistic discipline. Send a brief inquiry (one to two pages maximum) describing your proposed project and funding needs. Do not send videotaped or email proposals.

Deadline

Deadline information will be detailed in specific brochures. You will receive a response from the fund within twelve weeks of receipt of your inquiry.

Approximate Cost of Program

Not applicable in this listing.

MATTRESS FACTORY   PA

Mattress Factory, 500 Sampsonia Way, Pittsburgh, Pennsylvania 15212-4444
Attention: Mattress Factory, Submissions
Phone: (412) 231-3169; fax: (412) 322-2231

Type of Facility/Award

Residency.

Who Can Apply

Visual artists.

Provisos

None listed.

Dates of Operation

Open year-round.

Location

Pittsburgh, Pennsylvania.

History

"The Mattress Factory is an alternative museum that commissions, presents, and collects site-specific installations in an environment whose resources are totally dedicated to that process."

What They Offer

Information provided by the Mattress Factory was light on detail, but if you are invited to work in residence, the Mattress Factory provides free housing, free studio space, free materials, transportation, and some meals.

Facility Description

The Mattress Factory provides work spaces and extensive resources "for artists and art forms that do not adapt easily to studio situations, but share a common need for a research and development environment."

How to Apply

Send an SASE for information. Submit either 35 mm slides or VHS video tapes (include an adequate SASE if you want these materials returned) that best represent your work. Résumés are optional.

Deadline

Rolling application process.

Approximate Cost of Program

Meals and incidentals.

THE MILLAY COLONY FOR THE ARTS   NY

P.O. Box 3, 444 East Hill Road, Austerlitz, New York 12017-0003
Attention: Martha Hopewell, Executive Director or Gail Giles, Director of
    Admissions
Phone: (518) 392-3103
Email: giles@millaycolony.org

Type of Award

Residency.

Who Can Apply

Writers, composers, and visual artists.

Provisos

None listed.

Dates of Operation

Open year-round.

Location

Austerlitz is two and a half hours north of New York City and two hours west of Boston.

History

"In 1925, Edna St. Vincent Millay and her husband bought a berry farm on a hill in Austerlitz, New York, and named it Steepletop for the flower of the Steeplebush which grows wild here." The house is a National Historic Landmark providing quiet and beauty—the perfect place for artists to work. When the poet died in 1950, the estate was inherited by her sister, Norma Millay, who incorporated the Millay Colony for the Arts as a nonprofit organization in 1973.

What They Offer

Month-long residencies include housing, studio space (if applicable), and all meals at no cost. Weeknight dinners are prepared; breakfast and lunch foods are available. Residents prepare their own weekend meals. There is no application fee and no fee for a residency. However, the colony does depend on gifts for its existence and welcomes contributions. Residents must provide their own transportation to the colony.

Facility Description

The Millay Colony is located on a 600-acre estate in Austerlitz, New York. The main building is handicapped-accessible and includes a kitchen, dining room, living room, music listening room/library, laundry room, phone rooms, one-station sitting-dark-room, and two studio suites. The Speinson Studio contains a 16' x 20' studio space, two bedrooms, a bath with a roll-in shower, and a door that opens to an adjoining carport. The Speinson Studio is ideal for an artist needing an aide or by two artists working on a collaborative project. The McClennen/Hope Studio contains a 15' x 22' studio space and an upright Steinway piano for a composer. The Steepletop Barn provides additional studios, bedrooms, shared bath facilities, a common room, and a phone room. All studios use full-spectrum fluorescent lights and adjustable incandescent lights and include a nearby sink, full-room ventilation fan, and source capture exhaust systems. The Nancy Graves Art Library is also available for residents' use. All buildings are smoke-free. No pets are allowed, except for guide dogs.

How to Apply

Send an SASE or check the Web site for an application and brochure. Applications are available in large-type format or on audio cassette for artists with visual disabilities. Return the completed application with a résumé, a description of past work, a description of the work you intend to pursue at the colony, one professional letter of reference, and examples of your work. Include an adequate SASE for return of your materials, as well as any documents you consider to be helpful to the admissions committee in making its decision. Include an SASP if you want acknowledgment of receipt of your application. Appropriate work samples follow. Writers: up to thirty pages in manuscript form. Poets: up to fifteen poems in manuscript form. Visual artists: between six and ten slides labeled according to instructions and with an accompanying descriptive sheet. Composers: one tape and standard-size scores (they will not process scores larger than 14" x 17").

Deadline

February 1 (received) for June–September residencies. May 1 (received) for October–January residencies. September 1 (received) for February–May residencies.

Approximate Cost of Program

Transportation, materials, and incidentals.

MORAVIAN POTTERY & TILE WORKS   PA

130 Swamp Road, Doylestown, Pennsylvania 18901
Attention: Head Ceramist
Phone: (215) 345-6722; fax: (215) 345-1361
Web site: bchs@philadelphia.libertynet.org

Type of Facility/Award

Artist-in-residence program.

Who Can Apply

Ceramic artists.

Provisos

Only professional ceramic artists from the mid-Atlantic region may apply (excluding Pennsylvania). This includes Delaware, the District of Columbia, Maryland, New Jersey, New York, Virginia, West Virginia, and the U.S. Virgin Islands.

Dates of Operation

The program begins the last Monday in April and lasts six weeks.

Location

Doylestown is approximately forty-five minutes north of downtown Philadelphia.

History

The Moravian Pottery and Tile Works, a National Historic Landmark, is maintained as a "living history museum" by the Bucks County Recreation and Park Department. The pottery's founder, Henry Mercer, was a major proponent of the Arts and Crafts movement in America. Handmade tiles are still produced there in a manner similar to that developed by Mercer. Since 1975, MPTW has offered apprentice workshops that teach, through practical experience in a production setting, Mercer's tile-making methods and relate them to the needs and interests of ceramists working today. The artist residency program, initiated in 1993, allows ceramists to explore a new body of work involving tile.

What They Offer

Over the period of six weeks, resident artists will be provided the opportunity to pursue an independent project and create new work using materials and studio space provided by MPTW. Artists can benefit from the exchange of ideas and sharing of expertise that occur among residents, members of MPTW, and the local arts community. The residency includes housing, round-trip transportation, and a stipend.

Facility Description

Country fields surround you as you approach the Tile Works, which is set in semi-rural Bucks County. Beautiful old stone buildings, complete with archways and turrets, are nestled within a partially wooded landscape. The north wing of the MPTW, which is a reinforced concrete structure in a Spanish mission style, houses the primary studio space. The clay available at MPTW "is an impure local terra cotta which when glazed is fired to cone 05 (1944 F). A variety of lead glazes and slips are provided for use. Smoked surfaces may be obtained through firing the clay in saggars. Plaster is provided for mold work. Molds which are the property of the Tile Works may not be used for personal work. Cement is available for setting of tiles and mosaics. All work is hand-built or mold pressed. There are no pottery wheels available."

How to Apply
Interested applicants should contact the head ceramist of MPTW (phone number provided above) for application procedures.

Deadline
Contact MPTW by late winter.

Approximate Cost of Program
Meals and incidentals—offset by stipend.

MY RETREAT   NY
Writers Colony and Bed and Breakfast, P.O. Box 1077, Lincoln Road, South
    Fallsburg, New York 10464
Attention: Cora Schwartz, Innkeeper
Phone: (800) 484-1255 ext. 2485 or (914) 436-7455; fax: (718) 885-0066
Email: MYRETREAT2@AOL.com

Type of Facility/Award
Retreat.

Who Can Apply
Poets, writers, and artists of life.

Provisos
Guests must be non-smoking adults.

Dates of Operation
Main house—year-round. Cottages—April through November.

Location
My Retreat is located ninety miles northwest of New York City in the foothills of the Catskill Mountains. It is an eight-minute walk from the town of South Fallsburg (a summer mecca for the Hasidic community and well-known ashram) on a quiet, dead-end road. The area is serviced by the ShortLine Bus Company out of Port Authority in New York City. The closest airport is Stewart International in Newburgh.

History

The colony opened on June 1, 1993, after owner Cora Schwartz purchased two cottages across the road from her house and renovated and furnished them to create a private place for writing. "My Retreat was founded in the spirit of Olga Kobylianskaia, a forerunner of the women's liberation movement and a member of the Writers' Union of the U.S.S.R. Olga's dominant theme was 'aristocratism of the spirit' and the necessity for woman's liberation from the bondage of primitive traditional laws. In her book, *Tsariva*, Olga portrays a woman of universal ideas who strives for greater enlightenment and desires to become a useful, independent member of society. In 1942, the Hitlerites decided to try Olga by court-martial. Only death from illness saved her from violence. May Olga's talent for the lyrical, her gift of observation, sensitivity and artistic taste live on at My Retreat."

What They Offer

My Retreat offers clean, quiet, private, rustic rooms with a low-tech, 1950s-style decor. Each has a desk and a lovely view of the woods. Light breakfast foods are provided. Guests are responsible for their other meals, but kitchen facilities are available for their use. In the summer, My Retreat offers workshops in fiction, poetry, publishing, photography, and other subjects of interest to writers and artists. During the rest of the year, workshops or lectures are offered monthly.

Facility Description

The colony consists of a main house and two cottages. The cottages have six furnished bedrooms, three kitchens, and four bathrooms. There are six screened and open porches. One of the cottages has a cool, basement library. Rooms are available with shared bath, kitchen, laundry room, and patios. There is a separate suite with a private entrance, bedroom, kitchen, and bath. My Retreat is smoke-free. No pets are allowed.

How to Apply

Call for a brochure and newsletter.

Deadline

My Retreat is booked on a first-come, first-served basis. A 50% deposit is required seven days before arrival. The deposit will be refunded, less a $10 fee, if cancellation is received at least five days prior to arrival date.

Approximate Cost of Program

One person, shared bath: $100–$125/two nights, $225/week, $500/month. Two people, shared bath: $125–$150/two nights, $300/week, $600/month. One or two people, private unit: $175–$200/two nights, $450/week. Rooms are $85 per person per weekend (two nights) and $185 per person per week (seven nights). Guests are also responsible for transportation, meals, materials, and incidentals.

PAINTING SPACE 122 INC.

PS 122 Project Spaces

150 First Avenue, New York, New York 10009
Attention: Susan Schreiber, Gallery Director
Phone: (212) 228-4249; fax: (212) 505-6854 (call first)
Email: PS122gal@interport.net

Type of Facility/Award
Artist-in-residence program.

Who Can Apply
Visual artists.

Provisos
Students are ineligible.

Dates of Operation
Open year-round.

Location
New York City.

History
"Painting Space 122 Inc. was founded in 1978 by two local artists in the former Public School 122. The members run and operate the PS 122 Gallery, a not-for-profit, alternative space providing an excellent showcase for emerging artists."

What They Offer
They have two programs that offer reduced-rate studio space. PS 122 offers three studio spaces that rotate on a yearly basis and several short-term project spaces for artists needing studio space for a limited period in order to install a special exhibition. Announcement cards and press materials are provided. Artists-in-residence are asked to donate a small amount of their time each month to help run the organization and gallery, installing shows and gallery-sitting on weekends.

Facility Description
Two studios are between 250 and 300 square-feet; the third is approximately 500 square-feet. All studios are well-lit and artists are permitted twenty-four-hour access. Workspace is private, so artists remain undisturbed except during the open house each spring.

How to Apply
Send an SASE for a current application.

Deadline
Early April. Inquire directly for specific date.

Approximate Cost of Program
Transportation, housing, meals, materials, and incidentals.

PALENVILLE INTERARTS COLONY   NY   **DISCONTINUED**

PETERS VALLEY CRAFT CENTER   NJ
19 Kuhn Road, Layton, New Jersey 07851
Attention: Associate Residency Program or Professional Residency Program
Phone: (973) 948-5200; fax: (973) 948-0011
Web site: www.pvcrafts.org
Email: pv@warwick.net

Type of Facility/Award
Artist-in-residence program.

Who Can Apply
Emerging artists, artists in transition, and professional artists in blacksmithing, ceramics, fibers, fine metals, photography, weaving, woodworking, drawing, watercolor, oil painting, and printmaking.

Provisos
None listed.

Dates of Operation
Open year-round.

Location
Peters Valley is located in rural northwest New Jersey in the Delaware Water Gap National Recreation Area, just a few minutes from the Delaware River and a one-and-a-half-hour drive west of Manhattan.

History
"Originally settled at the turn of the nineteenth century and formerly known as the town of Bevans, Peters Valley's name is derived from Peter Van Ness, an early land owner and original settler of the area. Today, the educational organization of Peters Valley occupies and administers the buildings in cooperation with the National Park Service."

What They Offer
There are two residencies available: associate residencies and professional residencies.

Associate residents stay for a period of time between October and April or for the entire seven-month period. An associate who plans to stay for less than the full period may request an extension. Those who stay for the full period may be able to exhibit their work at Peters Valley's store and Sally D. Francisco Gallery (in conjunction with the store manager). The residency includes studio space and shared housing at a nominal rate. All residents are required to participate in critiques of the work they create during the residency. Associates must donate one piece of artwork for the Peters Valley permanent collection or benefit auction.

Professional residencies include access to equipped studios, material, technological resources, and housing for one to three months. Studio space is provided within the seven existing studios: blacksmithing, ceramics, fibers, fine metals, photography, weaving, and woodworking. Supplemental studios include drawing, watercolor, oil painting, and printmaking. Residents may work in a single discipline or with other studios and artists on interdisciplinary projects. Depending on the length of stay, residents may be provided an exhibition venue in the Sally D. Francisco Gallery. Residents must donate one piece of finished work for the Peters Valley permanent collection.

Facility Description

Peters Valley offers facilities for the following disciplines: blacksmithing/metals (including forging, knife-making, metal sculpture, forged furniture, and engraving), ceramics (including techniques for English slipware, raku, earthenware, tile-making, and anagama firing), fibers (including basketry, weaving, looming, quilts, silk painting, beadwork, book- and paper-making), fine metals (including filigree jewelry-making, enameling, casting, die-forming, chasing and repoussé, stonesetting, metal textures, metalsmithing, and embellishment), photography (including sun-printing, ilfochrome classic printing, black-and-white, color landscapes, infrared, pinhole photography, composition, darkroom tutorials, and multiple images), and woodworking (including volutes and "C" scrolls, veneers and inlays, furniture-making, small and large containers, and the making of acoustic guitars).

How to Apply

Send an SASE for a brochure and application. For the associate residency program, submit a completed application indicating which track you are choosing, a detailed letter of intent including an outline of how you will use your time at Peters Valley, the number and type of critiques you would like, other resources that you might utilize, your current résumé, two letters of academic or professional recommendation, ten to twenty slides of your most recent work, and an SASE for return of your application materials. For the professional residency, please send an SASE for current guidelines.

Deadline

Associate residency applicants: July 15 for those who wish to come from October through December or for the entire seven-month period; December 15 for those who wish to come from January through April. No deadline listed for the professional residency program.

Approximate Cost of Program
Transportation, reduced-rate housing and studio space, meals, some materials, and incidentals.

POETRY SOCIETY OF AMERICA   NY
15 Gramercy Park, New York, New York 10003
Phone: (212) 254-9628; fax: (212) 673-2352
Web site: www.poetrysociety.org

> *Notice: The PSA holds ten writing competitions, three of which are currently open to nonmembers: the Louise Louis/Emily F. Bourne Student Poetry Award, the George Bogin Memorial Award, and the Robert H. Winner Memorial Award. For a complete list of guidelines and current award amounts, send an SASE for a brochure.*

PRINCETON UNIVERSITY   NJ
Alfred Hodder Fellowship
The Council of the Humanities, 122 East Pyne, Princeton University, Princeton,
    New Jersey 08544
Attention: Alfred Hodder Fellowship Director
Phone: (609) 258-4717; fax: (609) 258-2783
Web site: www.princeton.edu/~humcounc

Type of Facility/Award
Fellowship.

Who Can Apply
Humanists.

Provisos
Humanists "with more than ordinary learning" and "much more than ordinary intellectual and literary gifts" are encouraged to apply. Preference is given to candidates outside of academia. Candidates for the Ph.D. degree are ineligible. The council seeks humanists in the early stages of their careers who have demonstrated exceptional promise but may not yet enjoy widespread recognition. The fellowship is designed to identify and nurture extraordinary potential rather than to honor distinguished achievement.

Dates of Operation
Academic year.

Location

Princeton, New Jersey.

History

"The Council of the Humanities was founded in 1953 to foster teaching and research in the humanities. Given the broad scope of its mission, the Council serves as a locus for many endeavors that bring together faculty, students, and distinguished visitors from many fields. Each year, the Council invites more than thirty guests for visits ranging from a day to a year. It is the home of a wide array of interdisciplinary courses and programs, including those in the Creative Arts."

The Hodder Fellowship was endowed by Mary MacKall Gwinn Hodder in honor of her husband, Alfred, who became an attorney at age twenty-three without any formal undergraduate education. He then went on to earn a Ph.D. in philosophy at Harvard University (in two years) and accepted a position at Bryn Mawr College, where he met his wife in 1898. They were married in 1904, but Alfred died three years later in 1907. Upon her death, she left her papers to Princeton and endowed the Charles John Morris Gwinn and Alfred Hodder Memorial Fund in honor of her father and her husband.

What They Offer

The award carries a stipend of $45,600 so that the fellow can undertake a significant new project in "studious leisure." The fellow spends an academic year in residence at Princeton pursuing an independent project.

Facility Description

University campus. No mention of on-campus housing.

How to Apply

Send an SASE for a brochure. Then submit a résumé, a sample of your work (maximum ten pages, not returnable), a project proposal (two to three pages), and an SASP for acknowledgment. Letters of recommendation are not required.

Deadline

November 1 (postmarked). Appointment is made in February.

Approximate Cost of Program

Transportation, housing, meals, materials, and incidentals—offset by $45,600 stipend.

SCULPTURE SPACE   NY

12 Gates Street, Utica, New York 13502
Attention: Gina Murtagh, Executive Director
Phone: (315) 724-8381; fax: (315) 724-8381
Web site: www.borg.com/~sculptur
Email: sculptur@borg.com

Type of Facility/Award

Artist-in-residence program.

Who Can Apply

Professional artists and sculptors.

Provisos

Primary criteria are quality, originality, and potential for growth. Sculpture Space can accommodate a great variety of projects, both in terms of materials and scale. Each case is assessed individually, and Sculpture Space defines sculpture in the broadest possible sense. There are no geographic or stylistic restrictions.

Dates of Operation

Open year-round.

Location

Utica is approximately 55 miles from Syracuse and 250 miles from New York City.

History

"Our program is funded by the New York State Council on the Arts, the National Endowment for the Arts, Oneida County, foundation grants and corporate sponsorships, and private donations. Sculpture Space is a founding member of the National Association of Artists Organizations (NAAO), the Alliance of Artists Communities, and is a member of the Alliance of New York State Arts Organizations."

What They Offer

Two-month residencies are designed to support professional artists by providing free use of a professionally equipped studio facility, access to industrial resources, and a support system to promote the development and presentation of sculptural projects. Artists accepted to work at Sculpture Space are given a key to the studio and are free to use the facility at any time, seven days a week. The studio manager is available to assist artists with an introductory orientation, to act as a liaison with suppliers, and to advise on technical problems. Artists are responsible for their own materials, specialized tools, fees for work done outside the premises, and for an assistant should they require one. Through its resources and contacts, Sculpture Space is able to help artists keep their expenses to a minimum. Residents spend an average of $1,000 per month. A three-bedroom house within walking distance of the studio is available at low cost to the artists. Artists are responsible for their own food, but there is a fully equipped kitchen in the house. Please note that pets are not allowed in the studio or the artists' apartments. In exchange for time spent at Sculpture Space, each artist is asked to contribute on some level to help support and promote the organization. There are several options that can be discussed on an individual basis, including providing slides of work for grant applications and contributing to the triennial art auction. Artists are advised to bring their own hand tools. A list of equipment available for artists' use will be mailed with the brochure and application form. Residents must provide their own transportation to the facility.

Facility Description

Sculpture Space is located close to scrap yards, light industry, and fabrication shops. The facility includes 5,500 square feet of open space and a 400-square-foot private studio for special projects. The space is outfitted with concrete floors, a two-ton system of traveling hoists, and extra-wide overhead doors for projects as large as you can imagine. The building is surrounded by three-quarters-of-an-acre of land that can supplement indoor studio space in the summer. There is an outdoor work pad with a 50-foot monorail and hoist. Depending upon the scale of the work, Sculpture Space can accommodate up to four artists at one time. The list of equipment available for artists' use is huge and includes hand tools (air and electric), steel, wood, and other miscellaneous tools and industrial equipment, though artists are advised to bring some of their own hand tools.

How to Apply

Send an SASE for an application and brochure. Applications should consist of no more than ten slides (labeled according to instructions) and a corresponding slide narrative with title, date, dimensions, and medium. Include an SASE for return of your materials. In addition, Sculpture Space would like a brief project description (half-page), a current résumé, and the names and phone numbers of three references. A personal visit is advisable before application; this can be scheduled by appointment from 10 A.M. to 6 P.M., Monday through Friday.

Deadline

December 15. Notification within three months.

Approximate Cost of Program

$1,000 (average amount spent by artists) plus transportation, meals, incidentals, and subsidized housing. A $2,000 stipend is possible; inquire at time of application.

SIENA COLLEGE   NY
International Playwright's Competition

Siena College, Department of Fine Arts, Theatre Program, 515 Loudon Road,
  Loudonville, New York 12211-1462
Attention: International Playwrights Competition
Phone: (518) 783-2384
Web site: www.siena.edu/theatre/playwrights.html

Type of Facility/Award
Opportunity for playwrights.

Who Can Apply
Playwrights.

Provisos
Scripts must be full-length, original, unpublished, unproduced, and free of royalty
and copyright restrictions. No musicals. Plays that have had staged readings are acceptable, but not plays that have had workshop productions. Plays must require a
unit set or minimal changes, be suitable for undergraduate performers, and require a
cast of three to ten actors.

Dates of Operation
This is a biennial program held in the spring.

Location
The college is located just north of Albany, New York.

History
"Siena College is a private undergraduate college of more than 2,700 full-time students founded by the Franciscan friars in 1937."

What They Offer
The winning playwright will receive an honorarium of $2,000 and full production
of the play by Siena College's theatre program in the spring as part of its Theatre
Series. Living expenses and transportation to and from the college (no more than
$1,000) will be awarded to the winning playwright for a four- to six-week residency
so he or she can participate in the rehearsal and design process, public discussions,
and the academic life of the Siena community.

Facility Description
Siena College has a 310-seat black box theater.

How to Apply
Send an SASE for an application and brochure. Return your completed application
with a typed, bound script and a business-size SASE. Include an adequate SASE if

you want your script returned. If you send more than one script, include an adequate return SASE for each. Entries will only be accepted between February 1 and June 30. If you are a finalist, you will be asked to submit a copy of your educational and professional credentials, three letters of reference, and a documented production history of the submitted script.

Deadline

June 30 (received). Notification by September 30.

Approximate Cost of Program

Transportation, housing, meals, and incidentals—offset by $2,000 honorarium.

SMITHSONIAN INSTITUTION   DC
Renwick Gallery

Smithsonian Institution, MRC-510, Washington, DC 20560-0510
Attention: Director, James Renwick Fellowship in American Crafts
Phone: (202) 357-2531; fax: (202) 786-2810
Web site: www.nmaa.si.edu
Email: jadamson@renwick.si.edu

Type of Facility/Award

Fellowship.

Who Can Apply

Scholars.

Provisos

Applicants must be graduate, masters, predoctoral, or postdoctoral students knowledgeable in the history of twentieth-century American art, craft, or design. The gallery is most interested in "research proposals concentrating on post-1930 craft developments or their historical antecedents."

Dates of Operation

Open year-round.

Location

Washington, D.C.

History

This award is funded by the National Museum of American Art and the James Renwick Alliance.

What They Offer

The Renwick Gallery offers research residencies of three to twelve months. Residents receive a cash award of $15,000 and $1,000 for research costs.

Facility Description

None provided.

How to Apply

Send an SASE for an application and brochure.

Deadline

January 15.

Approximate Cost of Program

Transportation, housing, meals, materials, and incidentals—offset by $15,000 stipend.

STUDIO MUSEUM IN HARLEM   NY

144 West 125th Street, New York, New York 10027
Attention: Pedra Chaffers, Director of Education
Phone: (212) 864-4500 ext. 215
Web site: www.studiomuseuminharlem.org

Type of Facility/Award

Artist-in-residence program.

Who Can Apply

Visual artists.

Provisos

Emerging African-American artists and other artists from Africa and the African diaspora, including sculptors, painters, printmakers, photographers, and fiber artists, are encouraged to apply.

Dates of Operation

Open year-round.

Location

Located in New York City between Lenox Avenue and Adam Clayton Powell Jr. Boulevard.

History

"Devoted to historical and contemporary works of art by black artists, the Studio Museum first opened its doors in 1967 in a rented loft at 125th and 5th. Since then the Museum has expanded greatly to offer a variety of valuable services to the community…. The Studio Museum in Harlem is a fine arts museum whose mission is the study, documentation, collection, preservation, and exhibition of the art and artifacts of Black America and the African Diaspora." For more than a quarter of a century, the museum has supported an artist-in-residence program while consistently avoiding stylistic or theoretical restrictions.

What They Offer

Three emerging artists are annually awarded studio space and a stipend for a period of four months. Artists have access to museum facilities during designated hours and are required to spend a minimum of twenty hours per week working in their studios. An exhibition of the artists' work will be presented toward the end of the residency in the museum's galleries. Resident artists must conduct two public workshops or presentations during their residencies and may occasionally be asked to meet with museum visitors.

Facility Description

The museum itself includes an impressive permanent collection of more than 1,500 objects acquired since 1979.

How to Apply

Send an SASE for an application form and brochure. Return a completed application with your résumé, two letters of recommendation, and supporting materials (which may include catalog cuts, reviews, etc.).

Deadline

Variable.

Approximate Cost of Program

Transportation, housing, meals, materials, and incidentals—offset by stipend.

UNITED STATES INSTITUTE OF PEACE   DC
Jennings Randolph Fellowships

1200 17ᵗʰ Street NW, Suite 200, Washington, DC 20036-3011
Attention: Jennings Randolph Program for International Peace
Phone: (202) 457-1700 Institute, (202) 429-3886 Program
Email: jrprogram@usip.org
Web site: www.usip.org

Type of Facility/Award

Fellowships.

Who Can Apply

Professionals in the early, middle, or late stages of their careers may apply for the senior fellowships.

Outstanding doctoral candidates are eligible for the Peace Scholar Dissertation Fellowships.

Provisos

The Peace Scholar Fellowship is intended for outstanding students enrolled in a recognized doctoral program in an American university. All course work and examinations (not the dissertation) must be completed before the beginning of the fellowship term. Peace Scholar awards may not be deferred or combined with any major award or fellowship unless approved in advance by the institute.

The senior fellowship is available for scholars, diplomats, public leaders, and professionals who have achieved exceptional international stature and recognition by virtue of their extraordinary academic or practical contributions to one or more fields. There is no specific degree requirement for this award, but applicants typically will have completed at least an undergraduate degree.

The institute welcomes applications from citizens of all nations and all walks of life. Women and members of minority groups are especially encouraged to apply, as are scholars, researchers, educators of students and citizens, and others who are practitioners in international security, peacemaking, and public affairs.

Dates of Operation

Fellowships are for one year each beginning in September, but shorter fellowships with a negotiable beginning date are available.

Location

The Peace Scholar works at his or her own university. The senior fellow spends his or her year in residence at the institute.

History

"The Jennings Randolph Program for International Peace enables outstanding scholars, practitioners, and students to focus their learning, practical experience, leadership abilities, and communication skills on a broad variety of issues concerning conflict and peace. It achieves this goal through providing fellowship support for individual research and education projects proposed by the fellowship candidate and through arranging program-wide activities designed to promote mutual learning, collegiality, and wider dissemination of the fellows' work. Named for the former United States Senator from West Virginia, whose efforts over four decades helped to establish the Institute, the Jennings Randolph Program has awarded 142 fellowships since it began in 1987."

What They Offer

The Peace Scholar Fellowship applies to doctoral students researching and writing their dissertations at their home universities and includes a stipend of $14,000 paid in three installments.

The senior fellow spends a year in residence at the institute participating in institute-sponsored conferences, outreach activities, and the collegial life of the institute.

The fellowship stipend is based on the recipient's salary for the preceding twelve months, but cannot exceed the GS-15/10 level of the federal pay scale (a maximum of $94,098 per year). It is expected that the fellow will devote full attention to completing his or her project within the agreed-upon time. This award also provides contributions toward health insurance (if needed), use of an office and a Macintosh word processor, a research assistant, and, subject to availability of funds, appropriate assistance to complete the fellowship project. Additionally, round-trip transportation to Washington, D.C., is provided (at the beginning and end of the fellowship period) for the fellow and any dependents who reside with the fellow during the entire fellowship period.

Facility Description
Federal office building.

How to Apply
Send a 9" x 12" SASE with adequate postage for an application and brochure. It is recommended you thoroughly familiarize yourself with the institute and the program before applying. Peace Scholar applicants: Return the completed application, a description of your proposed dissertation work, a letter of support from your primary dissertation adviser, graduate transcripts, and two current letters of reference. Senior fellowship applicants: Return the completed application, a résumé, a description of your proposed project, a writing sample, and three letters of reference.

Deadline
December 1 for the Peace Scholar Fellowship. October 16 for the senior fellowship.

Approximate Cost of Program
Housing, meals, some materials, and incidentals—offset by stipend.

WOMEN'S STUDIO WORKSHOP   NY
P.O. Box 489, Rosendale, New York 12472
Attention: Ann Kalmbach
Phone: (914) 658-9133; fax: (914) 658-9031
Web site: www.wsworkshop.org
Email: wsw@ulster.net

Type of Facility/Award
Fellowships and grants.

Who Can Apply
Visual artists.

Provisos

Applicants must be female artists working in intaglio, water-based screen printing, photography, letterpress, or papermaking.

Dates of Operation

September through June. Fellowships consist of two- to six-week sessions. Grants are for four- to six-week allotments.

Location

Rosendale, New York.

History

"We are one of the only artists' spaces especially interested in women's work. We have grown to be one of the largest publishers of hand printed artists' books in the country, but we keep hanging on to our grass roots in order to make every artist who works here come to a new understanding about their work."

What They Offer

The program offers women two- to six-week fellowships "designed to provide concentrated, uninterrupted work time for artists to explore new ideas in a dynamic and cooperative community of women artists in a rural environment." Artists pay $200 per week, which includes on-site housing and unlimited studio access. Artists are given a studio orientation but must be able to work independently and provide their own materials. Technical assistance is available for a fee. Fellowships begin on Mondays and conclude on Sundays.

There are also two types of book-production grants. (1) The Artists' Book Residency Grant enables an artist to produce a limited edition bookwork at WSW. The grant provides a stipend of $1,800 for the six-week period, materials up to $450, housing, and access to all studios. The artist will be involved in all aspects of the design and production of her new bookwork. WSW will provide technical advice and, when possible, help with editioning. (2) The Artists' Book Production Grant is for artists working off-site. This grant is designed for artists working in their own studios on projects of a smaller scale. Funds cover production costs of up to $750. The grant is not intended for the reissue of previously published material or partial funding of a larger project.

Facility Description

The Binnewater Arts Center is home to the program's studios and classrooms.

How to Apply

Send an SASE for a brochure. For fellowships: Send a résumé, six to ten slides of your work, a letter of interest that addresses the purpose of your proposed residency and explains areas of proficiency and studio skills, and an SASE for return of materials.

For grants: Return your completed application, résumé, six to ten slides, a one-page description of the proposed project, the medium or media to be used to print the book, the number of pages in the proposed book, the page size, edition size (an edition of at least one hundred copies is preferred), a structural dummy, a materials budget, and an adequate SASE for return of materials.

Deadline

May 15 for fall fellowships (September 1 through December 15), November 1 for spring fellowships (February 1 through June 30), November 15 for book arts grants.

Approximate Cost of Program

Fellowships: $200 per week plus transportation, meals, materials, and incidentals. Grants: Transportation, meals, and incidentals—offset by stipend.

WOODROW WILSON CENTER FOR SCHOLARS   DC

1000 Jefferson Drive SW, SI MRC 022, Washington, DC 20560

Contact:

The Fellowships Office, The Woodrow Wilson Center, One Woodrow Wilson
  Plaza, 1300 Pennsylvania Avenue, NW, Washington, DC 20004-3027
Phone: (202) 691-4170; fax: (202) 691-4001
Web site: wwics.si.edu
Email: fellowships@wwic.si.edu

Type of Facility/Award

Fellowship.

Who Can Apply

Scholars.

Provisos

Applications from any country are welcome, although all participants are expected to be fluent in English. Applicants must possess strong capabilities and experience in government, corporate, professional, or academic backgrounds.

"For academic participants, eligibility is limited to the postdoctoral level, and normally it is expected that academic candidates will have demonstrated their scholarly development by publication beyond the Ph.D. dissertation." Nonacademic applicants are expected to have an equivalent degree of professional achievement.

"The Center normally does not consider projects that represent essentially the rewriting of doctoral dissertations; the editing of papers and documents; the preparation of textbooks or miscellaneous papers and reviews; anthologies, memoirs, or translations. Because the Center has no laboratory facilities, primary research in the natural sciences is not eligible. However, projects that seek to relate the natural sciences to broader intellectual and social issues are welcomed. Proposals that represent essentially advocacy are not eligible."

Dates of Operation
One academic year (September through May or June), although occasionally fellowships are available for shorter periods (minimum four months).

Location
Washington, D.C.

History
Created by Congress in 1968 as the official memorial to the United States' twenty-eighth president, Woodrow Wilson, the center fosters communication between the world of learning and the world of public affairs. Wilson wrote, "The man who has the time, the discrimination, and the sagacity to collect and comprehend the principal facts, and the man who must act upon them, must draw near to one another and feel that they are engaged in a common enterprise."

What They Offer
The center awards approximately twenty residential fellowships each year to individuals with exceptional project proposals that intersect the humanities and/or social sciences with questions of public policy. Additionally, the center fosters the diversity of political views by encouraging free and lively debate among fellows and publishing selected meetings and research. Each fellow is provided with a furnished office available round-the-clock and access to a number of research facilities, including the Library of Congress. Also available are IBM-compatible PCs, manuscript-typing services, and the services of a part-time research assistant.

Stipends average $44,000 per year. Included are travel expenses and 75% of health insurance premiums for fellows, their spouses, and dependent children. The center encourages participants to seek supplementary sources of funding. Fellows will also be expected to interact with policy makers in Washington and with the center's staff on key issues relevant to their research.

Facility Description
The center's principal offices are located in the original Smithsonian Institution building on the Mall in central Washington. The smoke-free building includes conference rooms, a reference library, and a dining area. Though housing is not provided, the center can help fellows locate appropriate housing arrangements.

How to Apply
The center holds one round of competitive selection each year. Contact the fellowships office with an SASE for an application form and brochure. Return five collated copies of the application, a list of your publications, and your project proposal (not

to exceed 2,000 words). Submit one copy of the financial information form. The center also requests three letters of reference from professionals familiar with you and your work. It is your responsibility to make sure the reference letters (sent directly by referee to the center) arrive by the deadline.

Deadline
October 1. Decisions are made by early April.

Approximate Cost of Program
Housing, meals, materials, and incidentals—offset by stipend.

WOODSTOCK GUILD   NY
Byrdcliffe Arts Colony
Woodstock Guild, 34 Tinker Street, Woodstock, New York 12498
Attention: Artists' Residency Program
Phone: (914) 679-2079
Web site: www.woodstockguild.org

Type of Facility/Award
Residency.

Who Can Apply
Visual artists, writers, and playwrights.

Provisos
None listed.

Dates of Operation
June through September.

Location
Byrdcliffe Arts Colony is a mile and a half from the Woodstock village center. Woodstock is in the Catskill Mountains—ninety miles north of New York City.

History
"The Woodstock Guild, founded in 1940 to promote the study and development of the arts, crafts, literature, drama, and music, was incorporated as a not-for-profit arts organization in 1951 to foster friendship and cooperation among artists in all fields." In 1975, the guild inherited the historic Byrdcliffe Arts Colony which was founded in 1902 and has been operating as an artists' colony ever since. The guild also offers concerts, theater, and literary events on a regular basis in both the Byrdcliffe Theater and the Byrdcliffe Barn.

What They Offer

The colony offers four one-month residency sessions each year between June and September. The cost per session is $500. Candidates may apply for additional weeks if space becomes available. Writers under the age of thirty-five who need financial assistance may apply for a $100 scholarship from the Patterson Fund. Upon acceptance, a nonrefundable deposit of twenty-five percent of your fee is due. The balance is due approximately three weeks prior to the session date. The colony can accommodate ten residents at a time. Residents are housed in the Villetta Inn, a spacious turn-of-the-century lodge with communal dining and living rooms. Each artist is provided with his or her own room and a private studio. Residents, with use of the inn's well-appointed community kitchen, must provide their own meals.

Facility Description

Set on the slopes of Mount Guardian, the Byrdcliffe Arts Colony consists of twenty-five buildings on six hundred acres of land. There are hiking trails nearby leading into thousands of acres of the Catskill Preserve. The Villetta Inn is a turn-of-the-century mountain lodge with communal living, kitchen, and dining rooms.

How to Apply

Send an SASE for an application and brochure. Return two copies of the completed application with a $5 nonrefundable handling fee, a professional résumé, a list of your requirements (for space, light, water, etc.), a list of your work habits, a description of your proposed project, two letters of reference from authorities in your field who are familiar with you and your work, a sample of your work, and copies of any reviews, catalogs, articles, etc. that may be appropriate. Appropriate work samples follow. Visual artists: eight to ten slides (packaged and labeled according to instructions). Literary artists: no more than twelve pages of poetry or one chapter or story-length prose piece. Include an adequate SASE for return of your samples.

Deadline

April 1 (postmarked). Late applications may be considered on a space-available basis.

Approximate Cost of Program

$500, $5 handling fee, transportation, meals, materials, and incidentals. Limited financial aid is available by application.

YADDO

The Corporation of Yaddo, P.O. Box 395, Saratoga Springs, New York 12866-0395
Attention: Lesley M. Leduc, Admissions Committee
Phone: (518) 584-0746; fax: (518) 584-1312
Email: yaddo@yaddo.org

Type of Facility/Award
Residency.

Who Can Apply
Writers, visual artists, composers, choreographers, performance artists, photographers, and film and video artists.

Provisos
Applicants must be working at a professional level in their fields. Applications are judged on the quality of the artist's work and professional promise.

Dates of Operation
Open year-round.

Location
Saratoga Springs is in Upstate New York, about thirty minutes north of Albany.

History
The Yaddo mansion was built by Spencer and Katrina Trask in 1893. When their four children died, leaving the Trasks with no heirs, they formed and endowed the Corporation of Yaddo "to administer a working community of artists in perpetuity." The first group of artists attended Yaddo in 1926. Recently, Yaddo's board of directors "reasserted Yaddo's original commitment to aesthetic daring, social egalitarianism, internationalism, and the support of artists at political risk."

What They Offer
Yaddo offers residencies of two weeks to two months. The average stay is five weeks. Small groups of collaborators (two or three people) may apply to work together. Yaddo can accommodate thirty-five people concurrently during their "large season" (mid-May through Labor Day) and fifteen people concurrently during their "small season." Each artist is provided with a private bedroom, a private studio, and three meals a day. Breakfast and dinner are communal; lunch is packed for artists to carry away. Linens are provided. Spontaneous and planned sharing of works-in-progress among guests is allowed after quiet hours (9 A.M. to 4 P.M. daily). No guests are allowed at dinner or overnight. No pets, except seeing-eye dogs, are allowed. There are no medical facilities and special diets cannot be accommodated.

Facility Description

"Besides the fifty-five room mansion, the chief residence in the summer, there are three smaller houses, as well as studio buildings and a building for administrative offices and maintenance shops. The estate's 400 acres feature four small lakes, a renowned rose garden (the only part of the property open to the public), and large areas of woodland." There are separate studios for "painting and drawing, intaglio printmaking, sculpture and welding, lithography, and photography. Composer's studios are equipped with pianos. Choreographers may request portable mirrors and barres, and the floors of their studios can be covered with marley." Writers are provided with table space. Yaddo has several small libraries (including one of Yaddo authors), laundry facilities, a tennis court, a swimming pool, a pool table, and a ping-pong table. Bicycles and cross-country skis are available for residents' use.

How to Apply

Send an SASE for an application and brochure. Return the original and two copies of the completed application with a $20 nonrefundable application fee, two copies of a professional résumé, a brief biographical note, a brief description of your proposed project, some samples of your recent work, two letters of support sent directly by the sponsors, and an SASP to acknowledge receipt of your materials. Collaborators must submit separate application packages but should indicate they are collaborating with others. Appropriate work samples vary by category as follows. Typescripts: Send three copies of no more than thirty pages of either a group of poems, a short story, a one-act play, or a portion of a novel, play, or other work accompanied by a synopsis if necessary. If your work is not in English, send the original and an English translation. Typescripts will not be returned. Slides: Send seven colored slides (packaged and labeled according to instructions). Music: Send two scores and a clearly labeled audio cassette of one of them. VHS video cassettes: Send two clearly labeled cassettes cued to a ten-minute segment and accompanied by a written explanation, if necessary. Include an adequate SASE for return of samples, except in the case of typescripts.

Deadline

January 15 for residencies from mid-May through February. August 1 for residencies from late October to May.

Approximate Cost of Program

$20 application fee, transportation, materials, and incidentals. Room, board, and studio space are provided.

YELLOW SPRINGS INSTITUTE   **PA**   ****DISCONTINUED****

ZEN MOUNTAIN MONASTERY   NY

P.O. Box 197PC, South Plank Road, Mt. Tremper, New York 12457
Attention: Joy Jimon Hintz, Information Officer
Phone: (914) 688-2228
Web site: www.zen-mtn.org/zmm
Email: dharmacom@delphi.com

Type of Facility/Award
Retreat.

Who Can Apply
All artists and writers.

Provisos
All artists interested in pursuing their creative work within the context of Zen practice and the daily Zen training schedule are encouraged to apply.

Dates of Operation
Winter and summer sessions are open to artists.

Location
The monastery is located on 230 acres of nature preserve in the foothills of the Catskill Mountains. It is two hours north of New York City and just over one hour south of Albany. The bus passes within easy walking distance of the monastery building. Mt. Tremper is easily accessible from any of the New York City, Albany, or Newburgh airports via Adirondack Trailways.

History
"Zen Mountain Monastery is a monastic training center dedicated to providing authentic and traditional, yet distinctly American Zen training to people of all ages and religious backgrounds. With a resident community of twenty to thirty male and female monastic and lay residents, ZMM offers a wide variety of programs and retreats geared toward both beginning and advanced practitioners."

What They Offer
Retreats for artists include the daily training schedule with free time in the afternoon for personal study. All residency fees are payable at the beginning of each month spent in residential training; fees cover meals, lodging, and all training costs. Prices listed are for accommodations in the main building; add $100 per month for a private cabin, if available. Full-time: $575–$675 per month (includes monthly sesshin and special weekend retreats). Couples: $975 per month. Monastery guests: $175 per week includes meals, lodging, and instruction but does not include special programs or retreats. Work scholarships are sometimes available if payment for resi-

dency is not possible. Applicants are asked to spend at least one month in full-time residence before applying for a scholarship. Financial assistance is sometimes available according to need, skill, and motivation.

Facility Description

Residents of one month or more are housed in private or semiprivate rooms, either in the main monastery building or in one of the rustic cabins located on the property. Residents may choose to live in a single cabin or in one of the monastery's A-frames when they are available, but the cost for those accommodations is greater. Cabins and A-frames are located in the woods, which are part of the monastery's 200 acres of forest preserve. Both are equipped with electricity and wood stoves for heat, and there is a nearby bath house with shower and toilet facilities which operates for most of the year. Living quarters at the monastery are simple and comfortable. Residents are encouraged to bring with them only what is necessary.

How to Apply

Send an SASE for a brochure and application. They are interested in those who have the ability to follow the daily monastic schedule, are sincere, show a willingness to fully engage in the training program, and are willing to make a commitment to the development of the student-teacher training relationship during the time they are in residency.

Deadline

Rolling application basis.

Approximate Cost of Program

$575–$675 plus transportation, materials, and incidentals.

Headlands Center for the Arts (Photo by Ed Beyeler)

International Colonies

FRANS MASEREEL CENTRUM   BELGIUM

Zaardendijk 20, 2460 Kasterlee, Belgium
Attention: Jenny Caers
Phone: 00-32-(0) 14-852252; fax: 00-32-(0) 14-850591

Type of Facility/Award
Residency.

Who Can Apply
Graphic artists.

Provisos
Established artists only. Applicants must be able to apply one or more graphic techniques autonomously and must respect the independent work of her or his colleagues.

Dates of Operation
Open year-round (except December).

Location
Kasterlee is about eighty kilometers from the Brussels airport. Buses and trains run
between the airport and the center.

History
"Frans Masereel was born in Blankenberge on July 30, 1889, and died in Avignon
on January 3, 1972. On January 8, a Saturday, the population was given the opportunity to pay their respects and greet the mortal remains, from 11 a.m. to 1 p.m., at
the 'Paleis voor Schone Kunsten' in Ghent. A great tribute was paid to Frans Masereel
at 2:30 p.m.. Afterwards, the burial took place at Campo Santo in Sint-Amandsberg.
In his memorial speech, Professor Doctor Frans Van Mechelen, the Dutch Culture
Minister, announced that the recently acquired artists' center in Kasterlee was hence-
forth to be called the Frans Masereel Center. Since then, the former workshop of
Fons Mertens, graphic artist, has grown into a graphic techniques' center, in which
artists from all over the world meet each other, exercise and exchange their graphic
skills, compare and extend their artistic ideals."

What They Offer
Two- or three-week residencies include access to workshops and accommodations in
an apartment. Housing may also be available for artists' companions based on availability. The center provides technical assistance when needed and organizes courses
and graphic arts exhibitions. Though artists are encouraged to meet and work together as a functioning community, residents must be able to work independently.

Facility Description
Residents have access to three workshops, a reception area, eight apartments, and the Frans Masereel Museum. Apartments consist of a sitting room, a kitchen, two bedrooms, and a bathroom and may hold no more than four people. Television is included, but residents must provide sheets, towels, and tablecloths. Pets are not allowed anywhere in the center.

How to Apply
Send an SASE for a brochure. Submit your current résumé, a statement concerning the graphic technique or techniques you would like to apply at the workshop, the graphic technique or techniques you can apply autonomously, slides of your latest graphic design work, and an indication of the dates you wish to stay.

Deadline
Rolling application process. Apply at least six months in advance of desired dates.

Approximate Cost of Program
Transportation, meals, materials, and incidentals.

THE BANFF CENTRE FOR THE ARTS   CANADA
Leighton Studios Independent Residencies
Leighton Studios for Independent Residencies Program Office, Box 1020 Station 28, 107 Tunnel Mountain Drive, Banff, Alberta T0L 0C0, Canada
Attention: Registrar
Phone: (403) 762-6270; fax: (403) 762-6236
Web site: www.banffcentre.ab.ca/registrar/leighton/
Email: registrars_office@banffcentre.ab.ca

Type of Facility/Award
Residency.

Who Can Apply
Writers, composers, musicians, and visual artists.

Provisos
Senior-level writers, composers, musicians, and visual artists engaged in the creation of new work are encouraged to apply.

Dates of Operation
Open year-round. The maximum duration of a residency is three months in a given year.

Location
Located in the mountains of Canada's first national park, the Banff Centre for Con-

tinuing Education is a major tourist destination. The closest major city is Calgary, 120 kilometers east on the Trans-Canada Highway. Regular bus service is available between Banff and the Calgary International Airport.

History

"The Banff Centre for Continuing Education is a unique Canadian institution playing a special role in the advancement of cultural and professional life, internationally recognized for its leadership in arts and management, and for developing and hosting conferences on contemporary issues."

What They Offer

The Leighton Studios offer a focused retreat environment for senior-level artists concentrating on the creation of new work. Residents receive studio space, accommodations, and cooking facilities or a flex meal plan. On-site accommodation consists of a private room with bath, telephone, and housekeeping service. Artists have full access to the Paul D. Fleck Library and Archives, fitness and recreation facilities, a dining room, and a small store. Performances, concerts, and exhibitions take place throughout the year. Artists may choose to participate in the artistic community at the Banff Centre, though there is no expectation that they do so. Costs per day are as follows (Canadian currencies). Studio: $48.00. Single room: $45.50. Flex meal plan: $10.80–$15.20. All studios are equipped with kitchenettes, and artists may choose to prepare their own meals. Individual meals may be purchased in the dining room on a cash basis. Artists may apply for a discount on the studio fee.

Facility Description

The Leighton Studios are set in a mountainside pine grove slightly apart from the main buildings of the center. There are eight studios specially designed as workspaces for composers, writers, and artists. Each of these eight studios is equipped with a kitchenette, washroom, telephone, CD/cassette player, and comfortable furnishings. The writing studios have ample desk space, and typewriters and drafting boards are available. Three of the studios have pianos. Two are designed for painters and are large enough for small collaborative groups. Studios are accessible twenty-four hours a day. Each studio has large windows, a skylight, and a large open space that allows for work on the walls or floors. They are all equipped with adjustable track lighting, studio sinks, large work tables, and movable equipment trolleys. Easels are available. A ninth studio for potters is located in Glyde Hall, the visual arts building. It provides potter's wheels, kilns (electric, gas, wood, soda, and raku), a slab roller, an extruder, a sandblaster, an outdoor working pad, a plaster room, a clay mixing room, and a glaze room.

How to Apply

Send an SASE for an application and brochure. Submit your completed application with a project description, bio, and support material. If you are a first-time applicant, also include references and detailed background information. They encourage you to apply six months in advance, although openings with a short lead time may become available.

Deadline
Applications are accepted year-round.

Approximate Cost of Program
Approximately $3,261.00 (Canadian) for one month plus materials and incidentals.

THE BANFF CENTRE FOR THE ARTS   CANADA
Playwright's Colony
Playwright's Colony, Box 1020, Station 28, 107 Tunnel Mountain Drive, Banff, Alberta T0L 0C0, Canada
Attention: Registrar
Phone: (403) 762-6180 or (800) 565-9989; fax: (403) 762-6345
Web site: www.banffcentre.ab.ca/theatre
Email: registrars_office@banffcentre.ab.ca

Type of Facility/Award
Residency.

Who Can Apply
Playwrights.

Provisos
Applicants are generally Canadian, although French and Australian playwrights are also welcome to apply. The Banff Centre encourages applications from artists of all backgrounds. Full-length plays, one-act plays, and plays for young audiences are all eligible. The colony is interested in works of an interdisciplinary nature; however, it is not equipped to deal with musical theater or works that require significant musical or dance dramaturgy.

Dates of Operation
Late August through early September. (Dates vary from year to year.)

Location
Located in the mountains of Canada's first national park, the Banff Centre for Continuing Education is a major tourist destination. The closest major city is Calgary, 120 kilometers east on the Trans-Canada Highway. Regular bus service is available between Banff and the Calgary International Airport.

History
"The Banff Centre for the Arts is a place for artists, and is dedicated to lifelong

learning and professional career development in the arts, acting as site and catalyst for creative activity and experience. Located in the mountains of Canada's first national park, the Banff Centre for Continuing Education is a unique Canadian institution playing a special role in the advancement of cultural and professional life, internationally recognized for its leadership in arts and management, and for developing and hosting conferences on contemporary issues."

What They Offer

A playwright may spend one to three weeks working on a final manuscript with the opportunity for consultation with and commentary from a dramaturge of his or her choice. The playwright may also work with a professional cast of actors to further explore and refine the text. If they desire, playwrights may also have shared access to a small company of professional actors and readers. The program supplies printers, a Mac and an IBM computer for printing purposes only, and can supply typewriters upon request. The cost of the colony is $336 per week for the program fee, $45.50 per day for the room, and $15.20 per day for the flex meal plan (Canadian currencies). Some full and partial fee abatement awards are available. In exceptional cases, some individuals may be provided with a travel allowance. Contact the center to apply for travel assistance.

Facility Description

Banff was Canada's first national park. At 1,383 meters above sea level and surrounded by mountains, the town of Banff (pop. 7000) is a major tourist destination. The Banff Centre has performance theatres, recital halls, art galleries, an extensive library, a well-equipped recreation and fitness complex, and a campus store.

How to Apply

Send an SASE for an application and brochure. Return your completed application with a nonrefundable fee of $50 (Canadian) or $42 (U.S.), a script (packaged and labeled according to instructions), and, if you are requesting a reduction in cost, your written request for an award or travel assistance with documentation of need.

Deadline

February 11. Notification by May 19.

Approximate Cost of Program

$2,312 (Canadian), plus transportation, materials, and incidentals.

THE BANFF CENTRE FOR THE ARTS   CANADA
Writing Studio Program

Writing Studio Program, Box 1020, Station 28, 107 Tunnel Mountain Drive,
   Banff, Alberta T0L 0C0, Canada
Attention: Registrar
Phone: (403) 762-6180 or (800) 565-9989; fax: (403) 762-6345
Web site: www.banffcentre.ab.ca
Email: registrars_office@ banffcentre.ab.ca

Type of Facility/Award
Residency.

Who Can Apply
Writers.

Provisos
Open to applications from all sectors of Canadian society. Successful applicants will
have published a body of work (books, stories, poems, or belles-lettres in magazines
or anthologies) and will be working on a book-length manuscript or manuscript-in-
progress and will be interested in working with an editor at Banff.

Dates of Operation
Early October through early November.

Location
Located in the mountains of Canada's first national park, the Banff Centre for Continuing Education is a major tourist destination. The closest major city is Calgary,
120 kilometers east on the Trans-Canada Highway. Regular bus service is available
between Banff and the Calgary International Airport.

History
"The Banff Centre for the Arts is a place for artists, and is dedicated to lifelong
learning and professional career development in the arts, acting as site and catalyst
for creative activity and experience. Located in the mountains of Canada's first national park, the Banff Centre for Continuing Education is a unique Canadian institution playing a special role in the advancement of cultural and professional life,
internationally recognized for its leadership in arts and management, and for developing and hosting conferences on contemporary issues."

What They Offer
Twenty-five people are selected to work independently on their projects and consult
individually with the resource faculty at the center as required. "The program is
designed to give support not readily available elsewhere to writers at a crucial stage of
their careers." Fees for the studio session are $1,674 for tuition plus $1,566 for the

room and $504 for the meal plan (Canadian currencies). Limited financial aid is available (by application) for a reduction of up to eighty percent of the cost.

Facility Description

Banff was Canada's first national park. At 1,383 meters above sea level and surrounded by mountains, the town of Banff (pop. 7000) is a major tourist destination. The Banff Centre has performance theatres, recital halls, art galleries, an extensive library, a well-equipped recreation and fitness complex, and a campus store. The Leighton Studios are set in a mountainside pine grove slightly apart from the main buildings; eight studios are specially designed workspaces for composers, writers, and artists. Studios are accessible twenty-four hours a day. Each is comfortably furnished and has a kitchenette, a washroom, large windows with private view, a skylight, and a large open space that allows for work on the walls or floors. They are all equipped with adjustable track lighting, studio sinks, large work tables, and movable equipment trolleys. Writing studios have ample desk space. Typewriters and drafting boards are available. Writers working with computers must bring their own computers and software. An IBM and a Macintosh computer are available for printing purposes only. Photocopying services are available.

How to Apply

Send an SASE for an application and brochure. Return your completed application with an application fee of $49 (Canadian) or $42 (U.S.), a résumé (list publication credits on a separate sheet), a description of your proposed project, a statement about what you hope to accomplish during the program, the names and addresses of two references, and a work sample. Appropriate work samples follow. Poetry: two copies of a segment of a book-length manuscript or work in progress, supported by a portfolio of published or unpublished work (total of twenty-five to forty pages). Prose: two copies of a segment of a book-length manuscript or work in progress, supported by a portfolio of published or unpublished work (total of fifty to seventy-five pages). Those requesting financial aid must supply appropriate documentation of need.

Deadline

April 30. Notification by June 30.

Approximate Cost of Program

$3,744 (Canadian) plus transportation, materials, and incidentals. Limited financial aid is available.

NORTH PACIFIC WOMEN WRITERS RETREAT   **DISCONTINUED**

SASKATCHEWAN WRITERS GUILD   CANADA

Saskatchewan Writers/Artists Colonies and Retreats, Individual Retreats,
c/o Saskatchewan Writers Guild, P.O. Box 3986, Regina, Saskatchewan S4P
3R9 Canada
Attention: Shelley Sopher, Colony Coordinator
Phone: (306) 757-6310; fax: (306) 565-8554
Web site: www.skwriter.com/colonies.html
Email: swg@sk.sympatico.ca

Type of Facility/Award
Residency.

Who Can Apply
Writers and artists.

Provisos
Writers and artists may apply for up to four weeks per year of combined colony and
individual retreat time. Individual retreats are limited to two weeks per year. Though
writers and artists from around the world are invited to apply to the colonies, only
Canadians may apply for individual residencies.

Dates of Operation
St. Peter's Abbey Colony: February, July, and August. Emma Lake Colony: August.
The Riverhurst Colony: September.

Location
The guild offers access to three different colonies. St. Peter's Abbey Colony is located
just outside the village of Muenster; Emma Lake is only a few miles from the town of
Christopher Lake, approximately twenty-five miles north of Prince Albert; and the
Riverhurst Colony is held at the Mainstay Inn near Riverhurst, about a mile from
Lake Diefenbaker.

History
"The Saskatchewan Colonies were established in 1978 to provide a place where
writers could write free from distraction. The colonies were soon expanded to include visual artists. Not only is the uninterrupted working time invaluable, but conversation after hours provides a stimulating exchange of ideas. The individual retreats make the program more flexible in response to the needs of writers."

What They Offer
St. Peter's Abbey Colony offers two-week sessions and year-round retreats. Emma
Lake Colony and the Riverhurst Colony each host one two-week session. All three
programs provide uninterrupted working time, a stimulating exchange of ideas at meal
times, and many recreational opportunities after working hours. These colonies are

not teaching situations; writers and artists are expected to work independently.

Facility Description

St. Peter's Abbey is a Benedictine abbey. Guests are accommodated in private rooms in a former convent on the abbey grounds or in Severin Hall. Meals are homegrown and served in the college facility. Studio space for visual artists is provided. The setting is serene and timeless, promoting both work and relaxation.

Emma Lake is located in a forest region. Accommodations include separate cabins or single rooms in a one-story building. Artists share a large studio space. Meals are served in the dining room of a central building, which also has a lounge.

The Riverhurst Colony is held at the Mainstay Inn. This colony is ideal for applicants interested in an isolated setting. The hotel, with a vast prairie view, sits between two deep forested coulees about a mile from the sandy beaches of Lake Diefenbaker.

How to Apply

Send an SASE for a brochure, indicating which colony interests you. Submit ten typewritten pages of a manuscript or ten slides of artwork (packaged and labeled according to instructions), a description of your proposed project, the names of two references familiar with your work, length of stay, preferred dates, and a brief résumé of past work, including publications and exhibitions. Applications received after the deadline are considered on a space-available basis. A check for the total due must accompany your application.

Deadline

January 1 for St. Peter's Abbey (winter residency). April 15 for St. Peter's Abbey (summer residency) and Emma Lake. July 1 for Riverhurst. Rolling application process for St. Peter's Abbey year-round retreat.

Approximate Cost of Program

$125 (Canadian currency) per week for Saskatchewan Writers Guild members and $175 per week for non-members plus transportation, materials, and incidentals.

CTTEE ON SCHOLARLY COMMUNICATION WITH CHINA   CHINA

Office of Fellowships and Grants, American Council of Learned Societies, 228
East 45th Street, New York, New York 10017-3398
Attention: CSCC National Program for Advanced Study and Research in China
Phone: (212) 949-8058 ext. 136/138; fax: (212) 949-8058
Web site: www.acls.org
Email: grants@acls.org

> *Notice: In addition to the Research Program, the American Council of Learned Societies (ACLS) and the Committee on Scholarly Communication with China*

(CSCC) offer a variety of competitions, fellowships, and awards programs for international and scholarly studies. Request a brochure from the address above or see the ACLS Web site for current listings.

Type of Facility/Award
Fellowships/grants.

Who Can Apply
Scholars in the humanities and humanistic aspects of the social sciences doing in-depth research on China.

Provisos
Support is available to post-doctoral scholars only—the graduate program has been canceled due to lack of funding. Applicants must be U.S. citizens or permanent residents and must demonstrate that they have fully utilized the available resources in the U.S. and are prepared, by virtue of study and planning, to take full advantage of this opportunity to do research in the People's Republic of China.

Dates of Operation
Four to twelve months between July and December.

Location
Variable.

History
"The American Council of Learned Societies was established in 1919 to represent the United States within the Union Académique Internationale (UAI) (International Union of Academies), which itself was established earlier that year 'to encourage cooperation in the advancement of studies through collaborative research and publications in those branches of learning promoted by the Academies and institutions represented in the UAI—philology, archaeology, history, the moral, political and social sciences.' At that time, no organization existed in the United States to perform this function. The ACLS has represented the nation in the UAI with distinction for nearly 80 years."

What They Offer
Funded by the National Endowment for the Humanities, the research program supports scholars performing research on China or the Chinese portion of a comparative study in the People's Republic of China, with the exception of Hong Kong and Macau. For a period of four to twelve months between July and December, fellows receive a monthly stipend and travel allowances.

Facility Description
Variable.

How to Apply

Send an SASE for an application and brochure. Your application must include information regarding which award program you are applying for, your highest academic degree and the date you received it, your country of citizenship or permanent residence, your position (academic or otherwise), your field of specialization, your proposed subject of research, and your preferred dates for fellowship.

Deadline

October 15.

Approximate Cost of Program

Transportation, housing, meals, materials, incidentals—offset by monthly stipend and travel allowances.

PRAGUE SUMMER WRITERS' WORKSHOP   CZECH REPUBLIC
P.O. Box 221, 110 01 Praha 1, Czech Republic

U.S. Office:

Writers Workshop International, 2618A St. Charles Avenue, New Orleans,
     Louisiana 70130-5945
Attention: Trevor Top
Phone: (888) 873-8867
Web site: www.terminal.cz/~psww/index.html

COMMISSION FOR EDUCATIONAL EXCHANGE BETWEEN DENMARK AND THE USA   DENMARK
(The Fulbright Commission), Fiolstræde 10, Second Floor, 1171, Copenhagen K,
     Denmark
Phone: 33-12-82-23

U.S. Office:

Institute of International Education, U.S. Student Programmes, 809 UN Plaza,
     New York, New York 10017-3580

ALTOS DE CHAVON   DOMINICAN REPUBLIC
Apartado Postal 140, La Romana, Dominican Republic
Attention: Stephen Kaplan
Phone: (212) 229-5370
Email: altos@codetel.net.do
     Notice: Contacting Mr. Kaplan by phone first is advisable.

NEWBERRY LIBRARY/BRITISH ACADEMY FELLOWSHIP FOR STUDY IN
GREAT BRITAIN   ENGLAND
Newberry Library Committee on Awards, 60 West Walton Street, Chicago, Illinois
60610-3380
Phone: (312) 255-3666; fax: (312) 255-3513
Web site: www.newberry.org
Email: research@newberry.org

SUMMER WORKSHOP IN LONDON   ENGLAND
Institute for Readers Theatre, P.O. Box 17193, San Diego, California 92177
Attention: Dr. William J. Adams
Phone: (619) 276-1948; fax: (619) 576-7369
Web site: www.readers-theatre.com
Email: info@readers-theatre.com

Type of Facility/Award
Residential workshop.

Who Can Apply
Anyone.

Provisos
None listed.

Dates of Operation
July.

Location
Wellington Hall in London, England.

History
The Institute for Readers Theatre was founded nearly thirty years ago, and the international workshops have been conducted for twenty-six years with London being the most popular venue.

What They Offer
Two-week-long workshops provide the participants with help in the areas of writing, direction, performance, methodology, oral interpretation, storytelling, and creative dramatics. Participants may take part in other activities led by faculty, such as a city tour, afternoon tea, theatre pub crawl, river cruise, Shakespeare walk/Globe tour, and more.

Facility Description
Wellington Hall is located on green, quiet Vincent Square and is within walking distance of neighborhood stores, banks, Victoria Station, and the bustling shopping

area of Victoria Street. Wellington Hall has two lounges with views of the gardens and square, a library, conference room, TV lounge, and bar. There are 105 places in single- and twin-bedded rooms. All have washbasins and nearby toilets and showers. Residents have access to round-the-clock reception, public telephones, laundry and ironing facilities, and cooking facilities. Breakfast is included.

How to Apply
Send an SASE for an application and brochure.

Deadline
June 1.

Approximate Cost of Program
$1,395 (U.S.) includes two weeks of twin accommodation (some singles available for an additional $120), traditional English breakfast, complimentary mid-morning coffee/tea break and all institute fees. Optional university credit is available at additional cost. Participants are responsible for transportation, some meals, materials, and incidentals.

THE CAMARGO FOUNDATION   FRANCE
The Camargo Foundation, BP 75, 13714 Cassis Cedex, France
Attention: Michael J. Pretina, Jr.
Phone: (04) 42-01-11-57; fax: (04) 42-01-36-57

U.S. Office:
Park Square Court, 400 Sibley Street, Suite 125, St. Paul, Minnesota 55101-1928
Attention: Dr. William Reichard, U.S. Secretariat
Phone: (651) 290-2237

Type of Facility/Award
Fellowship.

Who Can Apply
Writers, visual artists, photographers, and composers.

Provisos
No guests are allowed, with the exception of spouses, adult partners, and dependent minors who are over the age of six and enrolled in school during the fellowship.

Dates of Operation
Fall and spring semesters annually.

Location
Overlooking both the Mediterranean Sea and Cap Canaille, the foundation is a five-minute walk from town and thirty minutes from Marseilles by train or bus.

History

"The Camargo Foundation, an educational trust established under the laws of the State of New York, was created by Jerome Hill in 1967 and endowed with his art collection, library, and land holdings in France and California. The Camargo Foundation maintains on Hill's former estate in Cassis, France, a center of studies for the benefit of scholars who wish to pursue projects in the humanities and social sciences related to French and francophone cultures."

What They Offer

Each fellow is provided with a fully furnished apartment complete with linens and towels, which are laundered by the foundation. Apartments are regularly cleaned by staff. Each apartment at the foundation has a view of the Mediterranean and Cap Canaille, the highest cliff in France. Fellows have access to the foundation's library, darkroom, music-conference room, and reading room. Studios are made available for composers and visual artists. Privacy is very important at Camargo, but the fellows do meet once a week to discuss the progress of their projects. The foundation also organizes a number of excursions for the fellows, including chamber music concerts, film screenings, poetry readings, and day trips. Only one composer, visual artist, and photographer can be accepted during each semester, as work space is limited. Fellows cannot be employed during the fellowship term and should apply for grants to cover living expenses prior to beginning the fellowship. A written report covering the project will be required at the end of the stay. Fellows are asked to give a copy of any completed work to the Camargo library. Any publication, exhibit, or performance resulting from the fellowship should give credit to the Camargo Foundation.

Facility Description

Private telephones are not available in individual apartments, but there are two phones at the center that fellows may use. Fax service and email access are available, though fellows should bring their own modems for email. A microfilm reader (35 mm) is available, as is a photocopier (for a charge). Fellows are responsible for providing their own writing instruments, including typewriters or computers.

How To Apply

Send an SASE to the U.S. office for a brochure and application. Submit your completed application form, vita, and a detailed description of your project, not to exceed one thousand words. If appropriate, the description should include a paragraph or two "designed to locate the project conceptually and/or bibliographically in the context of the most important works available in the field." Any research should be at an advanced stage and should not require the use of any facilities outside the Marseilles-Cassis-Aix region. Visual artists: Submit ten slides of your work. Composers: Submit a score, cassette, or CD. Writers: Submit ten to twenty pages of text or a copy of your publication. Also include three letters of recommendation to be provided by those who are familiar with your professional work, with at least two references coming from outside your institution (where applicable). The letters should be current and addressed to the Camargo Foundation.

Deadline
February 1 for the following academic year. Awards announced by April 1.

Approximate Cost of Program
A residential grant is available for writers and composers. Visual artists and photographers receive travel funds and a monthly stipend from the Andy Warhol Foundation. Contact the foundation for the specific amounts of these stipends. Living, material, and incidental expenses are the responsibility of the fellow.

CHATEAU DE LA GARENNE-LEMOT   **DISCONTINUED**

CHATEAU DE LESVAULT   FRANCE
Writers' Retreat Program, Margaret Ancker Fellowship, Onlay 58370,
    Villapourçon, France
Phone: (33) 86-84-32-91; fax: (33) 86-84-35-78

International Headquarters:
P.O. Box 15746, San Diego, California 92175-5746
Phone: (619) 589-1885; fax: (619) 589-1886

Type of Facility/Award
Fellowship or Retreat.

Who Can Apply
Fiction writers and poets.

Provisos
Applicants should be U.S. citizens.

Dates of Operation
From April through October, the château acts as a bed and breakfast, and artists may stay on a retreat basis. For the remaining months of the year the château hosts the Margaret Ancker Fellowship for selected guests.

Location
Nestled within the alluring setting of Le Morvan National Park in the Burgundy countryside, Château De Lesvault is located near many regional restaurants as well as historical and cultural sites (such as Vezelay and Autun). The surrounding regions of Côte D'Or, Beaune, and Sancerre may be of interest to wine enthusiasts.

History

The château is a French country manor that was built in 1860. It has undergone extensive remodeling and general upgrading during the last ten years and has been acclaimed in prominent publications as an inspirational haven for promising writers.

The Margaret Ancker Fellowship was first made available in 1998.

What They Offer

The fellowship provides an American writer of poetry or fiction a one-month residency, all expenses paid ($1,000 plus), at the Château de Lesvault Writers' Retreat. Full meal and beverage service is provided from April through October when the château is open as a bed and breakfast retreat space.

Facility Description

The château's ten acres of property are adorned with flowering trees, fragrant rosebeds, and a two-and-a-half-acre spring-fed lake. There is a curved greenhouse of year-round cultivation that includes colorful flowers and freshly grown vegetables. Guests enjoy panoramic views of the rolling French countryside.

Indoor facilities are composed of thirty rooms on four levels. The first floor features a fully equipped kitchen, dining room with a large fireplace, wine cellar, and storage and laundry facilities. The second floor includes an entrance hall, living salon, casual breakfast room, kitchen with bar, two bathrooms, and a private guest suite. Ten private guest suites and eight bathrooms are found on the third and fourth floors. The surrounding country roads offer plenty of room for walking, hiking, and recreational biking.

How to Apply

Send an SASE for a brochure. Send your résumé, project description, a representative sample of work, the names and addresses of two references, and an application fee of $15 (U.S.) made out to the Margaret Ancker Fellowship. Manuscripts will not be returned.

Deadline

November 1. Notification December 15.

Approximate Cost of Program

$15 application fee, housing, and meals—offset by $1,000 stipend.

ECOLE DES CHARTRES EXCHANGE FELLOWSHIP   FRANCE

c/o Newberry Library Committee on Awards, 60 West Walton Street, Chicago, Illinois 60610-3380
Phone: (312) 255-3666; fax: (312) 255-3513
Web site: www.newberry.org
Email: research@newberry.org

FONDATION ROYAUMONT   FRANCE

F-95270 Asnières-sur-Oise, France
Attention: Nathalie Le Gonidec
Phone: 33 (01) 30 35 59 88; fax: 33 (01) 30 35 39 45
Web site: www.royaumont.com
Email: semrecep@royaumont.com

GUILLY GLAS (Writer's Retreat)   FRANCE

Brittany, France

U.S. Address:

6621 Ascot Drive, Oakland, California 94611
Attention: Mark Greenside
Phone: (510) 530-4341; fax: (510) 482-9330
Email: MGDONNA@AOL.com

Type of Facility/Award

Retreat.

Who Can Apply

Writers, composers, and visual artists.

Provisos

Car rental is necessary.

Dates of Operation

Open year-round.

Location

Port Launay is in western France. The house at Guilly Glas is ten miles from ocean beaches, four and a half hours from Paris by train, and one hour from the Plymouth-Roscoff ferry to England and the Cork-Roscoff ferry to Ireland. There is also an airport in Brest, thirty minutes away.

History

None provided.

What They Offer

Guilly Glas offers private workspace in a secluded and inspiring environment. Rates are as follows (U.S. currencies). July and August: $1,700 per month. May, June, September, October: $1,300 per month. November through April: $1,100 per month. Residents must supply a fully refundable $100 security deposit for use of the phone. Long-term rates are negotiable.

Facility Description

Guilly Glas is located at the edge of a small village (pop. 600) that is right next to a larger town (pop. 7,000). The town has everything one might need, including a swimming pool, movie theater, and tennis courts. The house at Guilly Glas faces the River Aulne, which runs from Brest (on the Atlantic) to Nantes. The house itself is over one hundred years old, three stories high, and made of stone. It is private without being isolated. There are ample grounds, a garden, and a terrace. Behind the house is open land with hills and trees. Beyond the River Aulne is hilly farm and pasture land. There are neighbors on either side of the house, but they are not visible. Each side is separated by a strand of cypress trees.

How to Apply

Contact Mark Greenside directly via mail or email for a brochure and application.

Deadline

None.

Approximate Cost of Program

$1,100–$1,700 per month plus transportation, meals, materials, and incidentals.

INSTITUT DES HAUTES ESTUDES EN ARTS PLASTIQUES   FRANCE
DISCONTINUED

JOURNALISTS IN EUROPE   FRANCE
Journalists in Europe Fund, 4, rue du Faubourg Monmartre, F-75009 Paris, France
Phone: (33) 1-55-77-20-00; fax: (33) 1-48-24-40-02
Web site: www.europmag.com
Email: europmag@europmag.com

LIVE ART   FRANCE
736 Pine Crest Avenue, Sebastopol, California 95472
Attention: Carol Watanabe
Phone: (707) 823-9663 or (415) 454-1754
Web site: www.artfully.com/new/splash.html
Email: liveart@sonic.net or artlives@hotmail.com

Type of Facility/Award
Retreat.

Who Can Apply
Anyone.

Provisos
None listed.

Dates of Operation
Summer months.

Location
Sorèze, where Live Art retreats are held, is a small village in the southern region of France, nestled at the base of the Montagne Noir. Sorèze is a one-hour drive east by rental car from Toulouse International Airport.

History
None provided.

What They Offer
This retreat offers summer adventures in a beautiful and inspiring location for those interested in a variety of art forms, including acrylic painting, pastels, writing, cooking, and dance. Hostess and founder Carole Rae Watanabe houses guests in her two 400-year-old homes, Le Villette and L'Art Vivant. The homes have been decorated to give guests the experience of living among the works of such famous artists as Matisse, Bonnard, Van Gogh, Chagall, and Gaugin. Rooms are luxurious and lavishly decorated. The small size of the community (no more than fourteen guests at a time) allows for personalized daily art instruction and feedback from teachers. The retreat includes candlelit meals prepared by the in-house chef and daily on-site picnics, with the exception of one lunch and three dinners to explore local restaurants. All ground transportation to nearby villages is provided in shared rental cars.

Facility Description
Surrounded by sunflower fields, clear lakes, streams, and valleys of farmland, Sorèze is just large enough to support two bakeries, a patisserie, a boucherie/charcuterie, two small markets, one café, and one restaurant. Live Art's two houses are situated on a cobblestone street in town. Le Villette has three bedrooms and comfortably sleeps six. Each of the ample-sized rooms on the second floor includes a double and single bed, as well as bath. The attic atelier is divided into a garret bedroom with two single beds and an art studio. A fully equipped kitchen with a fireplace and grill opens onto a courtyard and fountain. L'Art Vivant includes Live Art's private gallery space as well.

How to Apply

Email or write for a brochure. After you mail your reservation check you will receive a handmade guide book with all the necessary information about what you need to bring, what materials are provided, a suggested reading list, etc.

Deadline

Reservations accepted year-round based on availability.

Approximate Cost of Program

Prices are variable depending on length of stay (at least one week) and number of guests.

N.A.L.L. ART FOUNDATION   FRANCE

(Nature Art and Life League), 232, Bd de Lattre, 06140 Vence, France
Phone: (33) 4-93-58-13-26; fax: (33) 4-93-58-09-00
Web site: www.nall.org
Email: nall@nall.org

U.S. Office:

511 Adams Street, Huntsville, Alabama 35801
Phone: (256) 512-0021; fax: (256) 512-0021

Type of Facility/Award

Residency.

Who Can Apply

Artists and writers (all mediums).

Provisos

None listed.

Dates of Operation

Variable.

Location

Vence, France.

History

The NALL Art Foundation was created in 1997 with the American artist and program director whose name is Nall. The goals of the foundation are to promote and sponsor the arts and to continue the cultural exchange between France and the United States.

What They Offer

Artists of all callings (painters, sculptors, writers, musicians, etc.) live and work together in ten available studios and attend exhibitions, conferences, concerts, and seminars.

Facility Description

The main facilities include a seventeenth-century farmhouse and eight buildings on nine acres of terraced olive groves. There is a museum designed and built by the artist Nall, who willingly describes himself as a "man of extremes." The Museum "vibrates with past centuries and styles" as well as modern works. "The floors, painted in trompe-l'oeil, blend with Indian sculpted doors from the 12th, 15th and 16th centuries. In the entrance to the Museum the beams of the ceiling and fireplace, overhung by Matisse mosaics and facing a stained glass window from the Cathedral of Algiers, are from the Gould residence in Cannes. In the courtyard, with Syrian mosaics dating from 2000 B.C., a mirrored wall reflects the olive groves, with the Mediterranean Sea shimmering over the foothills of the Alps."

How to Apply

Contact the NALL Art Foundation directly for application information.

Deadline

None provided.

Approximate Cost of Program

Transportation, meals, materials, and incidentals.

LA NAPOULE ART FOUNDATION   **DISCONTINUED**

PARIS WRITERS' WORKSHOP   FRANCE

20 Boulevard de Montparnasse, 75015 Paris, France
Attention: Rose Burke or Marcia Lebre, WICE/PWW Co-Directors
Phone: (33) 1-45-66-75-50; fax: (33) 1-40-65-96-53
Web site: www.wice-paris.org
Email: pww@wice-paris.org

Type of Facility/Award

Retreat/workshop.

Who Can Apply

Fiction writers, poets, and nonfiction writers.

Provisos:

None listed.

Dates of Operation

End of June to beginning of July.

Location

Paris, France.

History

"In its 12th year, the Paris Writers' Workshop has established a reputation for providing high-level instruction in a supportive and intimate environment. PWW is held at WICE, a nonprofit organization founded in 1978, offering innovative educational programs for English speakers of many countries living in the Paris area. The Paris Writers' Workshop, a member of Writers Conferences and Festivals, is a special event organized by WICE."

What They Offer

Enrollment is on a first-come, first-served basis, with twelve people per class. Each participant chooses a workshop: fiction, poetry, nonfiction, or tapping creativity (a multi-genre class for new writers or those interested in exploring the creative process). Workshops include readings, group discussions, critiques, and in-class or take-home writing assignments. In addition, each participant receives a one-on-one half-hour consultation with his or her writer-in-residence. All writers-in-residence at the Paris Writers' Workshop have extensive teaching and writing experience and are committed to sharing their skills and perspectives on the craft of writing. Financial assistance is available. See "Approximate Cost of Program" for details.

Facility Description

None provided.

How to Apply

Send an SASE or email your request for an application. Submit a clean copy of your typed, double-spaced, single-sided manuscript (no more than fifteen pages) stapled in the upper left-hand corner, along with the completed application. Include a large SASE if you would like your manuscript returned. Manuscripts may be used by writers-in-residence as class material for discussion, as well as in individual consultations, so bring a copy for yourself. No manuscript revisions will be accepted. Because the focus in tapping creativity workshops is on in-class writing, submissions for those classes are optional. To secure your place at the workshop in any class, send the completed application form along with full payment or a nonrefundable deposit of 500 FF or US$100 before June 1.

Deadline

June 1, though applications will be accepted after June 1 if space is available. If you are paying a deposit first, the balance is due by registration night before the opening reception.

Approximate Cost of Program

2,000 FF or US$370 for one week plus transportation, housing, meals, materials, and incidentals. Paris Writers' Workshop does not offer any stipend, but there is the possibility of a scholarship. Two half-tuition merit scholarships are available through a fund created in the memory of Patricia Painton, a founding member of WICE. Send a manuscript (following the same guidelines listed above) to WICE/PWW Scholarship Fund by April 30. Finalists will be notified by May 15.

SUMMER IN FRANCE WRITING WORKSHOP   FRANCE
Bettye Given, Director, Paris American Academy, HCO1, Box 102, Plainview, Texas 79072
Phone: (806) 889-3533
Web site: www.parisamericanacademy.edu/writing.htm
Email: bettye@parisamericanacademy.edu

AMERICAN ACADEMY IN BERLIN   GERMANY
In Germany:
The Hans Arnhold Center, Am Sandwerder 17–19, 14109 Berlin, Germany
Phone: 011-4930 804 83-0; fax: 011 4930 804 83-111
Email: mailbox@americanacademy.de

U.S. Office:
14 East 60th Street, Suite 606, New York, New York 10022
Attention: Dr. Everette E. Dennis
Phone: (212) 588-1755; fax: (212) 588-1758
Web site: www.amacberlin.com
Email: amacberlin@msn.com

Type of Facility/Award
Fellowship.

Who Can Apply
Scholars, artists, and professionals in a wide variety of fields who wish to engage in independent study in Berlin for an academic semester or year.

Provisos
Applicants should be affiliated or associated with a Berlin institution such as a museum, library, archive, university, government agency, architecture firm, film studio, or media organization. Appointments are for U.S. citizens or permanent residents of the United States who are faculty members at a university, artists, or practicing professionals at early, mid-career, or senior levels of achievement.

Dates of Operation
Academic year (mid-September through the end of May).

Location
Berlin, Germany.

History

"When U.S. troops left Berlin in the mid-1990's, a new post Cold War institution was conceived to build upon the long-standing links between Berlin, Germany and the United States in a new enterprise aimed at promoting cultural and commercial understanding. That idea was translated into the American Academy in Berlin, which opened its doors at an historic villa, now called the Hans Arnhold Center, in September 1998."

What They Offer

Fellowships run one to two academic semesters in length. Fellows receive a monthly stipend (amounts vary), housing and meals at the Hans Arnhold Center, and round-trip airfare.

Facility Description

The Hans Arnhold Center, named for the German-American banker and cultural leader Hans Arnhold, is a forty-room historic lakeside villa in the Wannsee district of Berlin. The villa includes public spaces, residential suites, conference and dining rooms, offices, studio space, and a library. It is fully wired with state-of-the-art technology.

How to Apply

Send an SASE to the U.S. address for a brochure and current application procedures.

Deadline

February 1 of every calendar year.

Approximate Cost of Program

Materials and incidentals—offset by stipend.

AMERICAN COUNCIL ON GERMANY   GERMANY

The John J. McCloy Fellowships, 14 East 60th Street, Suite 606, New York, New York 10022
Attention: Dr. Robert Dahlberg
Phone: (212) 826-3636; fax: (212) 758-3445
Web site: www.acgusa.org
Email: acggen@aol.com

Type of Facility/Award

Fellowship.

Who Can Apply

Museum curators.

Provisos

The John J. McCloy Fellowships are specifically intended to allow American curators to become acquainted with and gain insight into German approaches to their field. Those who are earlier in their careers are preferred.

Dates of Operation

Variable.

Location

The location of the fellowship varies according to the interests of the fellow. Multiple locations may apply to a single fellowship.

History

"The American Council on Germany was founded in the early 1950s to promote reconciliation between Germans and Americans. The ACG today promotes open communication and understanding between the two nations. The John J. McCloy Fund was established in 1975 as a tribute to Mr. John J. McCloy—soldier, lawyer, banker and former U.S. military governor and high commissioner in Germany."

What They Offer

McCloy fellows receive a per diem of $100 for up to twenty-eight days and transatlantic airfare. Domestic transportation costs are covered if pre-approved.

Facility Description

Facilities vary according to location.

How to Apply

Send an SASE for a brochure. Submit a curriculum vitae, a statement outlining what you expect to gain from your fellowship in terms of personal and professional development, and two letters of recommendation to Dr. Robert Dahlberg.

Deadline

There is no specific deadline, though application materials are preferred by the first of the year.

Approximate Cost of Program

Housing, materials, food, and incidentals—offset by per diem of $100 for up to twenty-eight days.

DEUTSCHER AKADEMICHER AUSTAUSCHDIENS (DAAD)   GERMANY

Jaegerstrasse 23, D 10117 Berlin, Germany

U.S. Office:

DAAD, German Academic Exchange Service, 950 Third Avenue, New York, New York 10022

Attention: Bernhard Ullrich, DAAD New York

Phone: (212) 758-3223; fax: (212) 755-5780

Web site: www.daad.org

Email: daadny@daad.org

Type of Facility/Award

Fellowship/grant.

Who Can Apply

Sculptors, artists, writers, composers, and filmmakers.

Provisos

Internationally renowned and exceptionally qualified artists are encouraged to apply.

Dates of Operation

Berlin fellowships last twelve months. In exceptional cases, the invitation will only involve a visit of six months. The grant for filmmakers is limited to six months.

Location

Berlin, Germany.

History

None provided.

What They Offer

The DAAD residencies focus on artists who wish to produce work in Berlin and play an active part in the cultural life of the city. Residents receive a grant (amount unspecified) which allows for a reasonable standard of living for Germany and which includes a portion of the rent for furnished accommodations and work areas in Berlin.

Facility Description

Variable.

How to Apply

Fine artists are not entitled to apply on their own behalf. Rather, they must be invited in person upon recommendation of an appointments committee. All those interested in other artistic fields should send an SASE to DAAD for a brochure and application. Submit the completed application with work samples that vary with art form as follows. Authors: Send no more than four to five books (German text is preferred, but English and French are fine). Composers: Send up to two scores, up to three records or tapes, and your own publications. Filmmakers: Send one to two filmscripts or videotapes (Super 8 and 16 mm formats are preferred). A synopsis in German, English, or French is required if the film has not been recorded or subtitled in one of these languages.

Deadline
January 1 of the year preceding the year for which the invitation will be issued.

Approximate Cost of Residency
Travel, materials, and incidentals.

GOETHE-INSTITUT CHICAGO   GERMANY
Berlin Fellowship Award, 150 North Michigan Avenue, Suite 200, Chicago, Illinois 60601
Phone: (312) 263-0472; fax: (312) 263-0476
Web site: www.goethe.de
Email: sipro@interaccess.com

HERZOG AUGUST BIBLIOTHEK WOLFENBÜTTEL FELLOWSHIP   GERMANY
c/o Newberry Library Committee on Awards, 60 West Walton Street, Chicago,
    Illinois 60610-3380
Phone: (312) 255-3666; fax: (312) 255-3513
Web sites: www.newberry.org and www.hab.de
Email: research@newberry.org

INSTITUT FÜR EUROPÄISCHE GESCHICHTE   GERMANY
Alte Universitätsstrasse 19, 55116 Mainz, Germany
Web site: www.inst-euro-history.uni-mainz.de/ieg.htm

WORPSWEDE ARTISTS COLONY   GERMANY
Worpsweder Touristik GmbH, Bergstraße 13, 27726 Worpswede, Germany
Phone: (0) 47-92-95-01-21/22; fax: (0) 47-92-95-01-23
Web site: www.worpswede.de
Email: info@worpswede.de or Worpsweder.Bahnhof@t-online.de

SKYROS CENTER   GREECE
92 Prince of Wales Road, London NW5 3NE, Great Britain
Phone: (44) 0-171-267-4424/284-3065; fax: (44) 0-171-284-3063
Web site: www.skyros.com/skyc.html
Email: connect@skyros.com

ART WORKSHOPS IN GUATEMALA

GUATEMALA

Callejon Lopez #22, La Antigua, Guatemala, Central America
Phone: 011-502-832-6403; fax: 011-502-832-6925
Web site: www.artguat.org
Email: info@artguat.org

U.S. Office:

4758 Lyndale Avenue South, Minneapolis, Minnesota 55409-2304
Attention: Liza Fourré, Director
Phone: (612) 825-0747; fax: (612) 825-6637

KJARVALSSTAOIR

ICELAND

The Reyjavik Municipal Art Museum, v/Flokagata, IS 105 Reykjavik, Iceland
Phone: +354-552-6131; fax: +354-562-6191

GILFELAGID

ICELAND

Cultural Society
Kaupvangsstraeti 23, IS - 600 Akureyri, Iceland
Phone: +354-461-2609; fax: +354-461-2928

SKRIDUKLAUSTUR

ICELAND

c/o Safnastofnun Austurlands, Skogarlond 4, IS 700 Egilsstadir, Iceland
Phone: +354-451-1451

DAVIDSHUS

ICELAND

c/o The Cultural Committee of Akureyri, Strandgata 19 B, IS 600 Akureyri, Iceland
Phone: +354-462-7245; fax: +354-462-5513

STRAUMUR ART COMMUNE

ICELAND

PO Box 33, IS 222 Hafnarfjordur, Iceland
Phone: +354-565-0128; fax: +354-565-0655

HAFNARBORG, MENNINGAR—or listastofnun
HAFNARFJAROAR INSTITUTE OF CULTURE AND FINE ART

ICELAND

Strandgata 34, IS 220 Hafnarfjordur, Iceland
Phone: +354-555-0080; fax: +354-565-4480

THE ICELANDIC GRAPHIC ART SOCIETY

ICELAND

Felagio islensk grafik, PO Box 857, IS 121 Reykjavik, Iceland
Phone: +354-552-2833; fax: +354-552-2866

THE HVERAGERDI CULTURAL COMMITTEE   ICELAND
Hverahlid 24, IS 810 Hveragerdi, Iceland
Phone: +354-483-4000; fax: +354 483 4802

THE UNION OF ICELANDIC WRITERS   ICELAND
Gunnarshusi, Dyngjuvegi 8, IS 104 Reykjavik, Iceland
Phone: +354 568 3190; fax: +354-568-3192

ANAM CARA   IRELAND
Republic of Ireland
Attention: Sue Booth-Forbes
Phone: 353-(0) 27-74441; fax: 353-(0) 27-74448
Web site (Anam Cara): www.ugr.com/anamcararetreat
Web site (Beara Peninsula): homepage.tinet.ie/~bearatourism
Email: anamcararetreat@eircom.net

Type of Facility/Award
Retreat.

Who Can Apply
Writers and artists.

Provisos
Applicants may be working at novice or professional levels. Residents should come already having done the advanced planning and preparation required to work on a specific project. Staff also recommends that residents stay at least one week.

Dates of Operation
Open year-round.

Location
Set high on a heather-covered hillside, Anam Cara overlooks Coulagh Bay and the mountains and farmlands of sub-tropical the Beara Peninsula in West Cork, Ireland. Travel by car from Cork City Airport takes approximately two hours. The Shannon Airport is approximately four and a half hours away.

History
Owner and hostess Sue Booth-Forbes is herself an established writer and editor. The name Anam Cara means "soul friend" in Irish. It was chosen, in part, in honor of the work and writing of John O'Donohue.

What They Offer
The daily schedule at Anam Cara is intended to nurture each individual resident and includes home-cooked meals featuring regional and local seafood and produce. Break-

fasts are taken either with others or on one's own, followed by full days of undisturbed seclusion with lunch delivered to each resident wherever he or she is working, and finally dinners, again, are taken with others or on one's own. Accommodations are both comfortable and inspiring. Room and board together are £300 (Irish) per person per week for a private working room with bath in the main house, and £600 (Irish) weekly to be shared by up to four people for the two-bedroom flat. Local taxi and mini-bus services provide transportation; residents may also make trips to town and farther afield with Sue when she goes.

Facility Description

There are two options for housing. Residents may choose a private working room and bath in the centrally heated main house with access to a sitting room and loft, each with turf/wood fires and a conservatory. A self-catering, centrally heated attached two-bedroom flat is also available, and includes a sitting room with a turf/wood fireplace, a fully-equipped kitchen, two bathrooms, and laundry facilities. The office space available for use is equipped with telephone, fax, email and Internet access, photocopier, and printer. All buildings are clean and smoke-free. Workshops and comprehensive editing services are also available. Other amenities include: jacuzzi and sauna, massage therapy, and access to several activities such as walking, hiking, cycling (two mountain bikes are available at Anam Cara), swimming, fishing, and golfing. In addition, Anam Cara provides "two acres of patio, lawn, and flower and vegetable gardens with private access to the Kealincha River, its cascades and swimming hole, an old stone mill, and a river island glen."

How to Apply

Contact Sue Booth-Forbes for availability, booking, and rates. Retreats are booked on a first-come, first-served basis.

Deadline

None.

Approximate Cost of Program

£300–£600 per week plus materials, transportation, and incidentals.

SUMMER WRITING WORKSHOP IN DUBLIN, IRELAND **DISCONTINUED**

SUMMER POETRY WORKSHOP IN IRELAND   **DISCONTINUED**

TYRONE GUTHRIE CENTRE   IRELAND

Annaghmakerrig, Newbliss, County Monaghan, Ireland
Phone: (353) 47 54 003; fax: (353) 47 54 380

HILAI: THE ISRAELI CENTER FOR THE CREATIVE ARTS   ISRAEL
P.O.B. 53007, Tel Aviv, 61530, Israel
Phone: (972) 3 478704

MISHKENOT SHA'ANANIM (PEACEFUL DWELLINGS)   ISRAEL
P.O.B. 8215, Jerusalem 91081, Israel
Phone: 02-6254321; fax: 972-2-6249987
Email: mishkenot@mishkenot.org.il

> *Notice: Mishkenot Sha'ananim is presently undergoing extensive renovations and will not reopen until the end of 2000 or beginning of 2001. Feel free to contact them after that time.*

AMERICAN ACADEMY IN ROME   ITALY
7 East 60 Street, New York, New York 10022-1001
Attention: Programs Department
Phone: (212) 751-7200; fax: (212) 751-7220
Web site: www.aarome.org

Type of Facility/Award
Fellowship.

Who Can Apply
Architects, design artists (including graphic design, industrial design, interior design, set design, urban design, and urban planning), historic preservationists and conservationists, landscape architects, writers, composers, visual artists, archaeologists, scholars, and art historians.

Provisos
Applicants for the Rome Prize Fellowships in the School of Fine Arts and for the predoctoral fellowships in the School of Classical Studies must be U.S. citizens. Permanent residents may apply for the post-doctoral fellowships in the School of Classical Studies. Undergraduates are not eligible. Graduate students may apply for pre-doctoral fellowships in the School of Classical Studies. Applicants must disclose all fellowships and awards they expect to hold during their proposed residency at the academy. Winners may not hold full-time jobs during their residency. Eligibility and submission requirements differ for each field.

Dates of Operation
Between mid-September and mid-August.

Location
Rome, Italy.

History

"The American Academy in Rome is the only American overseas center for independent study and advanced research in the fine arts and the humanities. Inspired by their comradeship in organizing America's contribution to the fine arts at the World's Colombian Exhibition in 1893, a group, including architects Charles Follen McKim and Daniel Burnham, painters John La Farge and Francis Millet, and sculptors Augustus Saint-Gaudens and Daniel Chester French, resolved to create a center to study art amid the classical traditions of ancient Rome. Rome was chosen as the site of the Academy because 'with the architectural and sculptural monuments and mural paintings, its galleries filled with the chef d'oeuvres of every epoch, no other city offers such a field for study or an atmosphere so replete with precedents.'"

What They Offer

Winners of the Rome Prize Fellowship pursue independent projects, which vary in content and scope, for periods ranging from six months to two years at the academy. Though the academy does not have a faculty, a curriculum, or a student body, it is composed of two historic schools: the School of Fine Arts and the School of Classical Studies. The specific terms of Rome Prize Fellowships depend upon which school the fellow's work falls into. Rome Prize winners are part of a residential community of sixty-five to seventy people each year at the academy. The artists have the opportunity to foster their work through exchanges with members of the Italian and newly united European artistic and scholarly communities. Stipends range from $9,000 to $17,800 (depending on the terms of the fellowships) and may not cover all expenses—this may especially be a concern for those bringing a spouse, companion, or child. Fellows are also provided with meals, a bedroom and private bath, and a study or studio. Fellows with minor children live in subsidized apartments. A series of walks, talks, and tours in and around Rome, Italy, and the Mediterranean is offered during the year.

Facility Description

The academy is housed in a series of buildings on the crest of the Janiculum hill in a setting of maintained gardens. The library of the academy contains over 120,000 volumes in the fields of classical studies and the history of art and architecture, many rare books, and imprints. The photographic archive contains documentation of Roman monuments, as well as a record of the work of past Rome Prize fellows. The academy also owns a small but varied collection of antiquities, ranging from statues and inscriptions to pottery and millstones.

How to Apply

Send an SASE for an application and brochure. Return your completed application form with a current résumé or curriculum vitae, project proposal, samples of your past work as specified for each discipline, three letters of reference, and a $40 application fee. All materials should be clearly marked with your field of application and submitted in English. Eligibility and submission requirements differ for each field and there are many fields of study at the academy, so make sure to read the specific guidelines before sending your application. Written materials will not be returned. Other materials will only be returned if accompanied by an adequate SASE.

Deadline
November 15 (postmarked).

Approximate Cost of Program
$40 application fee plus transportation, materials, and incidentals—offset by stipend.

ART WORKSHOP INTERNATIONAL   ITALY
463 West St. 1028H, New York, New York 10014
Attention: Bea Kreloff
Phone: (212) 691-1159; fax: (646) 486-4701
Web site: www.artworkshopintl.com
Email: bkart@workshopintl.com

Type of Facility/Award
Retreat/workshop.

Who Can Apply
Visual artists working in all media (including paint, pencil, video, photography, and found sculpture), art historians, and writers of fiction, poetry, and nonfiction.

Provisos
Artists of all levels of accomplishment and experience are welcome to apply. Participants must speak English.

Dates of Operation
June 13 through July 24.

Location
Assisi, Italy.

History
Art Workshop International began as a workshop for painters in 1975. It moved to the walled city of Assisi in 1983 and began including writers in 1992.

What They Offer
Three-week courses are available in June and July. Two-, four-, and six-week sessions are also available. Courses in a variety of disciplines are taught by professional visiting artists. Past faculty have included Frank McCourt, Grace Paley, Tony Kushner, and

Vivian Gornick. Advanced and professional participants have the option to participate in an independent program.

Facility Description
Participants are provided with private rooms in a hotel located within the walled city of Assisi. Each room has both a view and a bath. Studio space is provided; outdoor studio space is available in the garden of the hotel. Writing classes are held in communal meeting rooms.

How to Apply
Send an SASE for an application.

Deadline
May 10. (Deadlines subject to change.)

Approximate Cost of Program
$3,870 for a three-week session includes half the cost for hotel accomodations, tuition, studio space, lectures, and readings. Participants need to pay for the remainder of hotel costs, meals, materials, and incidentals.

BELLAGIO STUDY AND CONFERENCE CENTER   ITALY
Bellagio Center Office, Rockefeller Foundation, 420 Fifth Avenue, New York,
    New York 10018-2702
Phone: (212) 869-8500
Web site: www.rockfound.org
Email: bellagio@rockfound.org

Type of Facility/Award
Residency.

Who Can Apply
Scholars, scientists, policymakers, practitioners, and artists in any field.

Provisos
Applicants should expect that their work at the center will result in publication, exhibition, performance, or some other concrete product. Applicants may be from any country and involved in any discipline, provided they have significant publications, compositions, exhibitions, productions, or other accomplishments to their credit. Those who have applied and been declined are ineligible for reapplication for two years. Those who have already been through the program may reapply after ten years. The center is not entirely handicapped accessible.

Dates of Operation

Variable. Individual residency periods are staggered, with arrivals scheduled almost each week. However, there are no activities between mid-December and the end of January.

Location

Bellagio is located on Lake Como in northern Italy.

History

"When expatriate Ella Holbrook Walker bequeathed the Villa Serbelloni to the Foundation in 1959, the first order of business was determining how to fulfill her wish that the Villa be used for the promotion of international understanding. The result was the Bellagio Study and Conference Center."

What They Offer

The foundation offers approximately 140 month-long residencies annually at the center for scholars, scientists, and artists. Each resident is provided with a private room and bath, meals, and a study in which to work. There are fourteen studies for residents, including one for a visual artist and one for a composer. With the exception of the residents' spouses, the center cannot accommodate extra bodies (children, family members, friends, or pets) and is not entirely handicapped accessible.

Facility Description

The center occupies a wooded promontory situated in the foothills of the Italian Alps. The main house and seven other buildings, parts of which date back to the seventeenth century, are surrounded by fifty acres of parks and gardens. "The Center is an ideal site to work on stages of a project that do not require laboratory or library resources. The Center's small library has a number of basic reference works but is not appropriate for anyone requiring a research facility. Scholars and scientists often are able to bring information and data sources with them and to use the uninterrupted time for formulating conclusions and preparing a manuscript. IBM-compatible and Macintosh laptop computers are available, and the Center has fax facilities. Access to the Internet is provided; residents may access their email through their server or through any of the Web-based email services."

How to Apply

Send an SASE or check the Web site for an application. Your typed, unbound application materials must include the original and one photocopy of a completed cover-sheet form; a half-page abstract (including your name(s) and project title) that summarizes the project and describes its purpose, goals, and objectives; a detailed description of your project, its importance to the field, and its innovative qualities (about ten pages for scholars/scientists/practitioners and one to two pages for artists/composers/writers/ etc.); your curriculum vitae, including a list of publications, performances, and exhibitions and a maximum of three reviews of your past work, if available; and one sample of a published work (artists send a labeled slide-projector page; composers send a tape or CD and a score; and video/filmmakers send one videotape).

Deadline
Deadlines vary depending on preference of dates for the residency.

Approximate Cost of Program
Transportation, materials, and incidentals.

THE BRITISH SCHOOL AT ROME   ITALY
BSR Awards and Fellowships, The British Academy, 10 Carlton House Terrace,
    London SW1Y 5AH
Phone: (0) 171-969-5202; fax: (0) 170-969-5401
Web site: britac3.britac.ac.uk/institutes/rome/bsr.html
Email: bsr@britac.ac.uk

THE HARVARD UNIVERSITY CENTER FOR ITALIAN
RENAISSANCE STUDIES   ITALY
Villa I Tatti, Via di Vincigliata 26, 50135 Firenze FI, Italy
Phone: (39) 55-603-251/608-909; fax: (39) 55-603-383
Web site: www.peabody.harvard.edu/Villa_I_Tatti

Type of Facility/Award
Fellowship.

Who Can Apply
Art historians, musicians, historians, and literary scholars who are devoted to aspects of the Italian Renaissance.

Provisos
Applicants must be post-doctoral scholars interested in advanced study of the Italian Renaissance. Ordinarily, preference is given to scholars embarking on a new research project rather than to those wishing to pursue the subject of their dissertations or applicants who have not previously enjoyed the advantages of prolonged residence in Florence. Because the committee wishes to make fellowship opportunities available to as many scholars as possible, renewals, though possible, are rarely granted.

Dates of Operation
Academic year.

Location
I Tatti is located on the eastern edge of urban Florence.

History

"In 1900, the eminent historian and critic of late medieval and Renaissance art, Bernard Berenson, took up residence at Villa I Tatti and continued to live here until his death in 1959. In his will, he bequeathed the estate, located in the outskirts of Florence, and his vast collection of books, photographs, and works of art to Harvard University, from which he had received an A.B. in 1887. In leaving I Tatti to Harvard, the donor wished to establish a center of scholarship that would advance humanistic learning throughout the world and increase understanding of the values by which civilizations develop and survive. He particularly wanted to give younger scholars at a critical point in their careers the opportunity to develop and expand interests and talents."

What They Offer

At I Tatti, scholars independently study and research at the Biblioteca Berenson and in other libraries, archives, and collections in Florence and throughout Italy. Fellowships are either non-stipendiary or stipendiary, based on individual need and availability of funds. The maximum grant is $30,000; most grants are considerably less. Each fellow receives a study in which to work and the opportunity to associate daily with other members of the I Tatti community as well as with the many distinguished Renaissance scholars who continually visit and use the library. The center also sponsors a regular series of lectures and international conferences. There is also an active publication program including the biennial journal, *I Tatti Studies: Essays in the Renaissance*.

Facility Description

The grounds are surrounded by seventy-five acres of Tuscan farmland planted with grapes and almond, fruit, and olive trees. The sixteenth-century villa and attached library found in the center of this farmland are marked by a cluster of dark cypresses and towering umbrella pines, as well as turn-of-the-century English gardens.

Facilities include the Biblioteca Berenson, an extensive library containing approximately 100,000 volumes and an archive of more than 300,000 photographs; the library also subscribes to over 400 learned journals.

How to Apply

Send an SASE for a brochure and application form. Submit your completed application with a curriculum vitae, a statement of no more than ten pages describing your proposed research, and three confidential letters of recommendation (mailed directly by their authors).

Deadline

October 15 for the following year's fellowships.

Approximate Cost of Program

Transportation, housing, meals, materials, and incidentals—offset by stipend.

WORKSHOPS IN ITALY   ITALY
4 Edgewood Terrace, Northampton, Massachutsetts 01060
Attention: Fred Wessel
Phone: (413) 586-0707; fax: (413) 584-2240
Web site: uhavax.hartford.edu/~wessel
Email: Wessel@mail.hartford.edu

ASIAN CULTURAL COUNCIL   JAPAN
437 Madison Avenue, 37th Floor, New York, New York 10022-7001
Phone: (212) 812-4300; fax: (212) 812-4299
Web site: www.asianculturalcouncil.org

> *Notice: The ACC supports several types of residencies, grants, and fellowships in Japan, including programs for visual artists, scholars, archaeologists, conservationists, museologists, architects, historians, dancers, designers, filmmakers, musicians, composers, photographers, and theater artists. Send an SASE for a brochure.*

THE JAPAN FOUNDATION   JAPAN

For applications from all states east of the Rocky Mountains:
152 West 57th Street, 39F, New York, New York 10019
Attention: Artists Fellowship Program
Phone: (212) 489-0299; fax: (212) 489-0409
Web site: www.us-jf.org

For applications from all states west of the Rocky Mountains:
The Water Garden, Suite 650-E, 2425 Olympic Boulevard, Santa Monica,
    California 90404-4034
Attention: Artists Fellowship Program
Phone: (310) 449-0027; fax: (310) 449-1127
Web site: www.us-jf.org

Type of Facility/Award
Fellowship.

Who Can Apply
Writers, musicians, painters, sculptors, stage directors, film directors, screenwriters, and liberal arts faculty members involved in creative projects.

Provisos
Applicants must be proficient in either Japanese or English. Citizens of countries that do not have diplomatic relations with Japan are not eligible to apply. There are restrictions for those who have recently benefited from a grant. Fellowships are not

granted to those who have been living in Japan for more than one year or who have done research in Japan for a period of more than two months.

Dates of Operation
Variable. Fellowships are calculated in units of months and last between two and six months for artists.

Location
Various locations in Japan.

History
"The Japan Foundation was established in 1972 as a special legal entity under the auspices of the Ministry of Foreign Affairs for the purpose of promoting mutual understanding and friendship on the international scene. It was the first specialist organization for international cultural exchange in Japan, and it carries out a broad variety of cultural-exchange programs with personnel exchange as their basic premise, ranging from such academic pursuits as Japanese studies and Japanese-language education to the arts, publication, audio-visual media, sports, and general life culture."

What They Offer
Fellows receive round-trip airfare and ¥370,000 or ¥430,000 per month for living expenses. The grant also includes a settling-in allowance upon arrival, research allowance, dependent allowance, enrollment fees, insurance fees, and departure allowance.

Facility Description
Variable.

How to Apply
Send an SASE for current application requirements.

Deadline
November 1 (postmarked). Notification by May.

Approximate Cost of Program
Materials and incidentals. Living expenses between ¥370,000 and ¥430,000 are covered by the fellowship. Various allowances cover additional expenses.

MINISTRY OF EDUCATION, SCIENCE, AND CULTURE   JAPAN
Mombusho Scholarships, 3-2-2-chome Kasumigaseki, Chiyoda-ku, Tokyo 100, Japan

> *Notice: They request that you contact the Japanese Embassy or Consulate closest to you for information and an application.*

NATIONAL ENDOWMENT FOR THE ARTS   JAPAN

United States/Japan Creative Artists' Program, Japan-U.S. Friendship
    Commission, 1120 Vermont Avenue NW, Suite 925, Washington, DC 20005
Attention: Creative Artists' Program
Phone: (202) 275-7712; fax: (202) 275-7413
Web site: www2.dgsys.com/˜jusfc/commissn/commissn/.html
Email: 72133.7433@compuserve.com or jusfc@dgs.dgsys.com

Type of Facility/Award

Residency.

Who Can Apply

Candidates must be creative artists (contemporary or traditional) working as architects, choreographers, composers, creative writers, designers, media artists, playwrights,
solo theater artists (including puppeteers, storytellers, and performance artists) who
work with original material, or visual artists. Multidisciplinary artists and artistic
directors of theater companies are also eligible.

Provisos

Candidates must be citizens or permanent residents of the U.S. Preference will be
given to those applicants for whom this will be a first-time residency in Japan.

Dates of Operation

Six months to be determined on an individual basis.

Location

Various locations in Japan.

History

None provided.

What They Offer

The United States/Japan Creative Artists' Program provides a maximum of five six-
month residencies in Japan for individual creative artists in any discipline. The residencies allow U.S. artists to create original work or to pursue their individual artistic
goals and interests by living in Japan, observing developments in their fields, and
meeting with their professional counterparts in Japan. There are no requirements for
artistic creation, teaching, or public demonstration while in Japan. In addition, there
are no structured institutional affiliations or living arrangements for residents, allowing each artist maximum flexibility in designing his or her own fellowship activities.
International House in Tokyo will help make introductions into the artistic community throughout Japan and will assist selected artists with the logistics of settling in
for their six-month stay.

Facility Description
Facilities depend upon location.

How to Apply
Send an SASE for current guidelines and an application. Applicants are judged by the following criteria: the artistic excellence of the applicant's work and artistic merit of the proposed project; the extent to which working in Japan is consistent with the applicant's vision and would contribute to his or her artistic growth; the applicant's ability to meet cross-cultural challenges successfully; the availability of resources in Japan that are necessary to the artist's proposed project; and the benefit of interaction with Japanese culture to the applicant at this time in his or her career.

Deadline
June 28.

Approximate Cost of Program
Transportation, housing, meals, and incidentals—offset by fellowship award.

CAMPO DE ARTISTAS   MEXICO   **DISCONTINUED**

LATIN AMERICA WRITERS' WORKSHOP   MEXICO
Latin America Writers' Workshop, 2261 Market Street 334, San Francisco, California 94114
Web site: www.gnofn.org/~writer/mexico

NATIONAL ENDOWMENT FOR THE ARTS   MEXICO   **DISCONTINUED**

EMERSON COLLEGE   THE NETHERLANDS   **DISCONTINUED**

KOSCIUSZKO FOUNDATION   POLAND
15 East 65th Street, New York, New York 10021-6595
Web site: www.kosciuszkofoundation.org

Grants and scholarships for research and publication of scholarly books of all types on Poland and Polish culture.

THE INTERNATIONAL RETREAT FOR WRITERS AT HAWTHORNDEN CASTLE   SCOTLAND
Hawthornden Castle, Lasswade, Midlothian EH18 1EG, Scotland
Attention: The Administrator

SCOTTISH SCULPTURE WORKSHOP   SCOTLAND

1 Main Street, Lumsden, Aberdeenshire, AB54 4JN, Scotland
Attention: Chris Fremantle
Phone: +44-1-464-861372; fax: +44-1-464-861550
Web site: www.ssw.org.uk
Email: enquiries@ssw.org.uk

Type of Facility/Award

Artist-in-residence program.

Who Can Apply

All visual artists. Facilities include workshops for those working with wood, metal, clay, stone, bronze, aluminum, and iron.

Provisos

Residents must comply with standard terms and conditions, which are available upon request.

Dates of Operation

January 7 through December 20.

Location

Huntly is a rural village in the foothills of the Highlands, halfway between Aberdeen and Inverness.

History

The Scottish Sculpture Workshop was initiated in 1979 by Frederick Bushe, O.B.E., R.S.A., to provide space for artists to make sculpture. Since that time, SSW has expanded its mission, seeking not only to create opportunities for making sculpture, but also for exhibiting, siting sculpture, and increasing the public understanding and appreciation of sculpture.

What They Offer

For £80.00 (UK currency) per week, residents receive self-catering accommodation in either double or single rooms, use of workshop facilities, and technical support. Technicians provide on-site help and advice, run the foundry, and organize materials. Accessory items and disposable stock (gas, oxygen, acetylene, grinding and cutting discs, sandpaper) are kept track of and must be paid for at the end of each month. In addition to the residency program, SSW hosts the Scottish Sculpture Open exhibition every other year to attract artists to create work for the unique location of Kildrummy Castle. They also hold symposia, fellowships, commissions, and bursaries and have undertaken outreach through specialist courses and work with schools.

Scottish Sculpture Workshop
Sculpture

George Beasley

In 1982 I happened to mention to my friend, site specific sculptor George Trakas, that I wanted to visit Scotland because my grandmother had immigrated from there. Actually, I asked him if he knew a way that I could go here and do a bit of sculpture. Money being a problem, the trip had to be cheap. George immediately responded that he had a friend, Arden Scott, in New York, who had just returned from a "kind of co-op studio in northern Scotland." One call to Arden and two months later, I found myself at the Scottish Sculpture Workshop (SSW) in Northeast Scotland. At that time, the workshop had been in existence only a few years. The Scottish sculptor, Frederick Bushe, M.B.E., R.S.A., grand in stature as well as vision and ingenuity, had quit academia to open his own studio which was converted from an old bakery. Fred wanted to establish a place that could become a crossroads for artists from around the world to create work while also experiencing the landscape and culture of Northeast Scotland. That goal has been realized with artists visiting from just about every continent.

Photo credit: Tim Lodzinski © 2000

Studios at the workshop are well-equipped for stone carving, casting in bronze and iron, and fabricating in steel and wood. This is not a school, and artists are "left to get on with it." If you need assistance, the able staff of foundry technician, Eden Jolly, and workshop manager, Peter Smith, will guide you through most problems. There doesn't seem to be any technical issue beyond the scope of their knowledge. Chris Fremantle is doing a terrific job managing the independent charitable trust backed by a board of directors made up of important artists and art administrators.

Since that first time in 1982, I have returned to the workshop often, meeting and making new friends from all over the world. After a full day of working in the studios, residents will often collaborate in the kitchen. A resident might prepare a specialty from his or her own country for the group. Sometimes all might join in to create a culinary mix as wild as the mix of languages spoken. Then it's down to the pub to challenge the locals to a game of pool or darts. A bit of advice: Bring lots of change, as small bets are sometimes made and the peculiarities of the pool table are not always as apparent to visitors as to the locals. Watch out for Albert. At 87, he is still a major contender.

Whether you are a first-time visitor or a returning regular, the friendliness of the villagers and the charm of the surrounding area make a lasting impression. As a result, a remarkable relationship has been built between the village and the workshop. With gorgeous sunsets, the changing skies, and beautiful landscapes around every bend and over every hill, you are sure to experience a renewal of ideas and a

Facility Description

The site is equipped for a wide range of sculptural practice. Woodworking materials include a large band saw (15" x 22"), sander, bench drill, planer/thicknesser (12" x 8"), and circular saw (18"). For metal, provisions are made for cutting and welding with oxy/acetylene, mig and tig welding, and manual arc welding. The metal workshop provides a mechanical hacksaw, hand guillotine, rollers, sandblaster and paint spray, and a large drill of up to 2" capacity. There is a 22-cubic-foot electric kiln (1300 oc) for claywork. For stonework, particularly granite, there are compressors and tungsten tipped tools, rock drills, Stihl saws, grinders, and more. Fixed and moveable gantries and a forklift truck are available, all of which are capable of moving up to two tons. SSW also includes an open-access foundry, available with technical support. For casting bronze and aluminum, there is an oil-fired furnace that holds up to 60 kg of bronze per firing. Processes include investment, ceramic shell, and resin-bonded sand, though they welcome non-traditional approaches to casting. For iron casting, there is a cupolette using coke. There is a wide variety of consumables and materials available, and SSW can order materials for residents. The library houses a small collection of sculpture catalogues and provides a database of international contacts, a Mac (200 mhz PPC, 96meg. RAM, CD-ROM, Zip, Video I/O card, 17" monitor), slide and flatbed scanners, color printer, and access to the Internet and email. SSW is currently upgrading the facilities; plans are in hand for new workshops, studios, library, and darkroom.

How to Apply
Write or check the Web site for an application form. To apply, return the booking form with slides and a CV. Include a deposit of £10.00 for every week you plan to stay. Twenty-eight-days' notice of cancellation must be given for a refund. You will need to note on your application any materials that will be necessary for your project.

Deadline
No deadline. Open year-round based on availability.

Approximate Cost of Program
£80.00 (UK currency) per week includes self-catering accommodation, use of workshop facilities, and technical help. Residents are charged for materials and tuition as they are used, and are also responsible for transportation and incidentals. Discounts are available for students, people with disabilities, OAPs, and unemployed residents. There are also discounts for long stays. Inquire at time of application if you are eligible for a discount. Residents must include with their applications a £10.00 deposit per week they plan to stay.

SWEDISH INFORMATION SERVICE   SWEDEN
One Dag Hammarskjold Plaza, (Second Avenue and 48th Street), 45th Floor, New York, New York 10017
Phone: (212) 583-2550; fax: (212) 752-4789
Web site: www.webcom.com/sis/
Email: requests@swedeninfo.com

LA MALADIÉRE   SWITZERLAND   **DISCONTINUED**

BERLLANDERI SCULPTURE WORKSHOP   WALES
Usk Road, Raglan, Monmouthshire, NP5 2HR, Wales, UK
Attention: Mr. H. Hood
Phone: 01291 690 268
Web site: www.berllanderi.freeserve.co.uk/whatis.htm
Email: sculpture@berllanderi.freeserve.co.uk

Type of Facility/Award
Residency.

Who Can Apply
Sculptors.

Provisos
None listed.

Dates of Operation
Open year-round.

Location
The workshop is located in the Usk Valley, just one mile from Ragland and two hours from London by train. Monmouth, Newport, Cardiff, and Bristol are within easy access.

History
Berllanderi, translated as "Orchard of Oaks," is a seventeenth-century farm complex. "It is the intention of the workshop to have a mixed balance of disciplines to foster debate across a range of disciplines and backgrounds. Such a combination of sculptors might comprise, for example, a sculptor executing a major commission and needing specialist facilities, a mature sculptor seeking a different studio environment, a visiting international artist wanting a ready-made studio and base, and a younger sculptor."

What They Offer
Residents may stay for any length of time for up to a year. Berllanderi provides accommodations for up to four sculptors at a time, as well as the newly converted Stable Cottage which has group or family accommodation for six people. For £55–70 (UK currency) per week, residents are provided with a self-contained apartment converted from the old granary, a private studio, and use of specialist workshops and tools.

Facility Description
The workshop covers 7,000 square-feet of covered studio space, open courtyards, and seven acres of land. There are communal workshops that focus on the traditional processes of sculpture, including modeling and carving. A large stone-carving studio is equipped with a range of hand and compressed-air tools, gantries, and other lifting equipment. The fully equipped wood workshop includes a band saw, circular saw, planer/thicknesser, pillar drill, and more. There are additional foundry, forge, and metal working facilities. The workshop provides specialized cast-iron and sand-casting facilities and has a small cupola. They pour approximately five times a year.

How to Apply
Send an SASE or check the Web site for an application. Submit the application with a proposal of your intended program and evidence of your past work.

Deadline
No deadline. Acceptance is based on availability.

Approximate Cost of Program
£55–70 (UK currency) per week plus transportation, meals, and incidentals.

Appendix

Architecture

Midwestern Colonies & Retreats

New England Colonies & Retreats

Pacific Coast Colonies & Retreats

Middle Atlantic Colonies & Retreats

International Colonies & Retreats

Book Arts

Midwestern Colonies & Retreats

Rocky Mountain Colonies & Retreats

Southwestern Colonies & Retreats

Southern Colonies & Retreats

New England Colonies & Retreats

Middle Atlantic Colonies & Retreats

Ceramics

Midwestern Colonies & Retreats

Rocky Mountain Colonies & Retreats

Southwestern Colonies & Retreats

Southern Colonies & Retreats

Performing Arts (Dance, Choreography, Theater, etc.)

Photography

Playwriting & Screenwriting